AF699885

Rebalancing Growth in Asia

Economic Dimensions for China

EDITORS

Vivek Arora and Roberto Cardarelli

INTERNATIONAL MONETARY FUND

Copyright © 2011 International Monetary Fund

Production: IMF Multimedia Services Division
Cover Design: Michelle Martin/Lai Oy Louie
Cover Photo Credits: World of Stock (left); Stephen Jaffe (right)
Typesetting/Composition: SPS

Cataloging-in-Publication Data

Arora, Vivek B.
Rebalancing growth in Asia : economic dimensions for China / Vivek Arora and Roberto Cardarelli. – Washington, D.C. : International Monetary Fund, 2010.
p. ; cm.

Includes bibliographical references.
ISBN: 978-1-61635-056-7
1. Economic development – Asia. 2. Economic development – China. 3. Saving and investment – Asia. 4. Investments – Asia. 5. Exports – China. 6. Employment – China. 7. Consumption (Economics) – China. I. Cardarelli, R. (Roberto) II. International Monetary Fund. III. Title.
HC412.A76 2010

Disclaimer: The views expressed in this book belong to the individual authors and should not be attributed to the International Monetary Fund, its Executive Board, or the governments of any of its members.

Please send orders to:
International Monetary Fund, Publication Services
P.O. Box 92780, Washington, DC 20090, U.S.A.
Tel: (202) 623-7430 • Fax: (202) 623-7201
Email: publications@imf.org
www.imfbookstore.org

MIX
Paper from responsible sources
FSC® C012947
FSC www.fsc.org

Contents

Figures

Tables

Boxes

Foreword

Asia's economic performance in recent decades has been remarkable. A region that was once among the poorest in the world is today a force that is leading the global economy as the world recovers from its most devastating economic crisis in over half a century. Asia's success is, of course, no accident. It is based on years of sustained effort to implement reforms and strengthen institutions that laid the basis for raising economic growth, improving resilience to crises, and harnessing the benefits of globalization.

It is well recognized across the region, however, that rapid growth cannot be taken for granted. Asia will need to build on its robust policy foundation with further reforms to address the challenges that the region still faces in both the near and the medium term. In the near term, the main challenge is consolidation of the recovery while maintaining macroeconomic stability amid a volatile global environment. Over the medium term, a key policy challenge for many Asian countries is how to sustain rapid growth in an environment where exports—a key engine of growth—may be weakened as a result of diminished demand from the industrial countries that have been particularly hard hit by the crisis. Indeed, compared with other regions, Asia has come to rely heavily on external demand for its growth.

A second, domestic engine of growth is surely the answer to this challenge, and the recent policy debate in Asia has turned to the question of how to strengthen private domestic demand. The IMF has been closely engaged in discussing this issue with Asian authorities in recent years, and in emphasizing it in our research efforts in order to try and draw some policy conclusions.

Against this background, this book brings together material and analysis prepared in 2009 and 2010 by IMF staff working on Asia. The author team, led by Vivek Arora and Roberto Cardarelli, included Steven Barnett, Ray Brooks, Marcos Chamon, Kai Guo, Sonali Jain Chandra, Adil Mohommad, Malhar Nabar, Papa N'Diaye, Nathan Porter, Murtaza Syed, and Olaf Unteroberdoerster.

Anoop Singh
Director, Asia & Pacific Department
International Monetary Fund

Acknowledgments

The authors would like to acknowledge the valuable comments and input of several IMF colleagues who have worked on Asian economic issues, particularly Nigel Chalk, Joshua Felman, Tarhan Feyzioğlu, Subir Lall, and Mahmood Pradhan, and the overall guidance of Anoop Singh.

The authors' work on Asia has benefited greatly from interactions over the years with many officials and analysts in the region who are too numerous to name individually. Their views and insights have been critical for thinking through the issues dealt with in this book.

We are grateful to Kessia De Leo, Lesa Yee, and Imel Yu for assistance with preparing successive drafts of the volume, and to Sean Culhane for editing the volume and managing its production.

The opinions expressed in this book, as well as any errors, are the sole responsibility of the authors and do not necessarily reflect the views of other members of the IMF staff, of Asian authorities, or the Executive Directors and Management of the IMF.

Introduction and Overview

VIVEK ARORA AND ROBERTO CARDARELLI

INTRODUCTION

A key feature of the world economy in recent decades has been Asia's emergence as an economic powerhouse. This emergence is by now well documented and its many dimensions have been extensively studied, but a reminder of even the most basic facts is still striking. Over the last 30 years, the economy of emerging Asia and the newly industrialized economies—a group that encompasses all of Asia except Australia, Japan, and New Zealand—has grown by over 7 percent annually on average, with the implication that it has doubled in size every decade.[1] The resulting eight-fold increase in output in just a single generation is virtually unprecedented in history, and it has had significant implications for people in the region. Many hundreds of millions of people have risen out of poverty, and living conditions have improved substantially in almost every country. Asia has come to account for over one-fourth of the world economy in terms of GDP at market exchange rates, a share that exceeds that of the United States and of the Euro area.

Asia's successful emergence has been based in large part on a strategy of outward-oriented growth. China's "reform and opening up" policy, launched in 1978, is perhaps the most prominent example, but the move toward giving market forces greater play in the economy and, in particular, encouraging the production of tradable goods has been a common theme across most of the region. The move over time from relatively inward-looking toward more outward-oriented policies has allowed countries to better exploit their comparative advantages, benefit from the economies of scale afforded by global markets, become more competitive, strengthen their technological base, and increase both income and jobs. Asia's share in world exports has trebled over the last three decades, and it currently accounts for nearly one-fourth of all the world's exports.

Over time, however, a growing recognition has developed, in Asia and elsewhere, that in order for Asia to sustain strong economic growth, the impetus provided by exports needs to be balanced with a second engine of growth.[2] The global financial crisis hastened the urgency of this transformation as

[1]The NIEs comprise Hong Kong SAR, Korea, Singapore, and Taiwan Province of China. In what follows we use "Asia" and "emerging Asia" interchangeably to mean emerging Asia plus the NIEs.

[2]See, for example, Park (2009), Prasad (2009), Singh (2010), Strauss-Kahn (2010), and Zhu (2010).

global demand was dramatically lowered. But even before the crisis, policymakers recognized that Asia may have become unduly reliant on external demand in comparison with other regions, that market shares for Asian exports in key products were approaching high levels by historical standards and could run into natural limits, and that the heavy orientation toward the tradable goods that fuel production and exports may often come at the cost of a relative neglect of nontradable sectors, particularly services. This internal imbalance leaves an economy both more vulnerable to swings in external demand than it would otherwise be and unable to draw fully on the potential of nontradable sectors.

The heavy reliance on exports in Asia has been reflected in a rise in the external current account imbalance in recent years. For emerging Asia as a whole, the current account was close to balance during the 1980s and 1990s, recording a deficit of around ½ percent of GDP during the 1980s and a surplus of roughly the same magnitude during the 1990s. The picture changed during the 2000s, when the surplus rose sharply to average nearly 4½ percent of GDP for the decade. Similarly, Asia accounted for around 11 percent of global saving on average during 1980–2000, but this share nearly doubled in the 2000s. These patterns have reversed somewhat since the onset of the financial crisis, with current account surpluses falling since 2008 as external demand collapsed. However, it is still too soon to say whether the reduction in surpluses will endure or whether it represents largely a cyclical change.

The second engine of growth that would help to address these imbalances and reduce the undue reliance on external demand is, of course, domestic demand, and in particular *private* domestic demand. Private demand comprises both consumption and investment, and here the story across Asia is somewhat heterogeneous. In some countries, such as China, consumption is relatively low, while in others, such as the larger ASEAN countries, it is investment that has been relatively low ever since the 1997–98 Asian financial crisis. The implication of this heterogeneity is that any discussion of rebalancing growth in Asia toward domestic demand has to pay attention to the various components of private domestic demand. Meanwhile, the counterpart on the supply side is that production needs to be reoriented from export sectors toward sectors that serve domestic markets. Such a reorientation does not in any way call for a reduction in countries' openness to trade. It does, however, require the development of hitherto neglected domestically oriented sectors that likely would entail faster growth in nontradable production and in imports.

How, then, to develop this second engine of growth? Many of the policy changes that could contribute have been widely noted in international policy discussion (Strauss-Kahn, 2010). They include measures such as strengthening social safety nets, which should help to reduce the need for precautionary saving and thus boost consumption; improving infrastructure, which can encourage more private investment; financial sector deepening, which can support private consumption as well as investment both by smaller firms and by larger firms that seek financing for large projects; and, where needed, more exchange rate flexibility. Reflecting in part the varied pattern of domestic demand across Asia, however, the general policy themes involved in rebalancing growth apply differently to different countries.

OVERVIEW

As the foregoing discussion makes clear, rebalancing growth is a complex challenge that involves multiple policy and analytical aspects. The IMF staff's work on Asia in recent years has discussed many of these aspects, and this book focuses on a few of the issues that this work has covered.[3] Much of the work has focused on the rebalancing challenge in China, which is of interest in its own right as Asia's largest economy.

Accordingly, the book first discusses some general themes in Asia's rebalancing, and then the bulk of the book focuses on China. Part I outlines Asia's relatively heavy reliance on external demand for growth and discusses the determinants of low investment and high corporate saving in much of the region. (Corporate saving is a particular point of interest because it has played an important role in the rise in national saving in Asia over the past decade, but it seems to have been less extensively studied in the literature than household saving.) Part II focuses on some of the challenges that China faces in seeking to rebalance its growth, both the overarching challenge of reorienting the growth model away from exports and the specific question of how to raise private consumption. In particular, the three chapters in Part I, "Rebalancing Growth in Asia: Some General Themes," focus on the following themes:

- *Asia's overall export dependence.* Chapter 1 documents the fact that Asia's dependence on external demand is higher than that of other regions in the world and also higher than a simple examination of net exports would suggest. The counterpart is domestic demand that is often too low, reflecting consumption in some cases and investment in others. The chapter analyzes quantitatively the potential implications for Asia of a package of measures aimed at rebalancing growth. The benefits of implementing these measures across the region as a whole are shown to be substantially larger than implementing them on a stand-alone basis.
- *Corporate saving.* High saving in many Asian countries reflects not only household saving but also corporate saving. Chapter 2 documents the rise in corporate saving across Asia over the past decade or so. The rise stands in sharp contrast to the relatively anemic trends in investment and has thus contributed to the growing external imbalance. The analysis in the chapter ascribes the high and rising trend in corporate saving to a need for financial market development and further improvements in corporate

[3]Previous versions of some of this work appeared in IMF (2010).

governance that would allow firms to meet more of their financing needs from capital markets and less from retained earnings.

- *Investment.* Two aspects of Asia's investment that stand out are, first, its relatively low level in much of the region (although not in China) and, second, a general orientation of investment toward tradable sectors and away from nontradable sectors. Chapter 3 presents an empirical analysis to determine the basis on which investment can be said to be too low in much of the region. It finds that the relatively low investment owes largely to fundamental factors such as low returns, uncertainty, the business climate, insufficient access to market finance, and shortfalls in infrastructure.

The five chapters in Part II, "Rebalancing Growth in China: Relying Less on Exports and More on Consumption," focus on two additional issues:

- *China's export-oriented growth: sustainability and employment consequences of rebalancing.* Chapter 4 assesses the sustainability of China's export-oriented growth strategy and concludes that it would require very large increases in market share in key industries as well as steep reductions in profit margins. Turning away from export-oriented growth, however, is often dismissed as implausible given the employment implications. But these implications have seldom been quantified Chapter 5 uses the IMF's global integrated monetary and fiscal (GIMF) model to run scenarios of rebalancing and concludes that while in the short term there could be employment losses, in the longer term employment would actually rise as the growth of the nontradable sectors generated additional jobs.
- *Household consumption.* Chapters 6–8 address various challenges associated with raising private consumption, which is usefully done by examining the situation of China. To set the stage, Chapter 6 assesses the determinants of private consumption. It finds that China's low share of private consumption in GDP can be mainly explained by the low share of household income and by economic factors that keep the saving rate high. An important point is that high household saving in China is not somehow preordained by cultural forces but may owe to a small set of relatively well understood economic variables that may in turn be responsive to policies. Chapter 7 examines the particular role of government spending on health and education in determining precautionary saving (and thus consumption) in China, and finds that government health spending can have a particularly significant effect on urban consumption. Chapter 8 looks at the potential for greater consumer finance to boost consumption in China drawing on empirical analysis as well as case studies from some other countries (Brazil, Korea) and concludes that innovations in consumer finance may help to increase household consumption.

Overall, we hope that these chapters add to the rich discussion underway in policy and academic circles on rebalancing growth in Asia.

REFERENCES

International Monetary Fund, 2010, *Regional Economic Outlook: Asia and Pacific—Leading the Global Recovery, and Rebalancing for the Medium Term* (Washington), April.

Park, Y., 2009, "The Global Economic Crisis and Rebalancing Growth in East Asia," Research Policy Brief No. 15 (Tokyo: Asian Development Bank Institute).

Prasad, E., 2009, "Rebalancing Growth in Asia," NBER Working Paper No. 15169 (Cambridge, Massachusetts: National Bureau of Economic Research).

Singh, A., 2010, "Asia: Leading the Way Forward," *Finance and Development,* April, pp. 5–7.

Strauss-Kahn, D., 2010, "Asia and the Global Economy: Leading the Way Forward in the 21st Century," Opening remarks at the Asia 21 Conference, Daejeon, Korea, July 12.

Zhu, M., 2010, "Interview on Asia's Economy," *Finance and Development,* April, pp. 12–13.

PART I

Rebalancing Growth in Asia: Some General Themes

CHAPTER 1

Rebalancing Growth in Asia

ADIL MOHOMMAD, PAPA N'DIAYE,
AND OLAF UNTEROBERDOERSTER

Despite the strong increase in intraregional trade over the last decade, Asia is heavily dependent on external demand—more so than other regions. In the post-crisis world, Asia will need to rely more on domestic sources of demand to sustain high growth and improve economic resilience. Rebalancing toward domestic demand in turn will require many regional economies to act across a range of areas. Some countries may need to raise consumption, others to increase investment, and many will need to boost productivity in their service sectors. Achieving all of this will require a comprehensive package of measures, including fiscal measures, reforms in product, labor, and financial markets, and more flexibility in exchange rates. A rebalancing of Asian growth toward domestic demand would contribute to rebalancing global demand, especially if it is implemented simultaneously across the region, which is now the single largest source of growth in the global economy.

INTRODUCTION

Asia and the world economy need a rebalancing of demand to return to sustained high growth (Blanchard and Milesi-Ferretti, 2009). The global financial crisis has put an end to the credit-fueled consumption boom that started in the United States and other advanced economies in the early 2000s. Lasting damage to households' and financial institutions' balance sheets, the need for sizeable fiscal consolidation in the future, and likely steps toward more stringent financial regulation all mean that domestic demand in these economies is unlikely to return to precrisis growth rates.

For Asia, weaker growth in the advanced economies would mean that an important source of external demand remains subdued. The increasing integration of trade across Asian economies over the last decade had raised hopes that Asia was becoming more resilient to advanced economies' business cycles and that regional economies could converge faster by trading more with each other. But the disproportionate response of Asia's export-dependent economies to the collapse of global demand at the end of 2008 showed that Asia's fortunes remain closely linked to the performance of the global economy and that this region, perhaps more than any other, would benefit from a global rebalancing of demand.

Against this background, this chapter addresses three main questions:

- Is Asia more dependent on external demand than other regions?
- What is needed to strengthen domestic sources of growth in Asia? Are there differences in the region?
- Which policies, both in Asia and abroad, would achieve a successful rebalancing of global demand?

To answer these questions, the chapter follows a three-step strategy. First, it quantifies Asia's growth dependence on external demand by looking at a value-added concept of trade flows—one that captures not only the direct but also the indirect trade linkages between Asian and advanced economies (such as Malaysia's export exposure to the United States through its exports of intermediate goods to China). Second, the chapter assesses whether consumption and investment in Asia are "too low" and the amount of resources employed in the tradable sector "too high" by comparing them with benchmarks, both model-based and empirical. Third, it uses the IMF's global integrated monetary and fiscal (GIMF) model to assess the impact of macroeconomic and structural policies that could be adopted in Asia and abroad to strengthen domestic sources of growth in the region.

The two main findings of the chapter are these:

- Asia depends on external demand for its growth more heavily than do other advanced economies and emerging market regions. This dependence is reflected in an unbalanced production structure that is heavily tilted toward industry and, more generally, the tradable sector. Rebalancing growth will thus also require boosting productivity in the services sector in most Asian economies. A few economies seem to have excessively low consumption-to-GDP ratios, most notably China, while several others may have room to increase their investment.
- Reforms in product, labor, and financial markets and in fiscal and exchange-rate policies could produce a successful shift in the pattern of growth. These reforms would be most effective if they were undertaken by all economies in the region. If only a few countries implemented reforms, rebalancing might still have some positive domestic and regional spillovers (especially if undertaken in larger economies such as China) but would be unlikely to compensate sufficiently for the weaker demand from advanced economies.

ASSESSING ASIA'S EXPORT DEPENDENCE

Structural changes in the nature of trade, notably the growing significance of cross-border supply-chain networks, complicate assessments of the extent to which a country's growth depends on external demand. Simple export-to-GDP ratios tend to overstate the degree of external dependence, since increasing vertical trade integration means that exports include a declining share of domestically produced value added (see for example Cui and Syed, 2007, on China). Vertical trade integration also masks the true exposure of an economy to the final source

Figure 1.1
Illustrative Example of the Effect of Vertical Integration on Trade

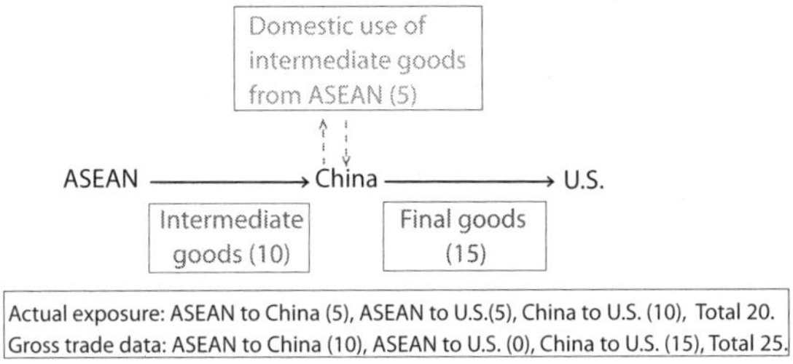

Note: Numbers in parentheses represent units of goods and are illustrative.

of demand (see the IMF's April 2008 *Regional Economic Outlook: Asia and Pacific*). For example, ASEAN economies depend on U.S. demand both through their direct exports to the United States and through their exports of intermediate goods to other countries that then re-export to the United States after processing them (Figure 1.1). To capture both direct and indirect exposure, we use Asian international input-output (AIO) tables that describe how Asian economies combine domestic and foreign inputs to produce goods. This provides a measure of the extent to which the value added that is produced in an economy can be attributed to domestic, intraregional, and extra-regional demand (see Technical Appendix for details).[1]

Using this methodology yields the following results:

- Asia's export "exposure"—defined as the share of value added linked to external demand—is high by international standards. For all Asian economies in the dataset (except Japan) it exceeds the OECD average, and for the most part this export exposure is even higher than for the highly integrated European OECD members (Figure 1.2).[2] Also noteworthy is that the gap generally has widened over time. About two-thirds of the exported value added goes to destinations outside Asia, although in some cases—such as Korea, the Philippines, and Taiwan Province of China—exposure to intra-Asian demand has increased.[3] By contrast, China's export exposure to the

[1]See also Kalra and others (2009). Input-output tables have been constructed for the years 1995–2008 based on the 2000 Asian Input Output Table provided by the Japan External Trade Organization using the methodology in Pula and Peltonen (2009).

[2]The OECD data are based on total external demand (as opposed to final external demand) for the Asian economies owing to data limitations. This makes final external demand an even more demanding benchmark.

[3]Calculations have been adjusted for Hong Kong SAR's entrepôt trade, which would otherwise lead to an overestimation of the contribution of Asian demand to value added in the region.

Figure 1.2
Share of Export Value Added in GDP, 2000 and 2005
(In percent)

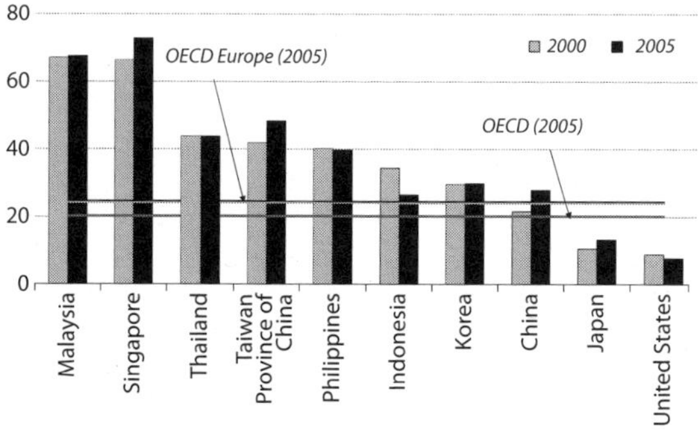

Sources: Japan External Trade Organization (JETRO), *Asian Input-Output Table* (2000); OECD; UN COMTRADE; CEIC Data Company Ltd.; and IMF staff estimates.

region has remained stable at a smaller base.[4] While India is not part of the value-added dataset used here, its low ratio of gross exports to GDP (19 percent in 2009) suggests that it is far less exposed than most of developing and emerging Asia.

- Even where export exposure is relatively low, exports are often the main engine of growth (Figure 1.3). In Japan, for example, where export exposure is only about 10 percent of value added, exports contributed about 40 percent to growth before the global recession—that is, between 2001 and 2007—when domestic demand growth was very weak relative to booming external demand (Figure 1.4). When exports are expressed on a value-added basis, their contribution to growth in Asian economies is much greater than what is suggested by the national accounts, often more than twice as high. The reason is that measures based on value added capture the share of income generated by exports. To the extent that this income is spent on imported final goods, it will reduce the contribution of net exports to the growth shown in the national accounts. Nevertheless, using the national-accounts measure as a widely recognized international benchmark, the contribution of net exports to growth across Asia has been consistently higher than in other emerging market regions, such as Latin America.

Asia's true dependence on external demand is in fact even greater than suggested by the value-added measure, for two reasons:

[4]China's exposure to external demand from outside Asia has increased from 15 percent of total value added (1995–2000 average) to over 19 percent (2001–08 average), while its exposure to demand from Asia has remained stable at about 6 percent of total value added. These trends mainly reflect China's rapid growth of exports to advanced economies as it has become a hub of the region's supply chain network.

Figure 1.3
Export Dependence and Exposure
(Average over 2001–08, in percent)

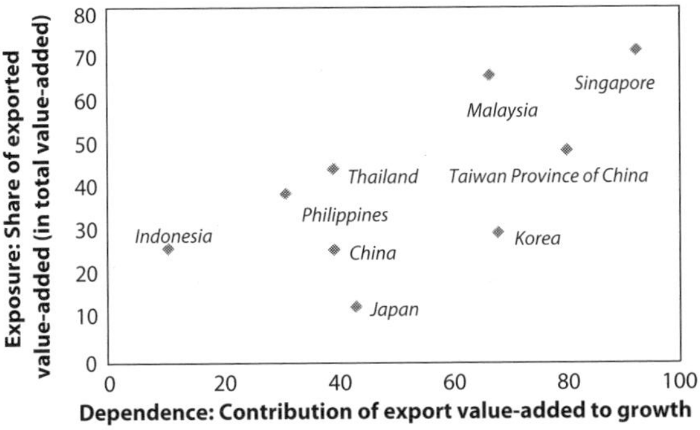

Sources: Japan External Trade Organization (JETRO), *Asian Input-Output Table* (2000); OECD; UN COMTRADE; CEIC Data Company Ltd.; Haver Analytics; and IMF staff estimates.

Figure 1.4
Average Contribution to Real GDP Growth, 2001–07[a,b]
(In percent of real GDP growth)

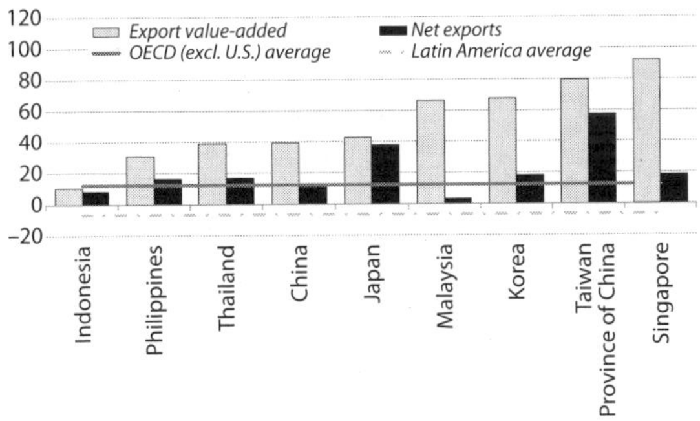

Sources: Japan External Trade Organization (JETRO), *Asian Input-Output Table* (2000); OECD; UN COMTRADE; CEIC Data Company Ltd.; Haver Analytics; and IMF staff estimates.
[a] Average of contributions to 3-year growth rates during 2001–07. Exchange rate adjusted deflator.
[b] Latin America includes Argentina, Bolivia, Brazil, Chile, Colombia, Mexico, Paraguay, Peru, Uruguay, and Venezuela.

- *Export-related investment.* Because a significant share of investment in Asia is linked to the export products, external demand also contributes to growth by affecting investment (see Guo and N'Diaye, 2009a, on China). Simple estimates based on the share of exports in manufacturing output and the share of machinery investment in total gross fixed capital formation suggest

Figure 1.5
Share of Export Value Added in GDP, 2000 and 2008
(In percent of GDP)

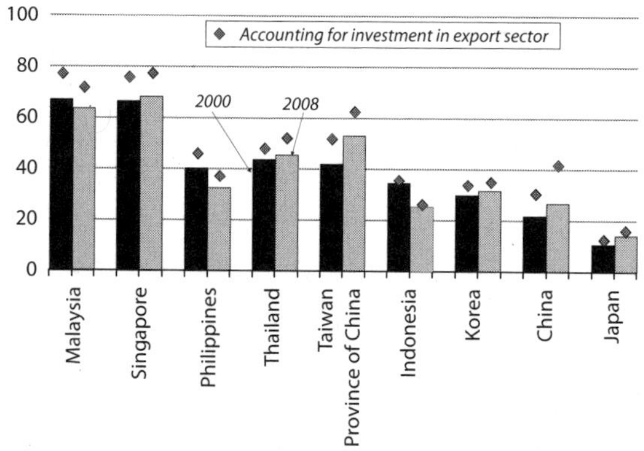

Sources: Japan External Trade Organization (JETRO), *Asian Input-Output Table* (2000); OECD; UN COMTRADE; CEIC Data Company Ltd.; Haver Analytics; and IMF staff estimates.

that about 30–40 percent of investment in Asia depends ultimately on exports. Taking this into account, our measure of external exposure increases by about 10 percentage points of GDP on average in the region, and China's export exposure rises to more than 45 percent of GDP (Figure 1.5). Thus, our measures of export dependence (reflecting the contribution of exports to growth) increase by about 5–10 percentage points on average.

- *Compositional effects.* Asia's dependence on exports is compounded by its specialization in highly cyclical manufacturing sectors—in particular information technology (IT) goods (Figure 1.6).[5] The global financial dislocation at the end of 2008 led to a collapse in demand for these goods, for which demand depends heavily on credit market conditions and consumer confidence. Over the four quarters up to 2009:Q2, U.S. imports from Asia fell about 10 times as much as U.S. consumption. Using our measures of export dependence, the fall in exports may have subtracted between ½ and 2 percentage points from GDP growth across Asian economies over that period (Figure 1.7).[6]

---

[5]For many Asian economies, the share of medium- and high-tech exports in total exports exceeds the OECD average (about 57 percent), and for all economies in our sample except Indonesia it also exceeds the average for Latin America and emerging Europe (about 45 percent). The definition of medium- and high-tech goods is based on International Standard Industrial Classification (ISIC) (Rev. 2) classifications.

[6]The estimated impact would have been even larger if the decline in U.S. import demand affected Asian imports disproportionately relative to imports from other regions (about 2–8 percentage points of GDP under the extreme assumption that it was all concentrated on imports from Asia).

Figure 1.6
Share of Medium and High-Tech Goods in Total Exports
(Average over 2000–08)

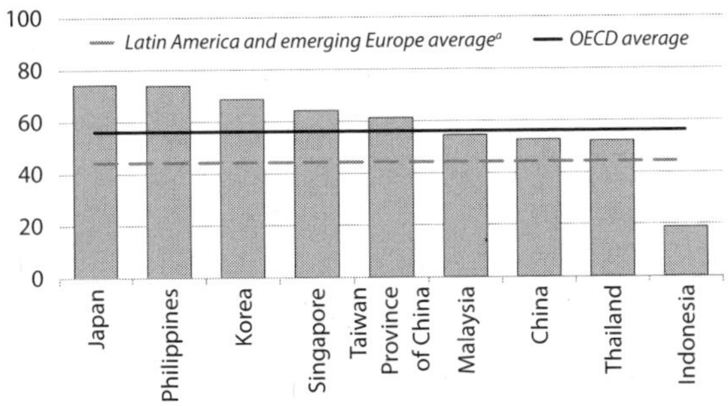

Source: UN COMTRADE database.
[a]Latin America includes Argentina, Bolivia, Brazil, Chile, Colombia, Mexico, Paraguay, Peru, Uruguay, and Venezuela. Emerging Europe includes Bulgaria, Croatia, Czech Republic, Estonia, Hungary, Latvia, Lithuania, Poland, Romania, Slovak Republic, and Slovenia.

Figure 1.7
Impact on Value Added of Actual Decline in U.S. Private Final Demand, 2008–09[a]
(In percent of GDP)

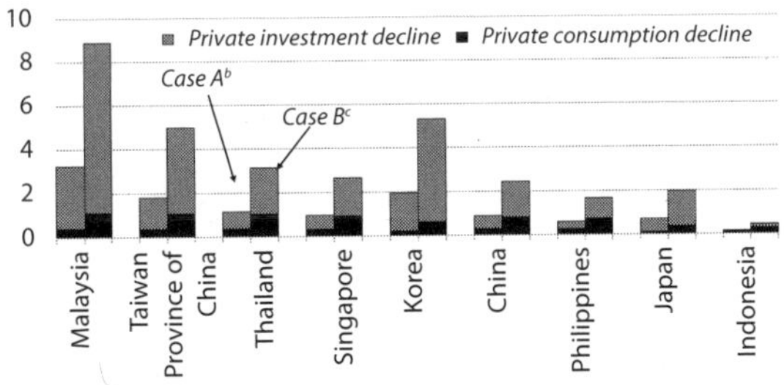

Sources: Japan External Trade Organization (JETRO), *Asian Input-Output Table* (2000); OECD; UN COMTRADE; CEIC Data Company Ltd.; Haver Analytics; and IMF staff estimates.
[a]Decline over 2008–09 in U.S. private durables expenditure, impacting imports in proportion to share of imports in durables consumption and investment in machinery and equipment.
[b]Decline in U.S. durable imports impacts U.S. imports from Asian countries in proportion to share of Asia in U.S. imports of consumer durables, and machinery and equipment respectively, based on COMTRADE data.
[c]Decline in U.S. durable imports concentrated in imports from Asian countries.

WHAT DOES REBALANCING MEAN FOR ASIAN ECONOMIES?

A different way of gauging whether Asia depends "too much" on external demand is by assessing whether its domestic consumption and investment are too low. In this section, these questions are tackled by using two different benchmarks for consumption and investment in Asia, one based on the values predicted by simple neoclassical growth models and the other based on the results of standard empirical models of investment and consumption.

Is Consumption Too Low?

Excessively weak consumption is often cited as the main driver of current account surpluses in Asia (see Bernanke, 2005). But consumption-to-GDP ratios vary substantially across Asia, ranging from less than 40 percent in China to about 70 percent in the Philippines (Figure 1.8). For many regional economies, consumption is close to OECD or other emerging market averages. This argues for some caution in a general characterization that consumption is weak in Asia. What do model-based and empirical benchmarks suggest?

- *Model-based estimates.* For a number of Asian economies, actual consumption does not appear to be out of line with our estimates of steady-state consumption levels (see Technical Appendix for details) (Figure 1.9). When compared to deviations in other emerging market economies, they tend to be within one standard deviation of the worldwide sample. There is one important exception: China's consumption stands out as relatively low—indeed, nearly two-thirds of the gross national saving of Asia (excluding Japan) in recent years is accounted for by China (Prasad, 2009).

Figure 1.8
Private Consumption
(In percent of GDP; 2004–09 average)

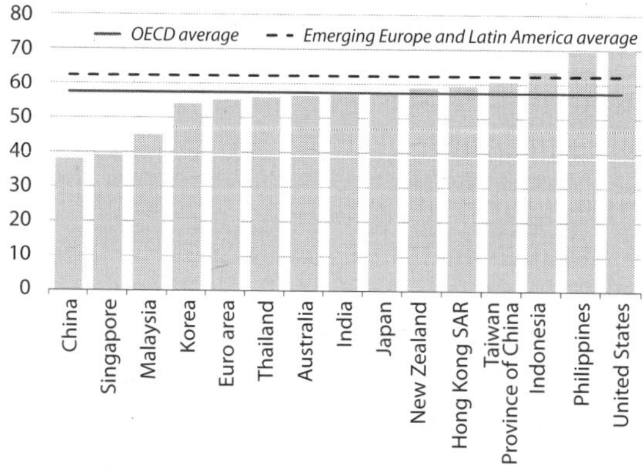

Source: IMF, WEO database.

Figure 1.9
Consumption Relative to Steady-State, 2004–08[a]
(In percent of GDP)

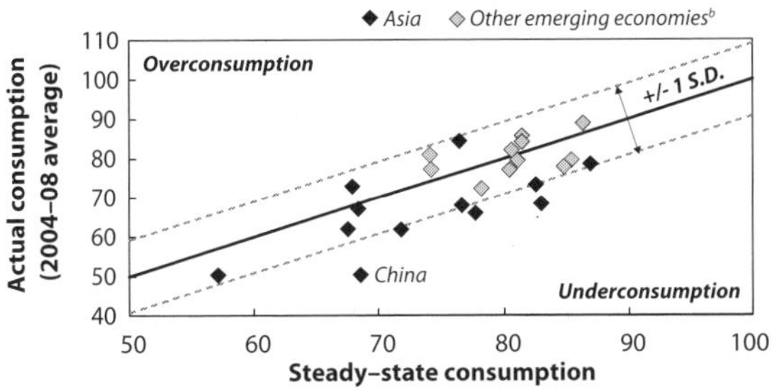

Source: IMF staff estimates.
[a]Uses savings-investment balance in the IMF CGER's Macroeconomic Balance approach.
[b]Other emerging economies include Argentina, Brazil, Chile, Colombia, Egypt, Israel, Mexico, Morocco, Pakistan, Peru, South Africa, and Turkey.

Figure 1.10
Cumulative Change in Ratio of Private Consumption-to-GDP (2000–07): Estimated Contribution of Disposable Income and Saving Rate
(In percent of GDP)

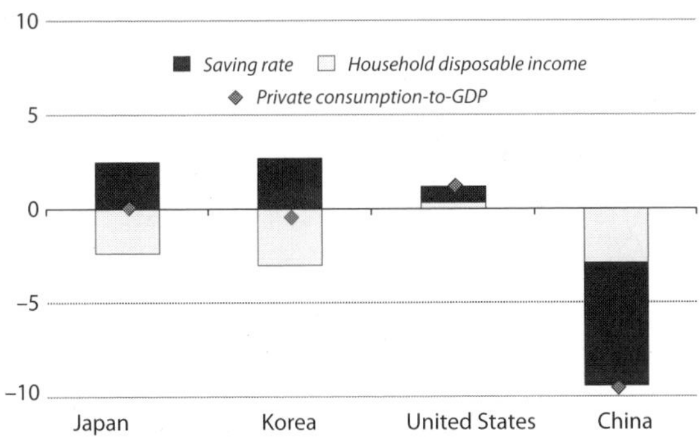

Source: Guo and N'Diaye (2010).

- *Empirical benchmarks.* Cross-country evidence from a structural consumption equation (see Chapter 6) suggests that the low consumption-to-GDP ratio in China has relatively little to do with country-specific behavioral factors. Instead, it can largely be explained by the low and declining share of household disposable income and a rising saving rate (Figure 1.10). The share of household disposable income in GDP also fell in Japan and Korea between 2000 and 2007, but households there responded by maintaining

Figure 1.11
Investment
(In percent of GDP, 2004–09 average)

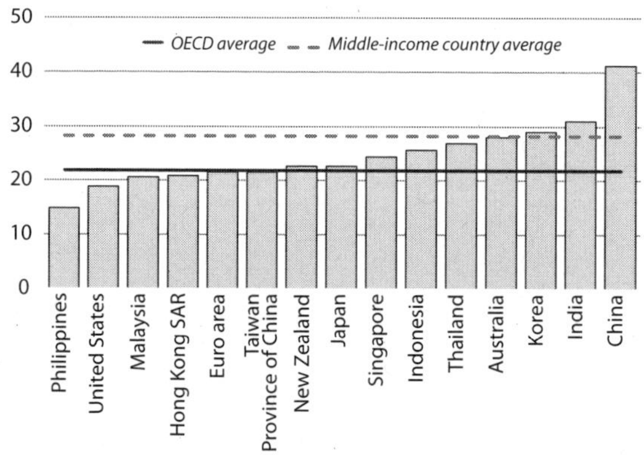

Sources: World Bank, *World Development Indicators*; and IMF, WEO database.

consumption and lowering their saving rates.[7] The high household saving rate in China in part reflects the need for precautionary saving to offset the lack of social safety nets and services and demographic factors like gender imbalances.[8] Limited access to financial services, including consumer credit and housing finance, may also have played a role. As discussed in Chapter 7, reforms that improve social insurance and services, notably healthcare coverage, could prove effective in boosting consumption in China. Measures that improve access to financial services, such as Korea's efforts to develop a mortgage market, also hold the promise of strengthening private consumption.

Is Investment Too Low?

Asia's high current account surplus may also be the result of an investment slump. In emerging Asia, investment-to-GDP ratios collapsed by about 10 percentage points of GDP immediately following the 1997–98 Asian crisis and have remained low (especially for economies hit most severely by the crisis), but saving remained broadly stable (see Chapter 8). While part of the decline can be attributed to overinvestment in the years leading up to the crisis, there are large differences in investment-to-GDP ratios across the region, suggesting caution against generalizations (Figure 1.11).[9] Except for Malaysia and the Philippines, most emerging Asian

[7]The declining share of household disposable income across Asia has been mirrored by rising corporate profitability and saving. This was analyzed in the IMF's October 2009 *Regional Economic Outlook: Asia and Pacific*.

[8]See for example Blanchard and Giavazzi (2005), Kuijs (2005), Chamon and Prasad (2010), and Wei and Zhang (2009).

[9]Eichengreen (2006), Hori (2007), and Guimaraes and Unteroberdoerster (2006).

economies have overall investment ratios that are higher than the OECD average and closer to the average for middle-income countries, consistent with their lower stage of development. For industrialized Asian economies, the investment ratio is close to the OECD average (about 20–25 percent), except for Korea where it is higher. In economies hit by the Asian financial crisis, the collapse of investment was mainly due to private investment; public investment, by contrast, rose after the crisis (notably for Korea, Malaysia, and Thailand), reflecting programs to upgrade infrastructure and partly offset the fall in private investment.

- *Model-based estimates.* In countries where the capital-output ratio is below its long-run level, investment rates should be above their long-run level since these countries are catching up with their trend levels. If they fail to do so, then investment rates are deemed "too low" and these countries can be said to have "underinvestment" (Figure 1.12). Based on our estimates of steady-state levels of capital and investment ratios for about 30 mainly emerging economies, some ASEAN economies (with the exception of Indonesia) moved deeper into the underinvestment quadrant in recent years (see Technical Appendix for details). By contrast, China and India are farthest out in the overinvestment quadrant. These model-based estimates should be treated with caution, however, because they do not reflect structural changes, such as a shift away from growth that is intensive in capital, infrastructure, or residential investment.[10]

Figure 1.12
Capital-to-Output and Investment-to-Output Ratio Relative to Steady-State Level in 2008
(Relative to steady-state level in 2008)

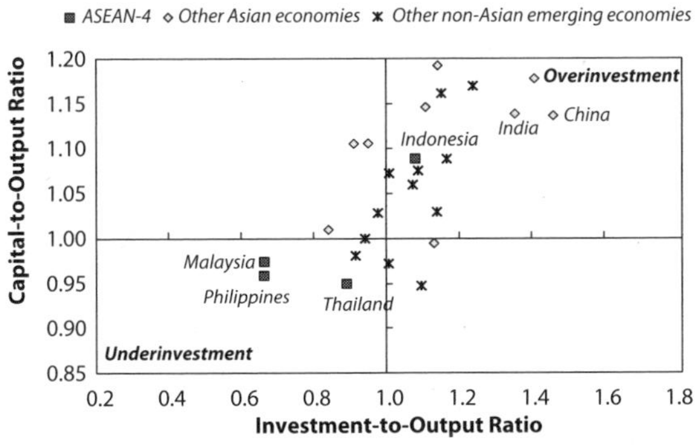

Sources: Penn World Tables; IMF, WEO database and staff calculations.

[10]Moreover, they do not control for changes in the efficiency of investment over time, although the fact that they are robust to a range of depreciation rates may in part address this issue. Excluding the Asian-crisis period, incremental capital-output ratios have remained relatively stable, averaging about 4.5 in the 1980s for emerging economies in Southeast Asia compared to 4 in the 2000s, suggesting that aggregate efficiency has also remained broadly stable.

Figure 1.13
Model-Based Determinants of Deviation of Investment-to-GDP Ratio from Sample Mean
(In percentage points from sample mean, 1980–2008)

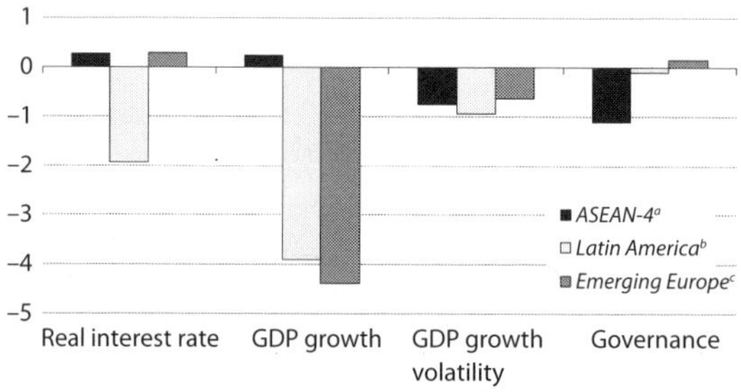

Source: IMF staff estimates.
[a]ASEAN-4 includes Indonesia, Malaysia, Philippines, and Thailand.
[b]Latin America includes Argentina, Brazil, Chile, Colombia, Mexico, and Uruguay.
[c]Emerging Europe includes Bulgaria, Croatia, Czech Republic, Estonia, Hungary, Latvia, Lithuania, Poland, Romania, Serbia, Slovak Republic, and Slovenia.

- *Empirical benchmarks.* Estimates based on an empirical model of investment suggest that weaknesses in the investment climate, notably governance, and macroeconomic uncertainty hinder private investment in the region, particularly among the ASEAN-4 economies (Figure 1.13).[11] Efforts to improve the business climate—including strengthening the rule of law, creditor rights, and transparency of government operations; reforms that facilitate access to finance; and efforts to level the playing field between foreign and domestic or private and public investors—have all been on the reform agenda (see Chapter 8) in many economies in the region as a way to boost both domestic and foreign investment. Yet, despite progress, investor perceptions seem to improve only slowly (see also Hori, 2008, and the IMF's May 2006 *Regional Economic Outlook: Asia and Pacific*).

In contrast, already high levels of investment in China and India present different challenges. China's unusually low level of consumption as a share of GDP and dependence on external demand point to a need to shift the composition of investment away from manufacturing and export industries and toward social and consumer sectors in order to reorient growth toward consumption. On the other hand, India, whose level of overall investment is between that of China and the ASEAN-4 and whose demand is already relatively well balanced between external

[11]This is indicated, for example, in an indicator for governance from the *International Country Risk Guide*, which largely reflects investor perceptions of corruption in the public and private sectors. As such, a worsening investment climate does not necessarily reflect an actual deterioration, but could also just reflect worsening investor perceptions triggered by severe economic shocks, like the Asian financial crisis.

and domestic sources, would benefit from financial reforms and fiscal consolidation to catalyze private sector participation in infrastructure investment.

ARE THERE ANY SUPPLY-SIDE IMBALANCES?

The supply-side counterpart of high dependence on external demand tends to be reflected in an overreliance on the tradable sector. For example, at about 50 percent, China's share of industry in GDP is nearly twice as high as the OECD average and more than 10 percentage points above the world average for low- and middle-income countries (Figure 1.14). ASEAN economies, Japan, and Korea also have a relatively high share of industry in GDP. As a mirror image, the share of services in GDP is generally lower in Asia, with the notable exception of India. Regression estimates confirm that the share of industry in GDP is above the "norm" in China and the ASEAN-4 economies (Figure 1.15). Similar results are obtained when looking at employment shares, broadly confirming the over- (under-) exposure of Asian economies to industry (services).

Industry and services broadly reflect the tradable and nontradable sectors, respectively. Service sector productivity has generally been low in Asia, and productivity growth in this sector has stagnated relative to the U.S. (Figure 1.16). According to empirical studies, deregulation and further opening to foreign competition would help in unlocking the services sector's growth potential (Nicoletti and Scarpetta, 2003; Conway and others, 2006). Indeed, in many regional economies policy efforts have already been directed at allowing greater competition in infrastructure-related services, further opening the retail and

Figure 1.14
Excess Share of Industry in GDP, 2000 and 2008[a]
(In percentage points; country industry share minus industry share of peer group)

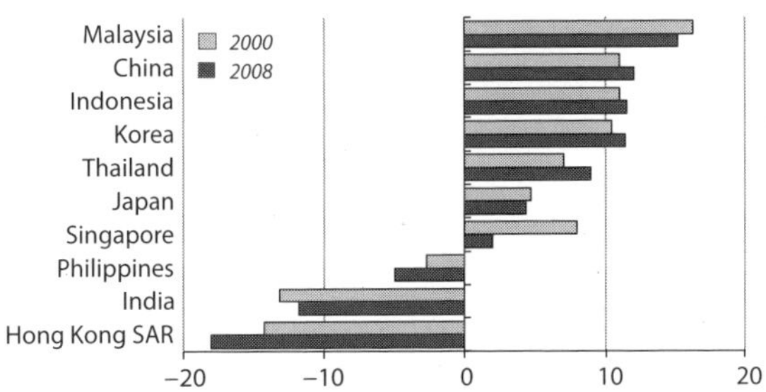

Sources: World Bank, *World Development Indicators*; and IMF staff calculations.
[a]Peer-group definitions are based on World Development Indicators. Countries were assigned the following peer-groups: Hong Kong SAR, Japan, Korea, and Singapore (OECD); China, Indonesia, the Philippines, and Thailand (low- and middle-income countries); India (lower-middle-income countries); and Malaysia (upper-middle-income countries).

Figure 1.15
Model-Based Excess Share of Industry in GDP, 2000 and 2008[a]
(In percentage points)

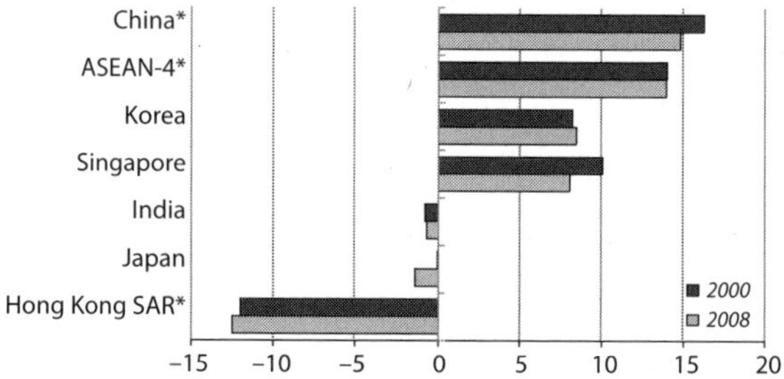

Source: IMF staff estimates.
[a]Estimated by country-specific dummy variable. Explanatory variables for industry share include per-capita income (PPP), population and geographic size. An asterisk mark next to the economies indicates statistical significance at the 5 percent level.

Figure 1.16
Asia: Productivity Levels, 1987–2008
(Relative to the United States)

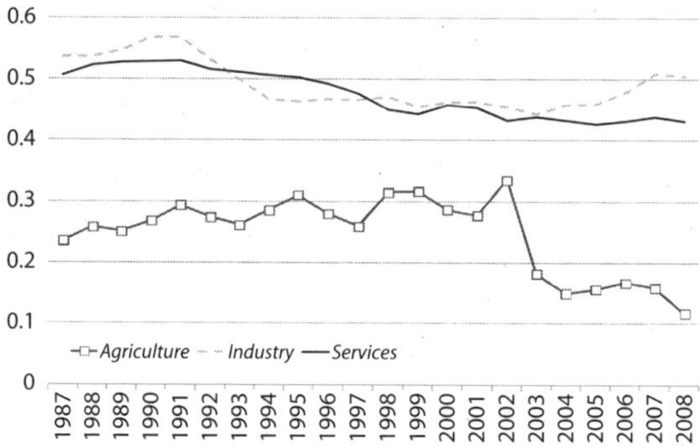

Sources: World Bank, *World Development Indicators*; and IMF staff estimates.

financial sectors, and lifting restrictions on entry into social services such as health and education.

India's vibrant services sector is an interesting counterpoint. In India, the services sector has been among the economy's most dynamic, in part reflecting higher productivity growth. India's services sector has led GDP growth for the last two decades. Yet formal employment has grown slower than in countries with growth led by manufactured exports. A broadening of infrastructure investment to improve connectivity to markets and liberalization of labor laws and other regulation would raise the prospects for growth in industry and agriculture, which are traditionally more labor-intensive.

IMPACT OF REBALANCING: ILLUSTRATIVE MODEL SIMULATIONS

How much can policies across the region contribute to sustained growth and what are the spillovers? This section uses multicountry simulations, based on the IMF's GIMF model, to help illustrate how successful implementation of structural and macroeconomic policies across the region could boost domestic sources of growth and bring about rebalancing. The set of policies considered here (see Box 1.1) ranges from structural reforms to boost productivity and thereby raise investment in the nontradable sector, to financial sector and fiscal policies that would help to reduce incentives for precautionary saving, to moves in the real effective exchange rate (REER). The combination of policies across economies in the region is guided by evidence on imbalances in demand and in resource allocation presented in the previous section. The policies are also generally consistent with medium-term reform plans being implemented or envisaged by authorities in the selected economies.

Main Scenario: Simultaneous Rebalancing by All Economies

The central scenario considered is one where Asia successfully rebalances in the face of weak demand from the United States. This scenario envisages an increase in the private U.S. saving rate of 2½ percent of GDP above the baseline and a protracted decline in private investment. This is combined with a fully fledged rebalancing scenario in Asian economies, in which all policy measures are simultaneously implemented across Asian economies to boost domestic demand and productivity in the services sector. As most reforms and their benefits will take time to materialize, this section focuses on their medium- to long-term impact.[12]

- Output rises in all Asian economies relative to baseline projections, reflecting the implementation of structural reforms and positive spillovers throughout the region and the rest of the world (Figure 1.17). U.S. output would still fall below the baseline, but the decline would be less than without rebalancing efforts in Asia. For example, GIMF model simulations by Blanchard and Milesi-Ferretti (2009) show that rebalancing efforts in emerging Asia (involving lower saving and a more flexible exchange-rate regime) would boost U.S. output by about 1 percent over a scenario without rebalancing.[13]

[12]However, rebalancing growth could entail short-term costs, including lower employment, which in turn depend on the degree of labor market flexibility and on policies put in place to smooth the transition (IMF *World Economic Outlook* (April 2010); Guo and N'Diaye, 2009b).

[13]According to these simulations, U.S. output after three years would remain about 2 percent below the baseline if rebalancing of global demand were to focus only on emerging Asia (and about 3 percent below the baseline with no rebalancing efforts in Asia).

BOX 1.1

The Asia GIMF Model and Policy Assumptions

The GIMF model used in this chapter includes eight regions: five Asian blocks (China, emerging Asia, Japan, Korea, and Australia and New Zealand), the United States, the Euro area, and the rest of the world.[a] Consistent with the opening section of this chapter, the model also incorporates several layers of production, distinguishing between manufacturing of intermediate goods, distribution of intermediate goods to domestic and foreign assemblers, and final production of consumption and investment goods. It thus captures a more comprehensive transmission (both direct and indirect) of external shocks and spillover effects from rebalancing.

Policy assumptions for rebalancing efforts of Asian economies in the main scenario are as follows:

- In China, the package of reforms assumed is similar to the one envisaged in N'Diaye, Zhang, and Zhang (2008) and includes (i) structural reforms in the services sector that raise productivity (e.g., enhanced competition between domestic and foreign firms, liberalization of retail services) accompanied by a shift in households' preference toward nontradable goods; (ii) fiscal reform aimed at reducing precautionary saving by increasing coverage of education, healthcare, and pensions and improving infrastructure in rural areas; (iii) further financial development and liberalization (including interest rates) to enable better smoothing of household consumption, capital allocation, and improved risk management by banks; and (iv) a gradual real effective appreciation of the renminbi—20 percent over 10 years for illustrative purposes—that supports the transition to greater reliance on the nontradable sector and stimulates private consumption by raising labor's share of income.
- In Japan, the reform package is geared toward improving productivity in the services sector (by ½ percentage point per year over five years), liberalizing labor and product markets, and putting public finances on a more sustainable path. Fiscal consolidation aims at lowering the fiscal deficit by 5 percent of GDP over five years (similar to the consolidation during 2002–07, albeit a period characterized by healthy growth), with half the burden falling on tax increases and the other half on expenditure cuts. The rise in taxes is achieved solely through a gradual hike in the consumption tax rate.
- In Korea and emerging Asia, structural reforms aim at raising productivity in the services sector by encouraging greater competition and leveling the playing field between the tradable and nontradable sectors, as well as enhancing flexibility in labor and product markets and further developing domestic capital markets, including reducing credit constraints for households.

---

[a] The emerging Asia group comprises Hong Kong SAR, Indonesia, Malaysia, the Philippines, Singapore, and Thailand.

Figure 1.17
Output (Main Scenario Projections)
(Deviation from baseline; in percent)

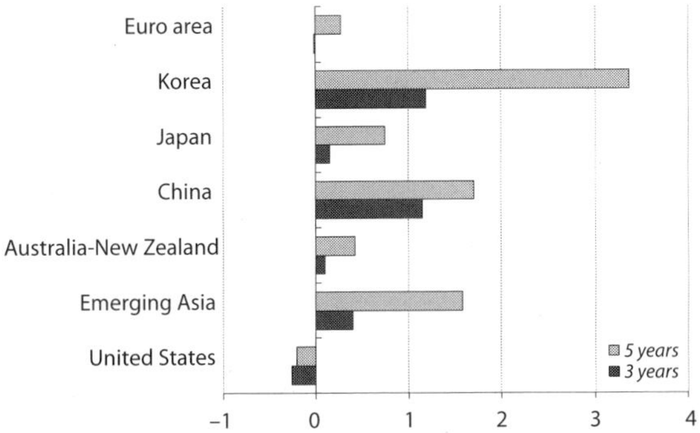

Source: IMF staff estimates.

Figure 1.18
Investment-to-GDP Ratio (Main Scenario Projections)
(Deviation from baseline; in percentage points)

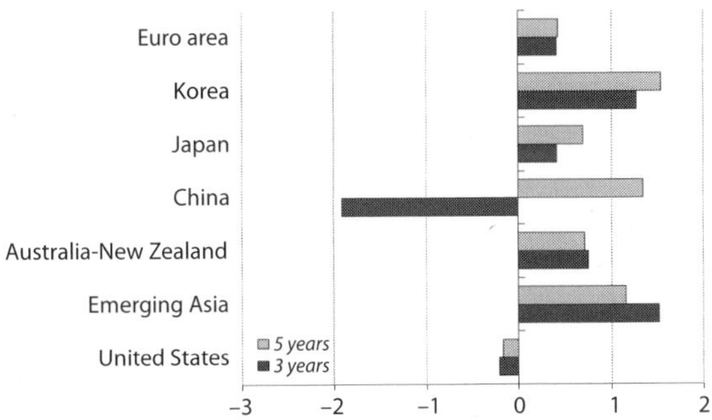

Source: IMF staff estimates.

- Investment rises relative to GDP in all economies in the short and medium term, except in China (Figure 1.18). The rise is primarily in the nontradable sector, as structural reforms lift productivity. In China, while firms in the nontradable sector invest more, those in the tradable sector invest less as the cost of capital increases and the exchange rate appreciates. The fall in investment in the tradable sector dominates initially. Over time, aggregate investment rises as firms' investment in the nontradable sector increases to meet growing demand.
- Private consumption-to-GDP ratios rise in Australia, China, emerging Asia, and New Zealand (Figure 1.19). The higher share of private consumption reflects financial sector reforms that result in better access to finance and

Figure 1.19
Consumption-to-GDP Ratio (Main Scenario Projections)
(Deviation from baseline; in percentage points)

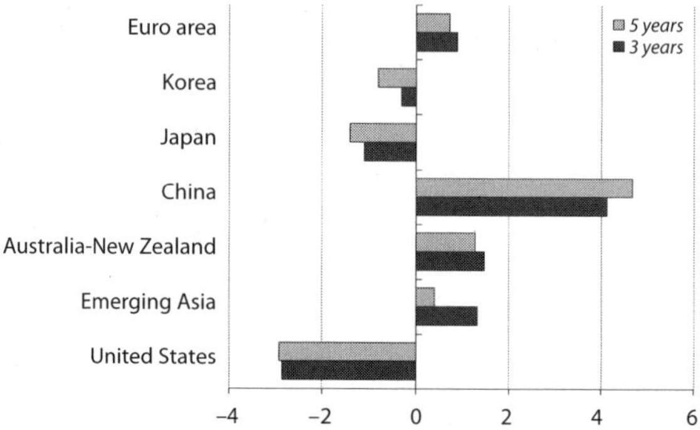

Source: IMF staff estimates.

reduced precautionary saving, higher labor income, and wealth effects from lower payments on foreign liabilities. In Australia and New Zealand, lower payments are enabled by lower interest rates and some currency appreciation.[14] Consumption relative to GDP falls in Japan and Korea but for different reasons, at least in the short-to-medium term. In Japan, the projected increase in the consumption tax rate to reduce the level of public debt dampens consumption initially, despite the positive impact of fiscal consolidation on risk premiums and the lowering of precautionary saving that results from such a consolidation. Consumption rises in the longer term as the benefits of structural reforms are felt and the tightening fiscal stance ends. In Korea, the fall in the consumption-to-GDP ratio reflects the fact that reforms mostly stimulate investment and that GDP rises faster than private consumption.

- Rebalancing Asia's growth would also lower global imbalances. Current account balances would be lower in most Asian economies, owing to stronger domestic demand, lower export demand from the United States, and an appreciating currency (Figure 1.20). In the short run, lower current account balances reflect lower exports and higher imports relative to the baseline, while in the long run, stronger import demand from China raises exports in Japan, Korea, and emerging Asia (Figures 1.21 and 1.22). Economies that benefit most from stronger demand from China are those whose production structure is ready to produce the final consumption goods that China will demand. Korea is a notable example.
- For India, spillovers from rebalancing in Asia would be relatively limited. As noted in the opening section of this chapter, India is much less export

[14]The valuation effects from currency changes may be overstated in the case of Australia and New Zealand because most banks' foreign liabilities are hedged.

Figure 1.20
Current Account Balance-to-GDP Ratio (Main Scenario Projections)
(Deviation from baseline; in percentage points)

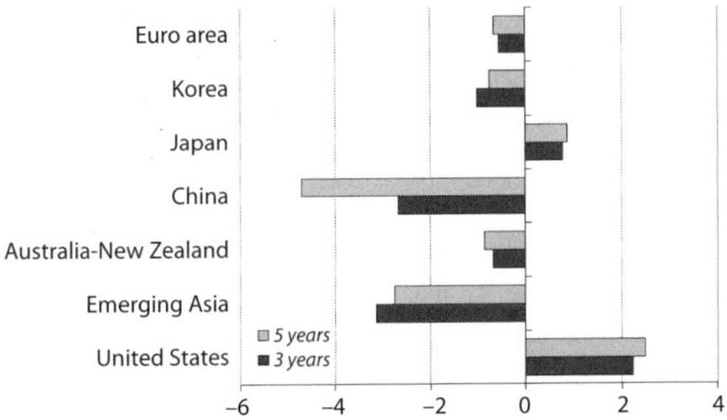

Source: IMF staff estimates.

Figure 1.21
Exports (Main Scenario Projections)
(Deviation from baseline; in percent)

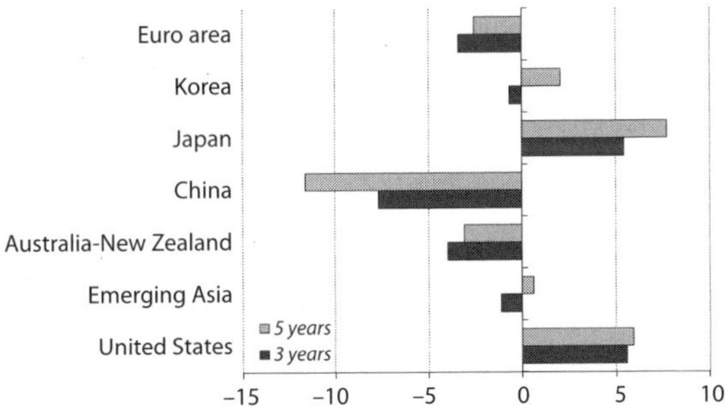

Source: IMF staff estimates.

dependent than the rest of Asia and thus would benefit less from strengthening domestic demand in the region. Moreover, India is less integrated with Asian trading partners. For example, the combined share of China, Japan, and Korea in India's capital and consumer goods exports is only about 2–3 percent, 5 to 10 times less than the respective shares for the United States. Spillovers from India's rebalancing to other Asian economies are also likely to be limited. India's growth is already reliant on domestic drivers, and rebalancing will not entail as much of a shift from external to domestic sources of growth as it will a focus on addressing structural bottlenecks like infrastructure. Improving connectivity to domestic and foreign markets

Figure 1.22
Imports (Main Scenario Projections)
(Deviation from baseline; in percent)

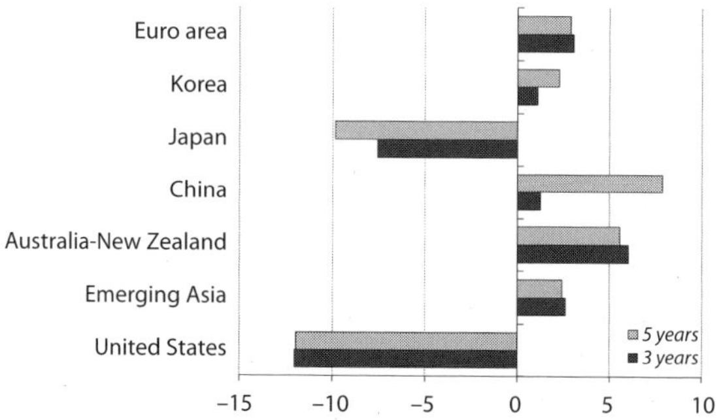

Source: IMF staff estimates.

would help redress India's overreliance on services and boost overall employment through better prospects for labor-intensive industry and agriculture. For other Asian economies, spillovers from the likely rise in capital goods imports would be limited, as India is only a marginal buyer on the world stage, accounting for 2 percent or less of their capital goods exports.

Alternative Scenarios: Partial Rebalancing

Rebalancing in some individual economies alone will have positive spillovers to other Asian economies, but it will not fully offset the lack of external demand. We focus on China, which has often been at the center of the debate on Asia's contribution to global rebalancing of demand. This may reflect, in addition to the large size of its current account surplus, at least two factors: first, the scope for boosting China's low consumption rate appears large by international standards (as shown in the third section of this chapter, "What Does Rebalancing Mean for Asian Economies?"); second, China's economic dynamism, including the fact that China has recorded very high import growth rates for consumer goods—about 15 percent per year over the last 15 years, compared with the world average of 10 percent.

Nevertheless, rebalancing growth in China alone will not fully offset the lack of external demand. For example, the negative impact on Asian exports of a rise in the saving ratio in the United States would not be offset by an equal decrease of that ratio in China. Positive spillovers to the region from greater Chinese demand would at best mitigate one-third of the adverse shock (see also the IMF's October 2009 *Regional Economic Outlook: Asia and Pacific*). One important reason is that, despite high growth, China has remained a marginal importer of consumer goods—accounting for only 3 percent of global imports—while the United States still dominates global imports, in terms of both direct and indirect trade linkages. Moreover, countries in the region, especially those that currently cater predominantly to demand in advanced economies, would need to adapt their production lines to the new Chinese demand for final goods.[15]

A faster appreciation of the renminbi than that considered in our central scenario would have only limited additional positive spillovers for trading partners, including the United States. A scenario analysis that adds increased exchange rate flexibility (with a 10 percent real effective appreciation of the renminbi over two years followed by a floating exchange rate) to the main scenario presented above, without accelerated reforms by China and other countries, shows that China's current account would only be lowered by an additional ¾ percent of GDP relative to the central scenario, while the U.S. current account would improve by ¼ percent of GDP. The ultimate impact on growth in China and elsewhere depends on how fast private consumption can be catalyzed. Exchange rate appreciation would help support private consumption by raising the labor share of income, but structural rigidities could slow the transition toward a more balanced economy.

CONCLUSION

How can Asia achieve a successful rebalancing? Asia's growth has depended heavily on external demand, according to various measures and by international comparison. This dependence has led to an unbalanced production structure, leaving the nontradable sector relatively underdeveloped. From the domestic demand side, ways to make growth more resilient are varied; a few economies need to raise private consumption and several need to promote investment.

Simultaneous implementation across the region of a package of measures, including a combination of reforms in product and labor markets, fiscal and exchange rate policies, and financial markets (where measures to improve access to finance are complemented by prudential policies to avoid excessive risk taking) has the potential to bring about a successful shift in the pattern of growth. When implemented on a stand-alone basis by individual economies, including China, rebalancing efforts will help increase growth in Asia but will not be sufficient to fill the void created by weaker external demand from advanced economies. In fact, the global slump has motivated a rethink of development strategy beyond the cyclical recovery across the region. In Singapore, for example, a high-level Economic Strategies Committee chaired by the minister of finance has laid out recommendations to make long-term growth sustained and inclusive. Singapore's 2010 budget implements some of these recommendations through measures to boost productivity growth and the role of domestic workers in the economy. In Malaysia, the government has unveiled a New Economic Model with an ambitious reform agenda to revitalize the economy by addressing long-standing structural and fiscal weaknesses. If implemented, Malaysia's plan could double its per-capita income in a decade.

[15]As measured by an import similarity index of more than 300 types of consumer goods, the consumer goods basket imported by China overlaps with that of other advanced economies by only about 35 percent.

TECHNICAL APPENDIX

Asian Input-Output (AIO) Tables

Updating the AIO 2000 Table and Data Sources

Our updating procedure follows Pula and Peltonen (2009). The AIO table is divided into three blocks: Intermediate demand (A), Final demand (F), and Exports (L), as shown below:

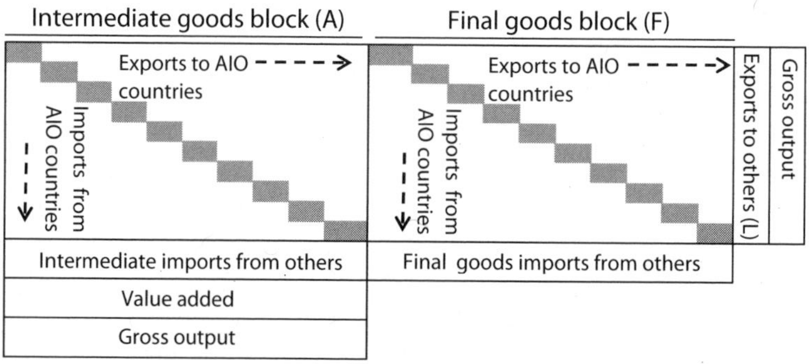

The elements in each of these blocks are updated as follows:

INTERMEDIATE DEMAND BLOCK (A)

- Value added (V^j_{t+1}): Growth rates of value added are calculated from National Accounts data for each country (data from CEIC Data Company Limited).
- Total output (X^j_{t+1}): Since total output data for the AIO countries is not available except for 2000 (with the exception of the United States), the ratio of output to value added in the manufacturing sector of each country is used as a proxy to estimate total output from GDP figures. Data on manufacturing value added come from National Accounts data, while data on manufacturing output are based on industrial production data (both from the CEIC database).
- Imported inputs ($A^{i,j}_{t+1}$): For imported intermediate inputs, we use two data sources. National Accounts data on imports were used to estimate the growth rate of overall imports, including goods and services. In order to capture changes in the direction of trade, we used COMTRADE data for intermediate goods. Since COMTRADE only covers merchandise trade, we assume that the changes in imports by direction and type are similar for goods and services. Let i and j stand for country of source and country of demand, respectively. Then

$$\text{int}\,M^{*ij}_{t+1} / \text{int}\,M^{*ij}_{t} = (M^{NA}_{t+1} / M^{NA}_{t}) * \frac{(\text{int}\,M^{COMij}_{t+1} / \text{int}\,M^{COMij}_{t})}{(M^{COM}_{t+1} / M^{COM}_{t})}, \qquad (1)$$

where *int* stands for intermediate, M for imports, and NA and COM for National Accounts and COMTRADE, respectively. The figures for 2000 are incremented by the growth rate of total imports, weighted by the change in the share of bilateral intermediate imports in total goods imports of country j.

- Freight, insurance, and import duties $(BA^{j}_{t+1}, DA^{j}_{t+1})$: Assuming the share of these items in total imports remains unchanged, the growth rates are set equal to the growth rate of total imports from National Accounts.
- Domestic intermediate inputs (A^{jj}_{t+1}): This is estimated as the residual, equal to total imports less total imported inputs, that is

$$A^{jj}_{t+1} = X^{j}_{t+1} - V^{j}_{t+1} - BA^{j}_{t+1} - DA^{j}_{t+1} - \sum_{i=1}^{n} A^{ij}_{t+1} \tag{2}$$

Final Demand Block (F)

The updating procedure for this block is similar to that described above. Final demand is updated separately for consumption and investment demand, as follows:

- Consumption and investment $(C^{ij}_{t+1}, I^{ij}_{t+1})$: National Accounts data are used to update these series. Consumption is taken as the sum of private and government consumption expenditure, while investment is defined as the sum of gross fixed investment and inventories.
- Imported final goods and investment goods $(cF^{ij}_{t=1}, iF^{ij}_{t=1})$: growth rates are calculated as follows:

$$cM^{*ij}_{t+1} / cM^{*ij}_{t} = (M^{NA}_{t+1} / M^{NA}_{t}) * \frac{(cM^{COMij}_{t+1} / cM^{COMij}_{t})}{(M^{COM}_{t+1} / M^{COM}_{t})}, \tag{3}$$

and

$$capM^{*ij}_{t+1} / capM^{*ij}_{t} = (M^{NA}_{t+1} / M^{NA}_{t}) * \frac{(capM^{COMij}_{t+1} / capM^{COMij}_{t})}{(M^{COM}_{t+1} / M^{COM}_{t})} \tag{4}$$

where c stands for consumption and cap for capital goods.

- Freight and insurance, and import duties $(cBF^{j}_{t+1}, iBF^{j}_{t+1}, cDA^{j}_{t+1}, iDA^{j}_{t+1})$: Same procedure as used for the intermediate block.
- Domestically produced final goods $(cF^{jj}_{t+1}, iF^{jj}_{t+1})$: This is the residual, estimated as total final consumption less sum of imported final goods, for each type of good.

Export Block (L)

Exports to Hong Kong SAR, EU-15, and rest of the world (RoW) $(L^{iH}_{t+1}, L^{iO}_{t+1}, L^{iW}_{t+1})$ are calculated in a similar manner, using both National Accounts and COMTRADE data. The formula is as follows:

$$(EX^{*ij}_{t+1} / EX^{*ij}_{t}) = (EX^{NA}_{t+1} / EX^{NA}_{t}) * \frac{(EX^{COMij}_{t+1} / EX^{COMij}_{t})}{(EX^{COM}_{t+1} / EX^{COM}_{t})}, \tag{5}$$

where $j = H, O, W$

Tracing Value Added to Domestic, Intraregional, and Extra-Regional Demand

Our exercise requires calculating the Leontief inverse matrix, as follows. From the supply side, the basic input-output equation can be written as $AX + Y = X$ where A is the matrix of input coefficients ($a_{ij} = \frac{A^{ij}}{X^j}$), I is the total output vector, and Y is the matrix of final demands. Rearranging this equation yields $X = (I - A)^{-1} Y = BY$, where B is the Leontief inverse matrix. Each element bij of B measures the units of output of country i required for 1 unit of final demand in country j.

For any final demand vector (or matrix) f^j the impact of fj on total output is given by $IF_X^j = Bf^j$.

The impact on value added is $IF_V^j = \hat{\upsilon} * Bf^j$, where $\hat{\upsilon}$ is a diagonal matrix consisting of the ratio of value added to gross output in each country.

The contribution ratio of final demand in country j to the value added in country i is given by $CR^{ij} = 100 * (IF_V^{ij} / \sum_{j=1}^{J} IF_V^{ij})$, where J is the number of final demand vectors.

Adjusting for Hong Kong SAR's Entrepôt Trade

Re-exports account for a high proportion of Hong Kong SAR exports (97 percent). If not accounted for, this will lead to an overestimate of the contribution of Hong Kong SAR final demand to value added in the AIO countries. To adjust for this, a part of the unadjusted contribution of exports to Hong Kong SAR to value added is reassigned to other countries and regions as follows:

$$CR_{t,HK}^{ij} = CR_t^{ij} + \mu_t^{Hi} * \lambda_t^{H} * CR_t^{iH}, \tag{6}$$

where $CR_{t,HK}^{ij}$ is the adjusted contribution ratio of exports to j in the value added of country i, CR_t^{ij} is the unadjusted ratio, μ is the ratio of Hong Kong SAR exports to country i in total Hong Kong SAR exports, λ is the ratio of Hong Kong SAR re-exports to total Hong Kong SAR exports in year t, and CR_t^{iH} is the unadjusted contribution ratio of Hong Kong SAR.

Steady-State Investment

We follow the approach set out in the IMF's September 2005 *World Economic Outlook*, Box 2.4 ("Is Investment in Emerging Asia Too Low?").

In a neoclassical growth model, the steady-state level of investment (i^*) is given by $i^* = k^*(g + d)/(1 + g)$, based on estimates of a steady-state capital-output ratio (k^*), the depreciation rate (d), and the rate of potential output growth (g).

The stock of capital is derived from the standard perpetual inventory method. Data on gross fixed real investment during 1950–80 are obtained from *Penn World Tables* and from 1980 onwards from the IMF's *World Economic Outlook*.

For a given depreciation rate, k^* is found as the maximum value of the capital-output ratio on average over long (15- and 20-year) periods between 1950 and

2008. This helps ensure robustness, particularly vis-à-vis boom and bust periods such as the Asian financial crisis.

Results reported here are the averages for two models, one with a depreciation rate of 5 percent and the other with a rate of 7 percent.

The rate for potential output growth is consistent with medium-term IMF *World Economic Outlook* projections.

Steady-State Consumption

Levels for steady-state consumption are derived from those for steady-state investment (see above) and country-specific saving-investment norms, exploiting the National Accounts identity for open economies: $Y^* - (S - I)^* - I^* = C^*$, with Y representing income, S saving, I investment, and C consumption.

The saving-investment norms $(S - I)^*$ are based on staff estimates using the IMF's Consultative Group on Exchange Rates' (CGER) macroeconomic balance approach. These are structural current account balances based on panel regression estimates that reflect country characteristics, such as level of development and demographic factors, and abstract from cyclical variations in current account balances.

REFERENCES

Bernanke, 2005, "The Global Saving Glut and the U.S. Current Account Deficit," Remarks by Governor Ben S. Bernanke at the Sandridge Lecture, Virginia Association of Economics, Richmond, Virgina (March 10).

Blanchard, O., and F. Giavazzi, 2005, "Rebalancing Growth in China: A Three Handed Approach," CEPR Discussion Paper No. 5403 (London: Centre for Economic Policy Research).

Blanchard, O., and Gian Maria Milesi-Ferretti, 2009, "Global Imbalances: In Midstream?" IMF Staff Position Note No. 09/29 (Washington: International Monetary Fund).

Chamon, M., and E. Prasad, 2010, "Why Are Saving Rates of Urban Households in China Rising?" *American Economic Journal: Macroeconomics,* Vol. 2, No. 1, pp. 93–130.

Conway, P., D. de Rosa, G. Nicoletti, and F. Steiner, 2006, "Regulation, Competition, and Productivity Convergence," OECD Economics Department Working Paper No. 509 (Paris: Organisation for Economic Co-Operation and Development).

Cui, L., and M. Syed, 2007, "The Shifting Structure of China's Trade and Production," IMF Working Paper No. 07/214 (Washington: International Monetary Fund).

Eichengreen, B., 2006, "The Blind Men and the Elephant," *Issues in Economic Policy*, January (Washington: Brookings Institution).

Guimaraes, R., and O. Unteroberdoerster, 2006, "What's Driving Private Investment in Malaysia? Aggregate Trends and Firm-Level Evidence," IMF Working Paper No. 06/190 (Washington: International Monetary Fund).

Guo, K., and P. N'Diaye, 2009a, "Is China's Export-Oriented Growth Sustainable," IMF Working Paper No. 09/172 (Washington: International Monetary Fund).

———, 2009b, "Employment Effects of Growth Rebalancing in China," IMF Working Paper No. 09/169 (Washington: International Monetary Fund).

———, 2010, "Determinants of China's Private Consumption: An International Perspective," IMF Working Paper No. 10/93 (Washington: International Monetary Fund).

Hori, M., 2007, "The Evolution of Trade in Emerging Asia," in *Regional Economic Outlook: Asia and Pacific* (Washington: International Monetary Fund), October.

———, 2008, "Investment Recovery from Financial Crisis: A View from Cross-Country Experiences" (unpublished; Washington: International Monetary Fund).

International Country Risk Guide, various issues. Available via the Internet: http://www.prs-group.com/icrg.aspx

Kalra, S., A. Mohommad, P. N'Diaye, and O. Unteroberdoerster, 2009, "Global Shifts in Demand: Making Up for Weaker Consumption in the United States," in *Regional Economic Outlook: Asia and Pacific* (Washington: International Monetary Fund), October.

Kuijs, L., 2005, "Investment and Saving in China," Policy Research Working Paper No. 3633 (Washington: World Bank).

N'Diaye, P., P. Zhang, and W. Zhang, 2008, "Structural Reform, Intra-Regional Trade, and Medium-Term Growth Prospects of East Asia and the Pacific—Perspectives from a New Multi-Region Model," Hong Kong Monetary Authority Working Paper No. 0817 (Hong Kong: Hong Kong Monetary Authority).

Nicoletti, G., and S. Scarpetta, 2003, "Regulation, Productivity and Growth: OECD Evidence," *Economic Policy*, Vol. 18, No. 36, pp. 9–72.

Palacios, R., and M. Pallarès-Miralles, 2000, "International Patterns of Pension Provision," World Bank Group Social Protection Discussion Paper Series No. 9 (Washington: World Bank).

Prasad, E., 2009, "Rebalancing Growth in Asia," NBER Working Paper No. 15169 (Cambridge, Massachusetts: National Bureau of Economic Research).

Pula, G., and T. Peltonen, 2009, "Has Emerging Asia Decoupled? An Analysis of Production and Trade Linkages Using the Asian International Input-Output Table," ECB Working Paper No. 993, (January). Available via the Internet: www.ecb.europa.eu.

Wei, S., and X. Zhang, 2009, "The Competitive Saving Motive: Evidence from Rising Sex Ratios and Savings Rates in China," NBER Working Paper No. 15093 (Cambridge, Massachusetts: National Bureau of Economic Research).

CHAPTER 2

Corporate Saving and Rebalancing in Asia

SONALI JAIN CHANDRA, MALHAR NABAR, AND NATHAN PORTER

INTRODUCTION

In recent years, the corporate sector in much of Asia has begun to save an increasing share of national income. This has been true in the regional powerhouses of Japan, Korea, China, and India, but also in the ASEAN region and among Asia's newly industrialized economies (Figure 2.1). Large profits and rising corporate saving have been a global trend through much of this decade (IMF, 2006a), but the increase in corporate saving in Asia has outstripped that in other regions of the world (Figure 2.2). As a result, corporate saving has come to account for not only an increasing share of the region's GDP but also a rising fraction of global saving (Figure 2.3).

High corporate saving becomes an important contributor to regional imbalances if investment is declining or if households fail to provide an offsetting increase in consumption. The decline in investment following the 1997–98 Asian crisis has been extensively studied (IMF, 2005 and 2006b; Chapter 3 in this volume). Less attention has been paid to whether Asian households have responded to the rise in corporate saving by increasing their consumption. This chapter investigates these interlinking themes and focuses on two questions that relate directly to the rebalancing debate:

- the extent to which Asian households offset corporate saving behavior and how the reaction to corporate saving has differed between Asia and elsewhere; and
- the impact of institutional and policy factors on corporate saving.

The chapter is structured as follows. The analysis in the next section shows that unlike in other regions, higher corporate saving in Asia has not been offset by higher household consumption over the past three decades. As a result, corporate saving has had a potent effect on national saving. Consequently, for a given level of investment, a decline in corporate saving should reduce regional imbalances and boost consumption. The following section finds that corporate saving is influenced by both corporate governance and the degree of financial market development and that these effects

Figure 2.1
Change in Saving since 2000
(In percent of GDP)

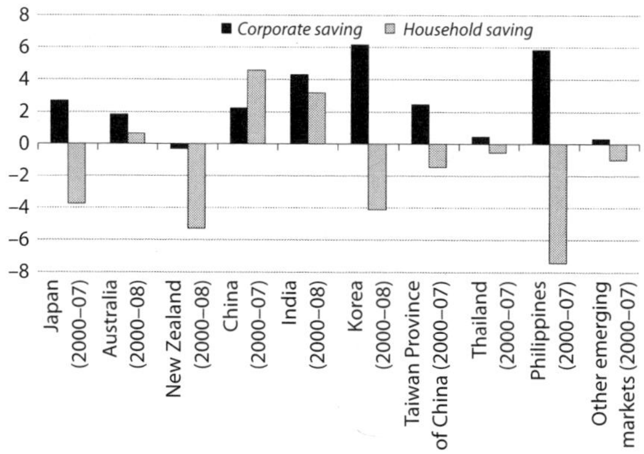

Sources: United Nations; CEIC Data Company Ltd.; and IMF staff calculations.

Figure 2.2
Difference in Mean Corporate Saving, Post-2000 versus Pre-2000
(In percent of GDP; regression coefficients and confidence intervals)

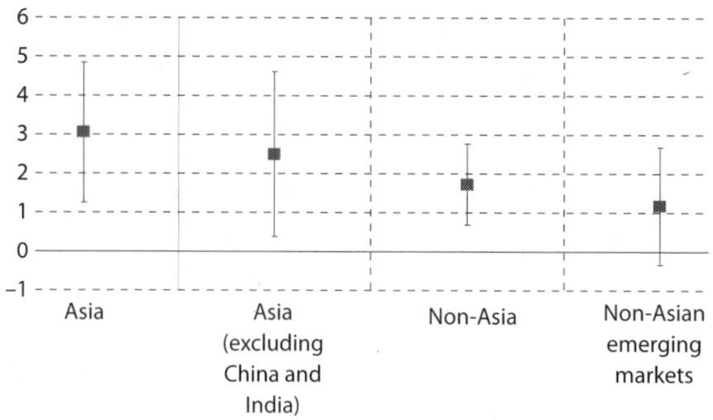

Source: IMF staff estimates.

are particularly strong in Asia. The final section draws out the policy implications of these results. Further improvements in corporate governance and financial reform will help to address the underlying structural incentives for high corporate saving. For example, if Asia can converge to the average level of financial development and corporate governance of the G-7, then corporate saving could fall by as much as 7 percent of GDP. The chapter's final section provides a brief conclusion.

Figure 2.3
Corporate Saving in Emerging Asia, 1993–2007
(Share in world saving, in percent)

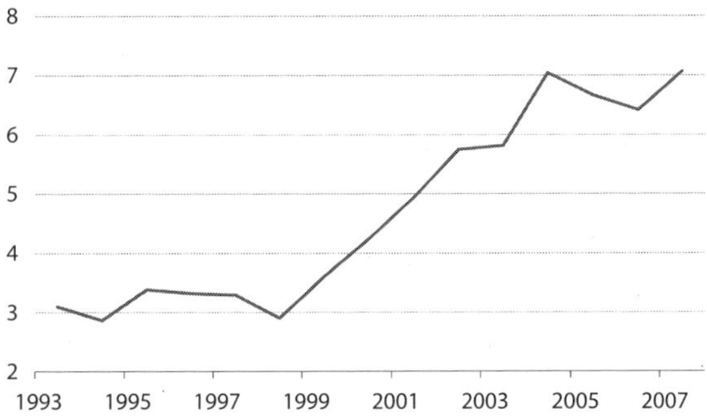

Sources: United Nations; CEIC Data Company Ltd.; and IMF staff calculations.

DOES HIGHER CORPORATE SAVING AFFECT HOUSEHOLD BEHAVIOR?

Economic theory suggests that, absent tax distortions, and assuming that households have easy access to well-functioning financial markets and that corporations are privately owned, the level of national saving should be relatively unrelated to the level of corporate saving. As households ultimately own the corporations, they should be indifferent between holding their saving directly or holding it indirectly via the saving of the firms that they own. If corporate saving increases, households should neutralize this by reducing their saving.

But there are a number of reasons why household saving might not, in fact, fall in response to an increase in corporate saving. For example, households might not realize any increase in their wealth from higher corporate saving, and therefore may not adjust their consumption and saving, if dividends are retained in order to finance low-rate-of-return projects. Similarly, if corporations are government owned and pay dividends to the state, but these revenues are then deployed in ways that have little direct benefit to households, the saving behavior of households might not offset the choices made by firms. Therefore, key to households' neutralizing the effect of corporate saving is the existence of an active corporate ownership culture and strong market discipline on managers so that their incentives are aligned with those of shareholders.

This section examines corporate and household behavior across a range of emerging markets, using a methodology developed by Poterba (1987), to assess how households react to changes in corporate saving. A panel of emerging market economies from 1979 to 2007 is used to test whether a change in the level of corporate saving has an impact on private (i.e., household plus corporate) saving.

If households are indifferent to the timing of dividends and the level of retained earnings, corporate saving should have no explanatory power in the regression.

Various factors such as age dependency (to capture life-cycle saving motives), the level of economic volatility (to capture precautionary motives), the real interest rate (to capture the financial incentive to save), the level of disposable income, and lagged private saving (to proxy for accumulated wealth) are also controlled for (Appendix 1). The results indicate that, in emerging markets as a whole, private saving is not significantly affected by the level of corporate saving (Figures 2.4 and 2.5). Changes in corporate saving are almost fully offset by changes in household saving. However, this result does not hold among the Asian economies.

Indeed, Asian households offset only around 20 percent of the increase in corporate saving. In other words, for every additional US$100 saved by Asian

Figure 2.4
Private and Corporate Saving, 1979–2007
(In percent of GDP)

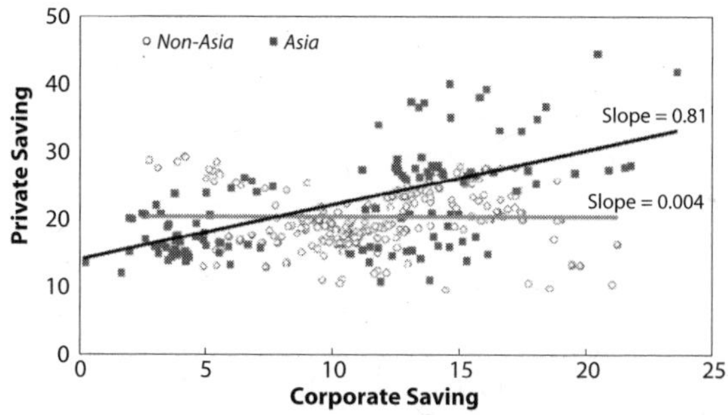

Sources: United Nations; CEIC Data Company Ltd.; and IMF staff calculations.

Figure 2.5
Household and Corporate Saving, 1979–2007
(In percent of GDP)

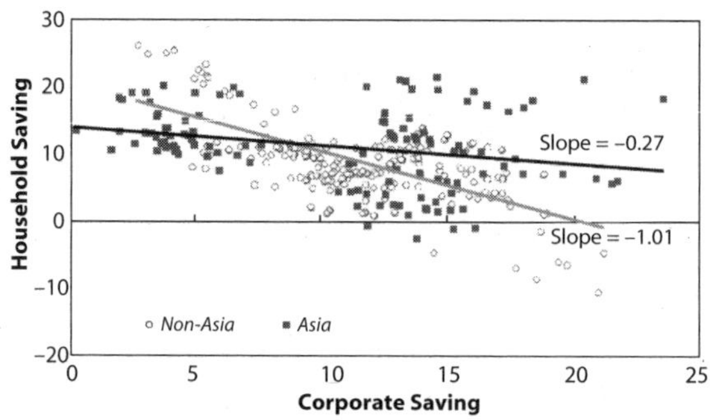

Sources: United Nations; CEIC Data Company Ltd.; and IMF staff calculations.

Figure 2.6
Corporate Saving Offset by Households, 1979–2007
(In percent of corporate saving)

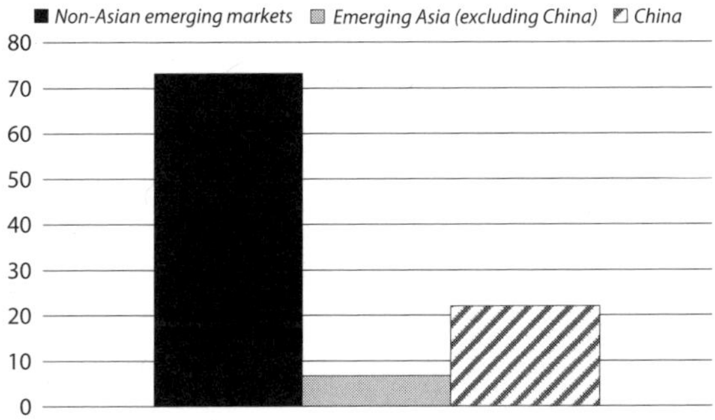

Source: IMF staff estimates.

firms, households in Asia reduce their saving only by US$20 (Figure 2.6). Moreover, these results do not just reflect the experience of China. Indeed, dropping China from the sample leads to the result that only 7 percent of higher corporate saving is offset by lower household saving. These results are robust to changes in sample period and the use of alternate measures of private saving (see Appendix 1 for detailed results).

An alternative approach to studying the interaction between household and corporate saving focuses on whether dividend income influences private consumption (Auerbach and Hassett, 1991). If households can access financial markets to liquidate assets or borrow against their wealth, consumption decisions should be independent of the flow of dividend income. Put differently, in the absence of liquidity constraints private consumption will not be affected by firms' decisions regarding whether to retain earnings or pay them out as dividends. Empirically, the marginal propensity to consume (MPC) out of dividend income should be zero.

Estimates of the MPC indicate that property income (encompassing interest, rent, and dividends) does influence household consumption and saving decisions (Figures 2.7 and 2.8). In particular, the MPC with respect to property income is significantly higher in emerging Asia than elsewhere, even though liquidity constraints seem equally binding. Asian households consume around US$7 more for every US$100 in property income they receive (compared with only US$1 for non-Asian emerging markets).

In sum, Asian households do not appear to offset the behavior of firms in making their consumption decisions. Therefore, the high levels of corporate saving in Asia are an important factor in regard to the size of national saving and have a clear role in determining the level of current account imbalances in Asia.

Figure 2.7
Households: Consumption and Disposable Property Income, 1979–2007
(Change in percent)

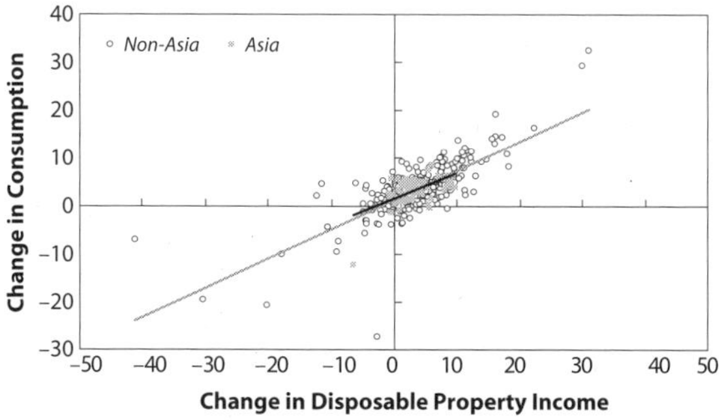

Sources: United Nations; CEIC Data Company Ltd.; and IMF staff calculations.

Figure 2.8
Marginal Propensities to Consume, 1979–2007
(Share of current real disposable income)

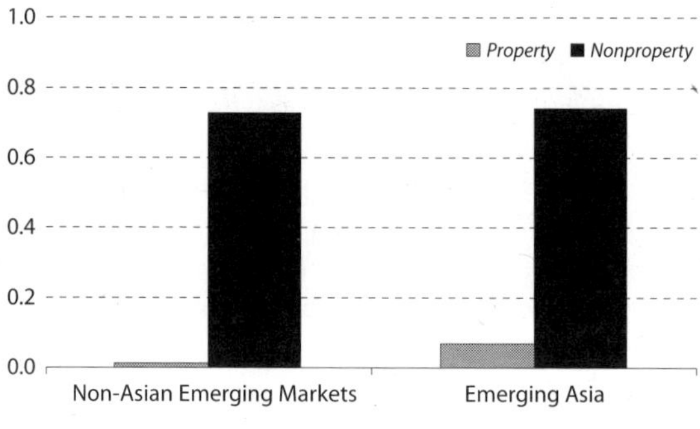

Source: IMF staff estimates.

WHAT INFLUENCES CORPORATE SAVING IN ASIA?

This section traces the influence of underlying structural and policy factors on corporate saving in Asia, using regression analysis at the aggregate cross-country level and at the level of individual firms.[1]

[1]For country case studies on the rise in corporate saving in Asia, see Porter (2009) and Asian Development Bank (2009). These studies link high corporate saving to energy and land subsidies, limited access (especially for SMEs) to capital markets, and low dividend payout ratios.

At the aggregate level, the rise in corporate saving in Asia in recent years can be attributed to efficiency gains from greater openness to trade, cheaper credit, and relatively strong economic growth in the years leading up to the recent crisis (Appendix 2). The most important of these factors in terms of economic magnitude appears to be the rising trend of openness to trade across the region. Compared with the 1990s, openness to trade (measured as the sum of imports and exports/GDP) increased in the period 2000–08. The regression estimates suggest that this increase in openness to trade accounts for nearly a fifth of the increase in corporate saving over this period.

Greater openness implies that firms are producing more in line with comparative advantage, while importing equipment and inputs at a lower cost from trading partners rather than sourcing these inefficiently at home. Reduction of trade barriers is also typically thought to reduce incentives for rent-seeking, which may help redeploy resources to more productive uses. Finally, the removal of trading restrictions may come as part of an overall structural reform (including the scaling back of licensing policies, such as in India) that boosts profitability and saving.

At the same time, greater openness may also leave firms more vulnerable to external fluctuations. In the absence of adequate hedging instruments, firms may build up a buffer stock of saving to guard against volatility. In order to assess whether openness induces higher saving as a residual from enhanced profitability or as an *ex ante* buffer against external volatility, an additional control (terms-of-trade volatility) is introduced in the regressions. The regression finds that terms-of-trade volatility does not influence corporate saving, nor does the relationship between openness and corporate saving depend on the degree of this volatility (see Appendix 2 for detailed results). This is consistent with the relationship between corporate saving and trade openness resulting from greater efficiency—and not from greater uncertainty—in a more open economy.

While structural factors have boosted efficiency and raised corporate saving in the region, at the same time there have been significant changes in corporate governance across the region following the Asian crisis. These changes may have also influenced the accumulation of corporate saving. The relationship between corporate saving and governance is tested using a data set (outlined in De Nicolo, Laeven, and Ueda, 2006) that looks at earnings opacity, the co-movement of stock prices, and the number of accounting regulations complied with in a particular country (Figure 2.9).

The overall effects of corporate governance reform on corporate saving may be ambiguous. Improvements in corporate governance, specifically transparency, may improve access to external funding and reduce the need to rely on internally generated funds. At the same time, firms may be influenced to a greater degree by shareholder demands and therefore find themselves paying out higher dividends. But corporate governance reform could also mean that firms can no longer rely on implicit intra-group cross-subsidies, and so have to rely more on corporate saving. Therefore, the net effect of corporate governance reform on corporate saving is an empirical question.

The empirical analysis suggests that at the aggregate level, corporate governance reform is associated with other structural changes, including greater openness to trade. In order to isolate the influence of corporate governance and to establish

Figure 2.9
Corporate Governance Quality, 2008
(Index)

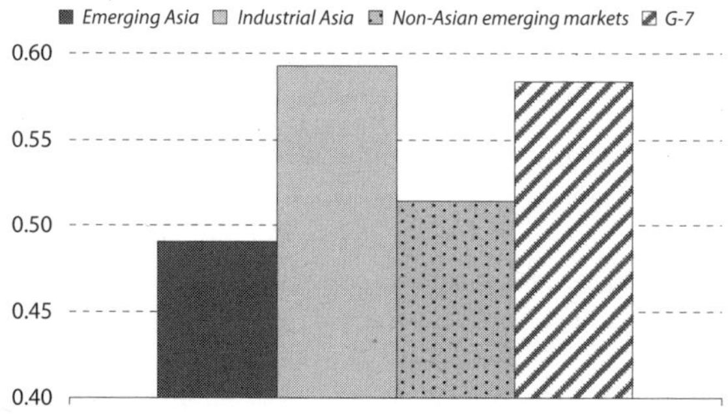

Source: DeNicolo, Laeven, and Ueda (2006).

whether there are any Asia-specific factors, a comparison is carried out across regions and over time. The results suggest that corporate governance reform has had an offsetting effect on the rising tide of corporate saving in the region (Appendix Table 2A.6). The increase in corporate saving is therefore tempered by the improvements in corporate governance that have taken place following the Asian crisis.

Similarly, improvements in the transparency of corporate operations also appear to have weakened the motivation for higher corporate saving at the level of individual firms (Figure 2.10). An attempt to confirm these results is made using the World Bank's *Doing Business* database, drawing on measures of shareholder protection, which capture the strength of protection for minority shareholders. Using these data,

Figure 2.10
The Effect of Corporate Governance Reform on Corporate Saving
(Regression coefficients)

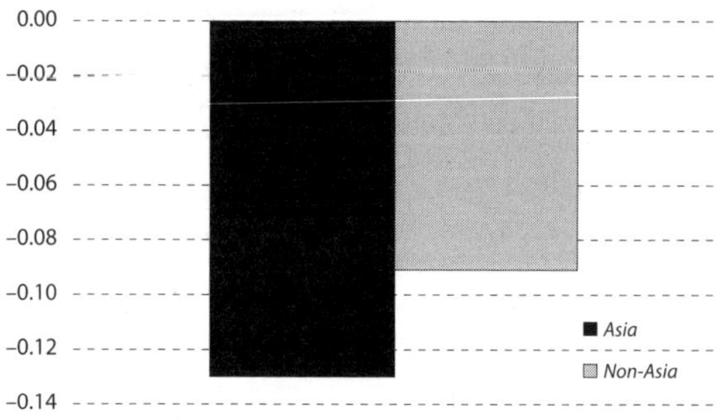

Source: IMF staff estimates.

Figure 2.11
Financial Reform, 2005
(Index)

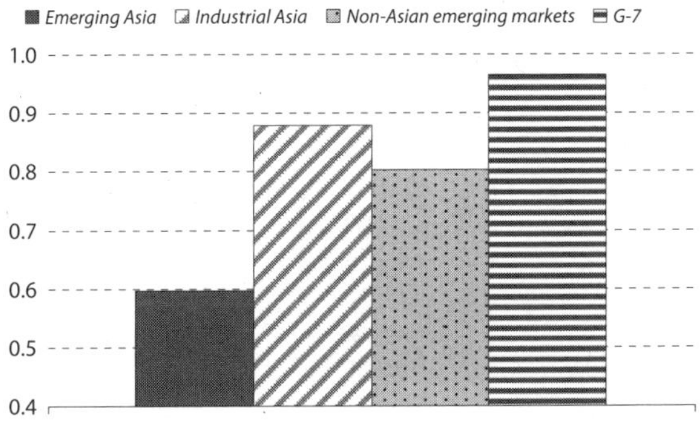

Source: Abiad, Detragiache, and Tressel (2008).

the analysis confirms the finding that improvements in corporate governance through stronger shareholder rights lead to a better alignment of the incentives of shareholders and managers, thereby moderating the tendency for corporations to save. The analysis is based on a firm-level data set that allows such fundamental drivers of corporate saving as profitability, Tobin's *Q*, the share of intangible assets, firm size, sales volatility, leverage, and capital expenditure to be controlled for. Additionally, an index constructed by Abiad, Detragiache, and Tressel (2008) is used that incorporates various dimensions of financial development, including banking supervision, privatization, barriers to entry, level of directed credit, credit ceilings, interest rate controls, and securities market reform (Figure 2.11).

As with improvements in corporate governance, corporate saving could either increase or decrease following financial reform. In a liberalized financial market, firms might have easier access to finance and so need to save less. But this may be counterbalanced by the fact that once close ties between firms and banks are severed, firms may no longer have access to relatively automatic credit lines and may therefore be induced to save more. The firm-level data suggest that financial reform has had a significant downward impact by slowing the rise in corporate saving across all emerging markets and, further, that this effect has been considerably larger in Asia than elsewhere (Figure 2.12).

POLICY IMPLICATIONS

Following the 1997–98 financial crisis, Asia was a fertile ground for financial market and corporate governance reform. The corporate governance measures and financial reform indicators used in the previous section all have improved significantly (Figures 2.13 and 2.14). As the financial system in the region has become more market driven, the options for firms to finance investment projects

Figure 2.12
The Effect of Financial Liberalization on Corporate Saving Post-2000
(Regression coefficients)

Source: IMF staff estimates.

Figure 2.13
Financial Reform Since the Asian Crisis
(Index)

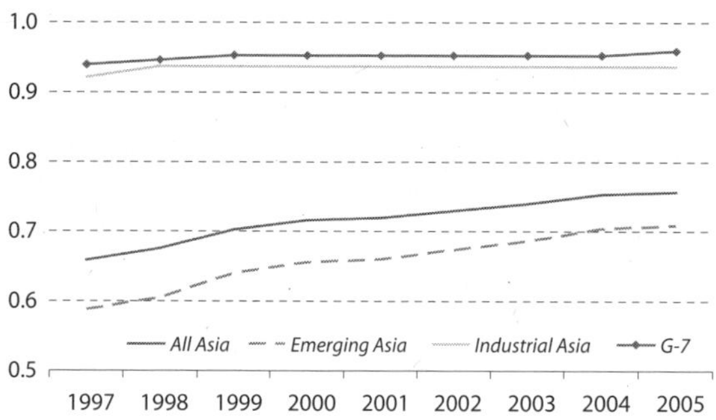

Source: Abiad, Detragiache, and Tressel (2008).

(including equity issuance, corporate bonds, and overseas financing) have grown. This, in turn, has limited firms' incentives to retain earnings as they have become more secure that market financing will be available for high-return projects. Consequently, firms have needed less to rely on self-financing. Similarly, improvements in corporate governance over the past decade have increased the discipline on corporations and lessened their tendency to hoard cash. This progress has had a significant effect in tempering the rise in regional corporate saving.

Nevertheless, despite the substantial progress in reforming the financial system and improving corporate governance, emerging Asia still lags behind competitors along a range of indicators. The difference has narrowed over the past decade but

Figure 2.14
Measure of Investor Protection in Asia, 2005–09
(Index)

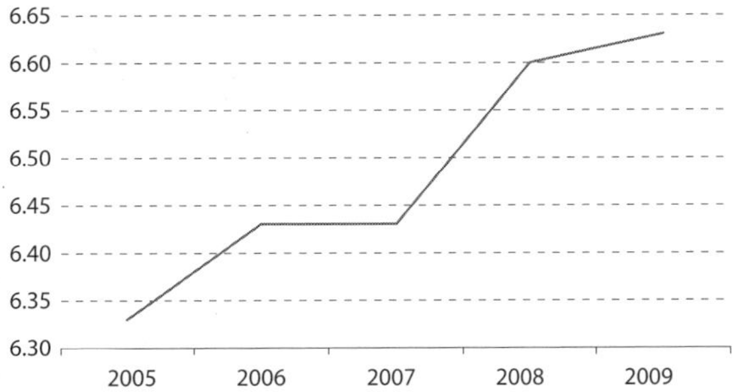

Source: World Bank, Doing Business database.

there is still much to do. Further reforms in corporate governance and finance would not only improve the allocation of capital and raise productivity but also have a significant impact on corporate saving. Such reform could be instrumental in reducing current account surpluses across the region, given how stagnant investment levels have been in most of Asia over the last decade. For example, if Asia were able to reach the average level of financial liberalization found in advanced economies, it would be able to lower corporate saving by as much as 5 percent of GDP. Similarly, improvement in corporate governance to bring Asia to the average levels prevailing in advanced economies could reduce corporate saving by 2.4 percent of GDP. Taken together, these results suggest that reforming corporate incentives and financial market institutions should be an integral part of regional rebalancing in the coming years.

CONCLUSION

In Asia, corporate saving has been a major contributor to national saving and to the increase in the saving-investment imbalance over time. Unlike in many other regions, Asian households have not offset the rise in corporate saving with higher consumption. Although high corporate profits and saving have been seen across the world, the rise in Asia has been particularly striking, especially given anemic investment demand. The rise in saving would have been considerably larger if the region had not made the important advances it did over the past decade in both financial market development and corporate governance. Further deepening these reforms would contribute to lowering corporate saving and raising consumption and would facilitate regional rebalancing. With the marginal propensity to consume from property income higher in Asia than elsewhere, a rise in property income that follows reform is likely to lead to a larger boost in private consumption and therefore likely to assist in rebalancing.

APPENDIX 1. CORPORATE AND HOUSEHOLD SAVING

Two tests of the interaction of households and corporate saving are considered:

- In the first, suggested by Poterba (1987), a saving function is estimated based on some fundamental drivers (X) of saving to test whether changes in corporate saving (S) are offset by households. In particular, the following equation is estimated:

$$S_t = \alpha + \beta^w S_t - 1 + \beta' X_t + \chi CS_t + \varepsilon_t, \tag{1}$$

where lagged saving proxies wealth. Generally, private saving (S) should be driven by life-cycle factors (such as aging) and precautionary motives. In light of this, the age dependency ratio, household disposable income, the (ex post) real interest rate, and a measure of aggregate volatility are used as fundamentals; disposable income is also included. Although the relationship may be biased by the holdings of equities outside the domestic market, this is unlikely to be a problem given the extent of home bias seen in equity holdings (well over 90 percent held domestically in emerging markets). To ensure robustness, the relationship is estimated using measures of both private saving and household saving. If the corporate veil is pierced, then χ should not be significantly different from 0 when a private saving equation is estimated and not significantly different from –1 when a household saving relationship is estimated. The relationship is estimated with generalized method of moments (GMM), using as instruments twice-lagged saving, a UN measure of the change in household financial assets, and the lagged value of the fundamentals to deal with possible endogeneity issues.

- The second set of tests, proposed by Auerbach and Hassett (1991), is based on determining whether consumption deviates from that implied by optimizing consumer theory, even after liquidity-constrained consumers are controlled for (by controlling for current disposable income). Specifically, the relationship between real consumption growth, interest rates, and both current disposable property and nonproperty income is estimated. Deviations based on consumption from current nonproperty income indicate the extent of liquidity constraints faced by households. However, because individuals who receive dividends (or other property income) are arguably not credit constrained, if consumption decisions depend significantly on dividend income, these households are arguably unable to realize the same wealth out of retained earnings (corporate saving) as out of disbursed earnings (dividends). In other words, instead of saving the expected part of dividend payments (adding it to their wealth to increase lifetime consumption), they consume a significant share of it today. The following equation is therefore estimated:

$$\Delta c_{t+1} = \sigma \ln(\beta) + \sigma r_{t+1} + \gamma^{Y} Y_{t+1}^{NPID} + \gamma^{PI} Y_{t+1}^{PID} + \eta_{t+1}, \tag{2}$$

where Y^{NPDI} is nonproperty disposable income, and Y^{PID} disposable property income. If consumers are credit constrained, then $\gamma^{Y} > 0$, and if $\gamma^{PI} > 0$ then households' saving behavior is unlikely to offset corporate saving behavior. We estimate this equation using GMM and instruments for twice and thrice lagged consumption growth, real interest rates, and income variables.

Empirical Results

Table 2A.1 shows the relationship between private saving (constructed as the sum of corporate and household saving using UN data), fundamentals, and corporate saving.[2] This is the analogous relationship to the baseline relationship estimated for the United States in Poterba (1987). In the pooled sample, corporate saving has no significant impact on total private saving—consistent with households' offsetting changes in corporate saving—thereby offsetting the impact of higher corporate saving with lower household saving. However, if the relationship for corporate saving in emerging Asia and elsewhere is estimated separately, it is found that private saving in Asia rises significantly with Asian corporate saving. Specifically, in emerging Asia, households offset (through lower saving) each additional dollar in corporate saving only by less than 20 cents, whereas elsewhere they offset almost three-quarters of the rise in corporate saving. The results are not an artifact of China's high saving and are robust even when Asian saving is broken down between China and the rest of

TABLE 2A.1

Private and Corporate Saving
(Regression results)

Constant	–2.83	–9.54	–8.89
Private saving/GDP	0.44 **	0.47 ***	0.48 ***
Age dependency	–0.19	–0.09	–0.09
Household disposable income/GDP	0.31	0.34	0.33 *
Real interest rate	–0.03	–0.05	–0.05
Volatility[a]	–19.80	–41.25	–41.72
Corporate saving/GDP			
Pooled	0.39		
Non-Asia		0.28	0.27
Asia		0.81 ***	
Asia (excluding China)			0.93 +
China			0.78 ***
R-squared	0.95	0.95	0.95
Adjusted *R*-squared	0.95	0.94	0.94

Source: IMF staff estimates.
Note: ***, **, and * indicate significance at the 1, 5, and 10 percent levels, respectively. + indicates significance at the 10.6 percent level.
[a]Standard deviation of Hodrick-Prescott filtered GDP cycles.

[2] These relationships are estimated using system GMM with fixed effects and lagged values as instruments to control for potential endogeneity. Significance is determined using robust standard errors.

TABLE 2A.2

Impact of Corporate Saving on Private Saving by Region
(Regression results)

Corporate saving/GDP	Private saving[a]		Private saving[b]		Household saving[c]	
Non-Asia	0.30	0.29	0.41	0.41	−0.05 ***	0.01 ***
Asia	0.29		0.77 ***		−0.09 ***	
Asia (excluding China)		0.68 **		0.96 ***		0.89 *
China		0.12		0.69 ***		−0.03 ***

Source: IMF staff estimates.
Note: ***, **, and * indicate significance at the 1, 5, and 10 percent levels, respectively.
[a]Private saving as measured in IMF WEO database.
[b]Private saving derived using national saving less government saving. Data obtained from IMF WEO database and the United Nations.
[c]Household saving as measured by the United Nations. The null hypothesis (pierce the corporate veil) is that the corporate saving coefficient is -1. The significance test is adjusted accordingly.

TABLE 2A.3

Private Consumption and Household Property and Nonproperty Income
(Regression results)

Constant	0.002	0.010 ***
Real interest rate (T-bill)	−0.103 ***	−0.067 ***
Disposable income growth		
Nonproperty (Pooled)	0.989 ***	
Property (Pooled)	0.033 **	
Nonproperty (Non-Asia)		0.729 ***
Property (Non-Asia)		0.013 **
Nonproperty (Asia)		0.740 ***
Property (Asia)		0.068 ***
Equity of disposable income coefficients (Asia= Non-Asia)[a]		
Nonproperty income growth		0.018
Property income growth		24.372 ***
R-squared	0.245	0.376
Adjusted *R*-squared	0.234	0.359

Source: IMF staff estimates.
Note: ***, **, and * indicate significance at the 1, 5, and 10 percent levels, respectively.
[a]Wald test for the null hypothesis that the disposable income coefficients in Asia and those outside Asia are equal.

emerging Asia. These results are also robust across measures of saving. Table 2A.2 shows the results of the test on corporate saving when various measures of private and household saving are used. The only substantial difference is that when the test is constructed using household saving directly, it seems that non-Asian households also fail to breach the corporate veil.

Following Auerbach and Hassett (1991), equation (2) is estimated using real disposable nonproperty disposable income and real disposable property income to test whether current consumption depends on property income (see Table 2A.3). The results suggest that households in all regions do not fully offset corporate saving. However, although all households have a similar propensity to consume out of nonproperty income (suggesting equally binding liquidity constraints), Asian households have a significantly stronger propensity to consume directly out of property income than households in other regions. This suggests that Asian households are much less likely to offset corporate saving decisions than households elsewhere.

APPENDIX 2. REGRESSIONS ON THE DETERMINANTS OF CORPORATE SAVING

This chapter relies on a series of regressions using macro-level and firm-level data to explain the impact of changes in the policy environment on corporate saving.

Macro-Level Regressions

At the aggregate level, the chapter uses a cross-country panel data set compiled from various sources: the United Nations Statistical Database, CEIC Data Company Limited, *World Development Indicators*, the Lane and Milesi-Ferretti (2006) database on financial openness, and two new data sets that construct indices for financial development (Abiad, Detragiache, and Tressel, 2008) and corporate governance quality (De Nicolo, Laeven, and Ueda, 2006). The covariates included are growth rate of GDP, real interest rate, trade openness (exports + imports)/GDP, and terms of trade volatility. Fixed-effects regressions are used to control for time-invariant country-specific factors.

Changes in the mean corporate saving/GDP ratio since 2000 relative to prior years are tested for. The results presented in Table 2A.4 indicate that corporate saving has increased in general across the world, with the increases ranging from 3.06 percent of GDP in Asia to 1.17 percent of GDP in non-Asian emerging market countries (the change is not, however, statistically significant for this latter group). The point estimates indicate that the magnitude of the increase is appreciably larger in Asia than it is outside Asia and that this result is not being driven entirely by China and India.

TABLE 2A.4

Difference in Mean Corporate Saving, Post-2000 versus Pre-2000
(Regression results)

	Asia	Asia (excluding China and India)	Non-Asia	Non-Asian emerging markets
Post-2000	3.06 ***	2.50 *	1.73 ***	1.17
	(0.90)	(1.06)	(0.52)	(0.75)
Constant	8.89 ***	9.61 ***	12.0 ***	13.3 ***
	(1.64)	(1.61)	(0.62)	(0.93)
Observations	208	166	684	305
R-squared	0.07	0.06	0.03	0.01

Source: IMF staff estimates.

Note: ***, **, and * indicate sigrificance at the 1, 5, and 10 percent levels, respectively. Robust standard errors are in parentheses.

To study the policy levers that influence corporate saving at the macro level, the earnings smoothing indicator of corporate governance constructed by De Nicolo, Laeven, and Ueda (2006) is used. This indicator tracks the degree to which managers are able to hide the true performance of firms by using accruals to smooth fluctuations of annual profits. It is calculated as the rank correlation between cash flows (before any accounting adjustments) and profits (after accounting adjustments) in a cross-section of firms within a country at each point in time.

Table 2A.5 reports the results from a country fixed-effects regression, which controls for time-invariant country specific factors that influence corporate saving. The three significant drivers of corporate saving are the growth rate of GDP, the real interest rate, and trade openness. Terms-of-trade volatility does not affect corporate saving, suggesting that openness raises corporate saving through efficiency gains rather than due to precautionary behavior by firms in an open environment.

Table 2A.6 reports the effect of corporate governance reform on corporate saving. As is indicated by the coefficient on the interaction term for Asia post-2000 and corporate governance quality, the association between corporate saving and corporate governance is significantly more negative than in the preceding years and when compared to that for the rest of the world. This is consistent with improvements in corporate governance in Asia having an offsetting negative effect on corporate saving (against the backdrop of an overall rising trend during this period).

TABLE 2A.5

Determinants of Corporate Saving-to-GDP
(Results from cross-country fixed-effects panel regression, 1979-2008)

GDP growth	0.209 ***	0.169 ***	0.115 **	0.115 **
	(0.056)	(0.057)	(0.056)	(0.056)
Real interest rate	−0.056 **	−0.049	−0.077 **	−0.076 **
	(0.026)	(0.030)	(0.036)	(0.037)
Trade openness		0.044*	0.067 **	0.065 **
		(0.023)	(0.026)	(0.025)
Terms-of-trade volatility			−0.059	−0.0935
			(0.044)	(0.174)
Trade openness x				0.001
terms-of-trade volatility				(0.003)
Constant	12.090 ***	8.89 ***	8.117 ***	8.227 ***
	(0.180)	(1.648)	(1.572)	(1.554)
Observations	607	605	370	370
Number of countries	49	49	32	32
R-squared	0.09	0.11	0.15	0.15

Source: IMF staff estimates.

Note: ***, **, and * indicate significance at the 1, 5, and 10 percent levels; respectively. Robust standard errors in parentheses.

TABLE 2A.6

Corporate Saving and Corporate Governance
(Fixed-effect regression results)

Post-2000	0.85 **
	(0.39)
Asia post-2000	4.24 ***
	(0.87)
Corporate governance quality	0.81 **
	(0.35)
Post-2000 x corporate governance quality	–0.24
	(0.38)
Asia x corporate governance quality	–1.52 ***
	(0.50)
Asia post-2000 x corporate governance quality	–1.70 **
	(0.84)
Constant	11.21 ***
	(0.25)
Observations	467
Number of countries	36
R-squared	0.23

Source: IMF staff estimates.
Note ***, ** and * indicate significance at the 1, 5, and 10 percent levels, respectively. Standard errors are in parentheses.

Firm-Level Regressions

The firm-level perspective controls for firm and industry characteristics in regard to overall corporate liquidity. The data are from the *Worldscope* database and are based on corporate balance sheets and income statements. The sample includes approximately 20,000 firms from 60 countries. It excludes financial firms, since they operate differently and hold cash and other liquid assets to meet statutory capital requirements.

The chapter analyzes the impact of financial liberalization on corporate saving, conditional on a number of firm-level determinants of corporate saving. The measure of financial liberalization used is an index of financial reform constructed by Abiad, Detragiache, and Tressel (2008), which looks at financial market development along seven dimensions (including banking supervision, privatization, entry barriers, directed credit, credit ceilings, interest rate controls, and securities market reform) and then takes an average across the seven indicators to compile the index.

The finding is that the lack of financial development has led to an external finance premium, forcing Asian firms to save more. The results suggest that financial liberalization does indeed lower the need for precautionary saving and tends to moderate the increase in corporate saving. The coefficient on the overall index is negative and significant, more so for Asia than for outside Asia.

This chapter uses the retained earnings-to-sales ratio as the measure of gross corporate saving. Retained earnings are defined as the accumulated after-tax earnings of a firm that have not been distributed as dividends to shareholders.

TABLE 2A.7

Results from Firm-Level Regression

Size	0.072
	(11.37) ***
Share of intangible assets	0.362
	(5.40) ***
Market to book value	0.018
	(3.16) ***
Return on assets	0.01
	(8.91) ***
Volatility	−0.001
	(0.40)
Capital expendture	−0.001
	(0.34)
Financial reform index	−1.181
	(4.93) ***
Asia x financial reform index	−3.416
	(9.51) ***
Number of observations	105897

Source: IMF staff estimates.
Note: *** indicates significance at the 1 percent level. Robust *z*-statistics are in parentheses.

Following the literature on corporate liquidity (Opler and others, 1999; IMF, 2006a), a number of determinants are considered in the chapter, in a dynamic-panel setting (using Arellano-Bond GMM estimation and robust standard errors). The firm-level control variables include firm size (measured by the log of the book value of assets); share of intangible assets in total assets, Tobin's *Q* (or the market-to-book value, defined as the market value of firms' assets to book value of firms' assets), rate of return on assets, volatility of sales (measured by the rolling standard deviation of sales), capital expenditure, and leverage. In addition to the above firm-level variables, the analysis controls for country, industry, and time effects by including dummy variables. Industries are defined at the two-digit Standard Industrial Classification level (Table 2A.7).

The effect of corporate governance reforms on corporate saving is also analyzed using two databases: De Nicolo, Laeven, and Ueda (2006) (discussed above) and the World Bank's *Doing Business* database. The latter database gauges the strength of minority shareholder protections against directors' misuse of corporate assets for personal gain. The indicators distinguish three dimensions of investor protection: transparency of transactions (extent of disclosure index), the extent of director liability, and shareholders' ability to sue officers and directors for misconduct (ease of shareholder suits index).

REFERENCES

Abiad, A., E. Detragiache, and T. Tressel, 2008, "A New Database of Financial Reforms," IMF Working Paper No. 08/266 (Washington: International Monetary Fund).

Asian Development Bank, 2009, *Asian Development Outlook 2009* (Manila).

Auerbach, A. J., and K. A. Hassett, 1991, "Corporate Savings and Shareholder Consumption," NBER Working Paper No. 2994 (Cambridge, Massachusetts: National Bureau of Economic Research).

Aziz, J., and L. Cui, 2007, "Explaining China's Low Consumption: The Neglected Role of Household Income," IMF Working Paper No. 07/181 (Washington: International Monetary Fund).

Balakrishnan, R., S. Danninger, S. Elekdag, and I. Tytell, 2009, "How Linkages Fuel the Fire: The Transmission of Financial Stress from Advanced to Emerging Economies," *World Economic Outlook: Crisis and Recovery* (Washington: International Monetary Fund, April).

Barnett, S., and R. Brooks, 2009, "China: Does Government Health and Education Spending Boost Consumption?" IMF Working Paper No. 10/16 (Washington: International Monetary Fund).

Beck, T., and A. Demirguc-Künt, 2006, "Small- and Medium-Size Enterprises: Access to Finance as a Growth Constraint," *Journal of Banking and Finance*, Vol. 30, pp. 2931–43.

Beck, T., L. F. Klapper, and J. C. Medoza, 2008, "The Typology of Partial Credit Guarantee Funds Around the World," Policy Research Working Paper No. 4771 (Washington: World Bank).

Carroll, C., 2001, "A Theory of the Consumption Function, with and without Liquidity Constraints," *Journal of Economic Perspectives,* Vol. 15, No. 3, pp. 23–45.

Cerra, V., and S. Saxena, 2008, "Growth Dynamics: The Myth of Economic Recovery," *American Economic Review*, Vol. 98 (December), pp. 439–57.

De Nicolo, G., L. Laeven, and K. Ueda, 2006, "Corporate Governance Quality: Trends and Real Effects," IMF Working Paper No. 06/293 (Washington: International Monetary Fund).

Dunn, J., 2007, "The Ready-Made Garment Industry in Bangladesh: An Update," IMF Country Report No. 07/230 (Washington: International Monetary Fund).

Espinosa-Vega, M., and A. Rebucci, 2003, "Retail Bank Interest Rate Pass-Through: Is Chile Atypical?" IMF Working Paper No. 03/112 (Washington: International Monetary Fund).

Estevão, M., 2009, "U.S. Potential Growth in the Aftermath of the Crisis—Selected Issues Paper for the 2009 Article IV Consultation with the United States" (Washington: International Monetary Fund).

European Commission, 2009, "Impact of the Current Economic and Financial Crisis on Potential Output," Occasional Paper No. 49 (Brussels).

Flavin, M., 1981, "The Adjustment of Consumption to Changing Expectations About Future Income," *Journal of Political Economy*, Vol. 89, No. 5, pp. 974–1009.

Furceri, D., and A. Mourougane, 2009, "The Effect of Financial Crises on Potential Output: New Empirical Evidence from OECD Countries," OECD Economic Department Working Paper No. 699 (Paris: Organisation for Economic Co-Operation and Development).

International Monetary Fund, 2006a. "Awash with Cash: Why Are Corporate Savings So High?" Chapter 4 in *World Economic Outlook* (Washington, April).

———, 2006b, "Asia's Investment Decline" in *Regional Economic Outlook: Asia and Pacific* (Washington, May).

———, 2008, "The Changing Housing Cycle and the Implications for Monetary Policy," Chapter 3 of *World Economic Outlook* (Washington, April).

———, 2009a, "Global Crisis: The Asian Context" in *Regional Economic Outlook: Asia and Pacific* (Washington, April).

———, 2009b, *Japan—Article IV Staff Report*, IMF Staff Country Report 09/210 (Washington, July).

———, 2009c, "What's the Damage? Medium-Term Output Dynamics after Financial Crises" Chapter 4 of *World Economic Outlook* (Washington, October).

———, 2009d, *Global Financial Stability Report* (Washington, October).

Kang, K., M. Syed, and K. Tokuoka, 2009, "Revisiting Japan's Lost Decade," in *Regional Economic Outlook: Asia and Pacific* (Washington: International Monetary Fund, May).

Lane, P., and G. M. Milesi-Ferretti, 2006, "The External Wealth of Nations Mark II: Revised and Extended Estimates of Foreign Assets and Liabilities, 1970–2004," IMF Working Paper No. 06/09 (Washington: International Monetary Fund).

Nakagawa, S., and T. Shimizu, 2000, "Portfolio Selection of Financial Assets by Japan's Households—Why Are Japan's Households Reluctant to Invest in Risky Assets?" (Tokyo: Bank of Japan).

N'Diaye, P., P. Zhang, and W. Zhang, 2010, "Structural Reform, Intra-Regional Trade, and Medium-Term Growth Prospects of East Asia and the Pacific—Perspectives from a New Multi-Region Model," *Journal of Asian Economics*, Vol. 21, No. 1, pp. 20–36.

Opler T., L. Pinkowitz, B. Stultz, and R. Williamson, 1999, "The Determinants and Implications of Corporate Cash Holding," *Journal of Financial Economics*, Vol. 52.

Organisation for Economic Co-Operation and Development (OECD), 2009, "Beyond the Crisis: Medium-Term Challenges Relating to Potential Output, Unemployment, and Fiscal Positions," Chapter 4 in *OECD Economic Outlook*, Vol. 85 (Paris).

Peltonen, T., and G. Pula, 2009, "Has Emerging Asia Decoupled? An Analysis of Production and Trade Linkages Using the Asian International Input-Output Table," ECB Working Paper No. 993 (Frankfurt: European Central Bank).

Porter, N., 2009, "Savings in China," in *Regional Economic Outlook: Asia and Pacific* (Washington: International Monetary Fund, October).

Poterba, J., 1987, "Tax Policy and Corporate Saving," Brookings Papers on Economic Activity No. 2, pp. 455–503 (Washington: Brookings Institution).

______, 1992, "Dividends, Capital Gains, and the Corporate Veil: Evidence from Britain, Canada, and the United States," NBER Working Paper No. 2975 (Cambridge, Massachusetts: National Bureau of Economic Research).

Prasad, E., 2009, "Rebalancing Growth in Asia," NBER Working Paper No. 15169 (Cambridge, Massachusetts: National Bureau of Economic Research).

Reinhart, C. M., and K. S. Rogoff, 2009, "The Aftermath of Financial Crises," *American Economic Review*, Vol. 99, No. 2, pp. 466–72.

Shim, I., 2006, "Corporate Credit Guarantees in Asia," *Quarterly Review* (Basel: Bank for International Settlements), December.

Sommer, M., 2009, "Why Are Japanese Wages So Sluggish?" IMF Working Paper No. 09/97 (Washington: International Monetary Fund).

Terrones, M., and R. Cardarelli, 2005, "Global Imbalances: A Saving and Investment Perspective," in *World Economic Outlook* (Washington: International Monetary Fund, September).

Tokuoka, K., 2009, "The Outlook for Financing Japan's Public Debt–Selected Issues: Japan," IMF Country Report No. 09/211 (Washington: International Monetary Fund, July).

Ueda, K., 2008, "Corporate Governance and Liquidity Management" (unpublished; Washington: International Monetary Fund).

CHAPTER 3

Investment and Rebalancing in Emerging Asia

MALHAR NABAR AND MURTAZA SYED

Ensuring stable growth in the postcrisis world economy will require a rebalancing of economic activity in several countries. In Asia's export-dependent economies, this entails relying more on private domestic demand as a driver of growth. While some countries need to raise consumption, several need to raise investment or reorient it from tradable to nontradable sectors. These changes in investment could be facilitated by financial reforms that enhance domestically oriented firms' access to credit and by improvements in infrastructure that raise the returns to private investment.

INTRODUCTION

Rebalancing Asia's growth model involves simultaneously reorienting both production and spending away from external drivers toward domestic drivers of growth. The domestic drivers include both consumption and investment, although the emphasis differs across countries. The IMF's April 2010 *Regional Economic Outlook: Asia and Pacific* examined the consumption aspects of rebalancing growth. In this chapter we discuss the investment aspects.

Although individual circumstances differ across economies, one common channel through which these objectives can be met is by promoting investment. In some parts of the region, notably the ASEAN-4 countries, aggregate investment, particularly private fixed investment, appears low. In other parts, including the newly industrialized economies (NIEs) and Japan, although aggregate investment is in line with comparators, the composition is skewed toward exporters and capital-intensive firms, crowding out domestically focused and labor-intensive enterprises. Added to this, rapid growth has stretched existing infrastructure close to the point where it severely constrains activity.

This chapter examines the case for rebalancing in Asia through the route of investment. In contrast with existing work (Guimaraes and Unteroberdoerster, 2006; and Hori, 2008), it focuses on investment at both the aggregate level and the level of individual sectors across major Asian economies.[1] The analysis is guided by the following questions:

[1]Guimaraes and Unteroberdoerster (2006) also look at investment trends at the aggregate and firm level, focusing on developments in Malaysia since the Asian crisis.

- What factors determine private investment spending at the aggregate level and at the sectoral level in Asia? What structural attributes help explain recent investment trends in the region? How do the patterns differ in Asia compared with other regions?
- Is investment in Asia constrained by the limited development of financial sectors and infrastructure in many countries?
- What policies could promote investment to rebalance Asian economies toward domestic demand-led growth and lift potential growth?

The analysis leads to two main findings. First, lower returns, greater uncertainty, and altered perceptions of the ease of doing business have held down investment in many regional economies over the past decade or so. But financial constraints also play a role, as small and medium enterprises (SMEs) and firms operating in the service sector appear to have limited access to external funding, particularly in Japan and the NIEs. In these economies, promoting financing on risk-based terms, supporting SMEs' restructuring through more private out-of-court workouts, and streamlining tax policies could help rotate the composition of investment toward nontradable sectors. Second, shortfalls in infrastructure also suppress private investment spending, particularly in the ASEAN-4. With most of the infrastructure in the region provided by governments, greater private participation through public-private partnerships and bond funds may help reduce the pressure on government budgets.

INVESTMENT TRENDS IN ASIA

Recent Developments

In the decade between the Asian crisis and the current global crisis, investment spending in Asia diverged across two groups of economies (Figure 3.1). In the economies with relatively large domestic demand bases, China and India, investment decreased slightly during the Asian crisis, but then increased appreciably starting in the early 2000s.[2] In the group of relatively more export-oriented economies (NIEs, Japan, Malaysia, the Philippines, and Thailand), the average decline in the investment share of GDP following the Asian crisis was about 7 percentage points. Combined with relatively stable saving in this group, the fall in investment as a share of GDP contributed to rising current account surpluses over this period.

A sharp fall in private spending on fixed capital explains most of the investment decline in export-oriented Asia (Figure 3.2). Outside of Taiwan Province of China, the bulk of the investment slowdown originated in the private sector. In particular, a sustained slump in fixed investment—in the form of factories and machinery—typically accounted for between half and three-fourths of the overall decline in countries for which a breakdown is available. In addition, excess investment in residential construction may have played some role in the precrisis boom and subsequent slump (Figure 3.3).

[2]Most of the subsequent discussion on private investment focuses on developments outside China and India, and emerging Asia is used to refer to economies excluding these two countries.

Figure 3.1
Asia: Gross Fixed Capital Formation (GFCF) and Gross Saving, 1993–2009
(In percent of GDP)

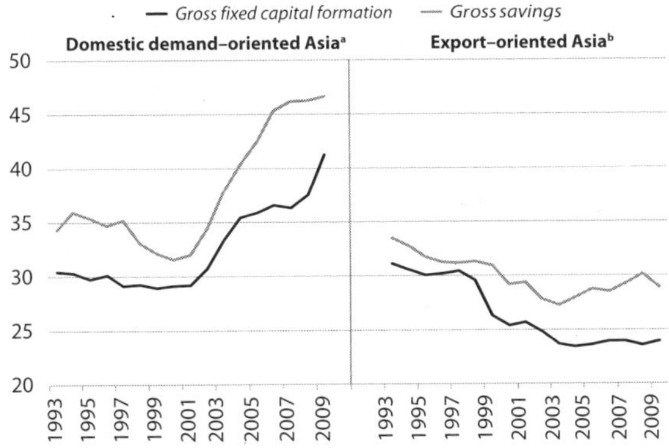

Source: IMF, WEO database.
[a]China and India.
[b]NIEs, Japan, Malaysia, the Philippines, and Thailand.

Figure 3.2
Export-Oriented Asia: Contribution to Change in Average Share of GFCF in GDP
(In percentage points; change in average shares between 1990–97 and 2000–07)

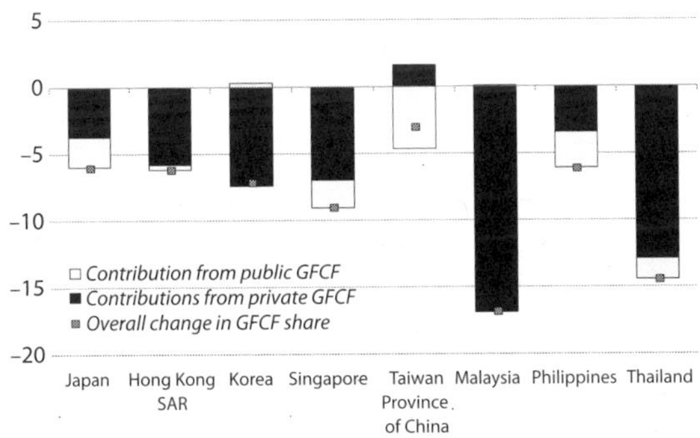

Sources: IMF, WEO database, and staff calculations.

Meanwhile, the decline in the public investment share has meant that an "infrastructure gap" persists between emerging Asia and the rest of the world, particularly in a few countries, such as the ASEAN-4 and India (Figures 3.4 and 3.5). The stock of infrastructure has increased since the 1990s along several dimensions, but still lags comparator emerging market regions in important respects. The median electricity-generating capacity in emerging Asia is approximately 90 percent of the median for Latin America (up from 50 percent in 1995). And despite the rapid spread of telephones, particularly mobile phones,

Figure 3.3
Selected Asia: Change in Investment by Type[a]
(2000–07 relative to 1990–97; in percent of GDP)

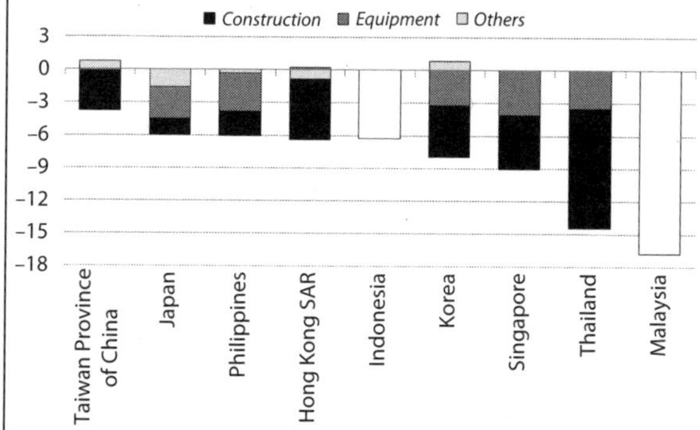

Sources: CEIC Data Company Ltd.; and IMF staff calculations.
[a]For Indonesia and Malaysia, change in overall gross fixed capital formation shown by all-white columns due to lack of sufficient data by type of investment.

Figure 3.4
Phone Connections, 1995, 2005, Latest[a]
(Median; number of connections per 100 people)

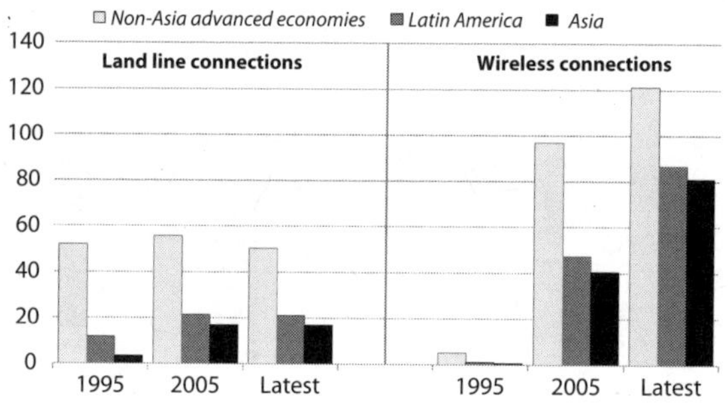

Source: World Bank, *World Development Indicators,* 2010.
[a]Asia includes ASEAN-5, China, India, and Korea. Latin America includes Argentina, Brazil, Chile, Colombia, Costa Rica, Ecuador, and Mexico.

in the region in the past decade, emerging Asia also continues to lag behind Latin America in its stock of telecommunications infrastructure. There is growing recognition among policymakers in the region that these infrastructure deficits impede private investment and growth.[3]

[3]India's National Economic Advisory Council, for example, has called the state of physical infrastructure a "binding constraint" on expansion and a "significant contributor to lower competitiveness" (Rangarajan, 2010).

Figure 3.5
Electricity Generation, 1995, 2005, Latest[a]
(Median; in kilowatt hours per capita)

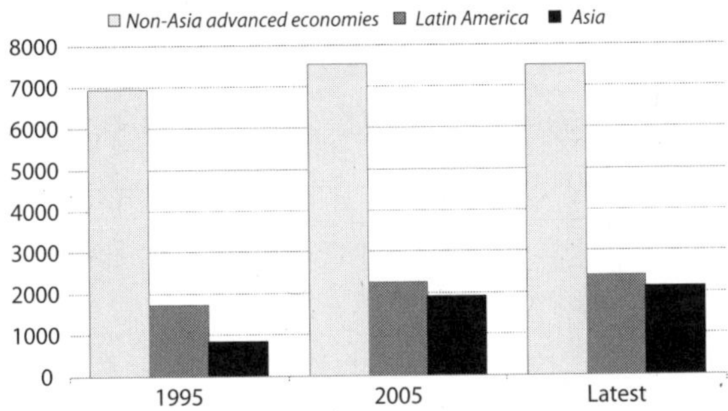

Source: World Bank, *World Development Indicators*, 2010.
[a]Asia includes ASEAN-5, China, India, and Korea. Latin America includes Argentina, Brazil, Chile, Colombia, Costa Rica, Ecuador, and Mexico.

Investment Levels and Composition in Asia

Investment is relatively low in some regional economies, notably the ASEAN-4. Previous research using macrolevel estimates from a standard neoclassical growth model demonstrated that most ASEAN economies have been investing well below the rate implied by their current capital-output ratios (see Chapter III in the IMF's October 2010 *Regional Economic Outlook: Asia and Pacific*). Firm-level data also support this view. Even as liquidity indicators have improved and leverage has decreased since the Asian crisis, operating margins and investment have fallen markedly over this period.[4] Investment rates in the ASEAN-4 economies are now lower than in other emerging economies and closer to those in economies with much higher per capita incomes and capital intensity, such as Japan, the United States, and the Euro area (Figure 3.6).

In contrast, in Japan and the NIEs, the issue is one of composition rather than the overall level of investment. In these economies, investment has shifted since the Asian crisis toward manufacturing and large firms, particularly in the export sector.

In Japan, for instance, the share of the nonmanufacturing sector in overall investment has fallen from 70 percent in 2000 to just over 50 percent in 2007 (Figure 3.7). Despite broadly similar economic structures, this decline contrasts sharply with developments in comparator economies, such as the United States, the United Kingdom, and Germany, where the starting share was similar but has now risen to about 80 percent. In particular, the share in total investment of the four main exporting sectors—automobiles, machinery, electronics, and steel—rose from 19 percent to 31 percent in Japan.

At the same time, investment has lagged behind for smaller firms and in the services sector (Figure 3.8). These divergent trends are clearly highlighted in

[4]See Appendix Table 3A.1 for details.

Figure 3.6
Firm-Level Investment Rate, 2000–07[a]
(Median investment-to-capital ratio)

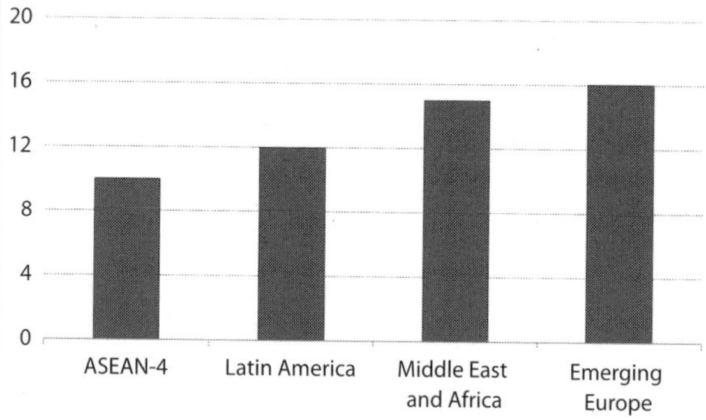

Sources: Worldscope; and IMF staff calculations.
[a]Latin America includes Argentina, Brazil, Chile, Colombia, Mexico, and Peru. Middle East and Africa includes Israel, Egypt, Morocco, Pakistan, and South Africa. Emerging Europe includes Czech Republic, Hungary, Poland, Russia, and Turkey.

Figure 3.7
Composition of Investment by Sector, 1990, 2000, and 2007[a]
(In percent of total, at constant 1995 prices)

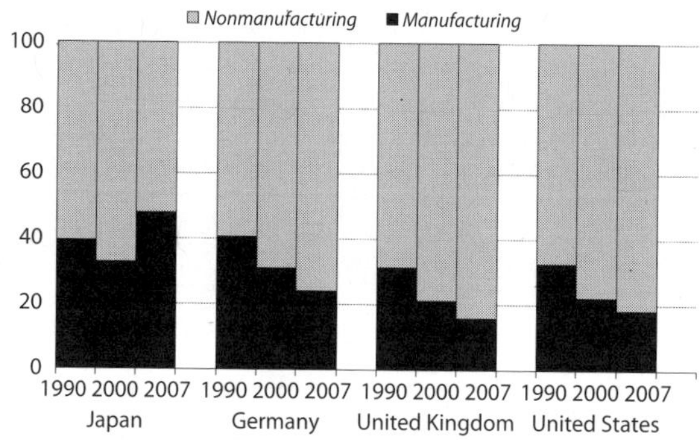

Sources: European Union, KLEMS Database.
[a]Excluding finance, insurance, real estate, and public utilities.

Korea, where rising regional competition has put pressure on labor-intensive SMEs, particularly in low-end manufacturing.[5] SMEs also seem to suffer from

[5]Country-specific experiences vary, but the rise of China has intensified competitive pressures, particularly on the SMEs in the region. In the case of Korea, for example, SMEs have either scaled down operations or shifted production to China (Kang and Kim, 2006). The sectors most directly affected appear to be textiles and basic manufacturing.

Figure 3.8
NIEs: Firm-Level Investment Rate, by Size and by Sector, 2000 and 2008
(Median investment-to-capital ratio)

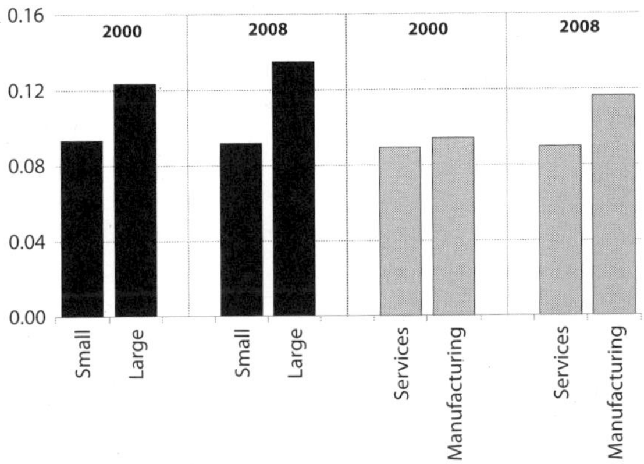

Sources: Worldscope; and IMF staff calculations.

excess capacity, while low productivity in the services sector, where many of these firms operate, has been a constraint on investment.

Therefore, even in Japan and the NIEs, where investment levels do not seem obviously low, there may be scope for supporting rebalancing by reorienting capital spending toward firms and sectors more directly linked to the domestic economy.

WHAT DRIVES INVESTMENT IN ASIA?

The two key aspects of investment in Asia—the fall in the share of investment in GDP in some economies and the shift in composition in others—are at the core of the rebalancing debate. This section attempts to explain both features of the data with a view to establishing what specific policies might help on the Asian side of the global rebalancing effort.

Explaining the Fall in Aggregate Investment

Could the fall in the private investment share simply reflect a decline in the relative price of capital goods? Following the Asian crisis, several economies introduced structural and financial market reforms that may have raised their efficiency in producing capital goods during the past decade.[6] Another question is whether, as the importance of IT capital has increased, the productivity gains

[6]More generally, Hsieh and Klenow (2007) document an inverse relationship between the relative price of capital goods and the level of development. This implies that as economies grow over time the relative price of capital falls as they become more efficient at producing capital goods.

in that sector have contributed to a decline in the relative price of capital (DeLong, 2002). In such a case, the decline in the share of nominal investment spending in nominal GDP may simply reflect a fall in the relative price of capital goods.

On balance, however, the evidence suggests that falling relative prices are unlikely to explain the decline in the investment rate. If that explanation were valid, we would expect to see a strong positive correlation between the change in the relative price of capital and the change in the investment share of GDP.[7] However, the evidence suggests that in Asia the opposite is true (Figure 3.9). In fact, the relative price of capital and the investment rate appear to be negatively correlated. The decline in the investment share was associated with lower relative prices in only half the cases, possibly reflecting the differential pace of structural and financial reforms across regional economies or, alternatively, compositional differences in the mix of IT and non-IT capital goods employed. Moreover, the economies that have witnessed the largest falls in the investment share of GDP have also seen the largest increases in the relative price of capital goods. And there is considerable variation across the region: Hong Kong SAR, Japan, and Singapore all experienced a similar decline in the investment share but differing declines in the relative price of capital goods. At the very least, this explanation cannot account for trends across the region as a whole.

Instead, estimates from a standard regression approach suggest that at the aggregate level, the decline in the investment rate may have been caused

Figure 3.9
Export-Oriented Asia: GFCF—Change in Share versus Change in Relative Price
(Comparison between 1990–97 and 2000–07)

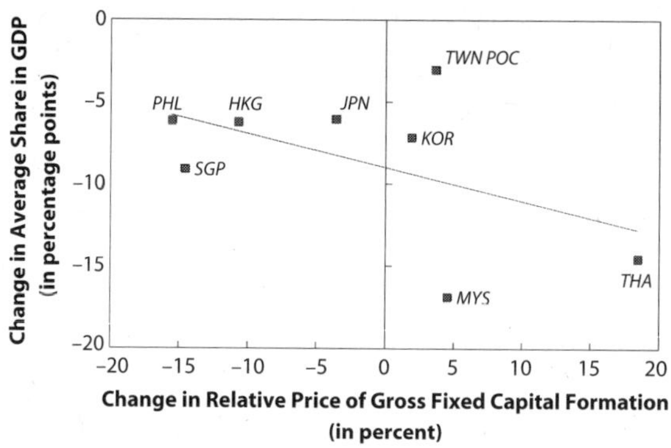

Sources: IMF; WEO database; and staff calculations.

[7]The relative price of capital is measured using the ratio of the investment deflator to the overall GDP deflator from the IMF's WEO database.

TABLE 3.1

Determinants of Private Investment Spending[a]

	(1)	(2)	(3)	(4)	(5)
Lagged private investment	0.772 ***	0.742	0.748 ***	0.745 ***	0.710 ***
	(0.039)	(0.040)	(0.040)	(0.045)	(0.036)
Real interest rate	0.0319 *	0.030 *	0.0328 *	0.014	0.006
	(0.017)	(0.018)	(0.017)	(0.011)	(0.011)
GDP growth	0.360 ***	0.328	0.340 ***	0.331 ***	0.299 ***
	(0.046)	(0.040)	(0.039)	(0.040)	(0.041)
Volatility		−0.224 ***	−0.241 ***	−0.250 ***	−0.310 ***
		(0.060)	(0.060)	(0.064)	(0.077)
Manufacturing share of value added			0.091	0.054	0.089
			(0.072)	(0.063)	(0.062)
Ease of doing business				0.244	0.343 **
				(0.157)	(0.174)
Financial development					21.270 *
					(12.210)
Financial development (squared)					−15.210 *
					(9.228)
Observations	412	412	369	338	260
Number of countries	44	44	42	39	37
Autocorrelation in first-differenced errors (p-value)[b]	0.8779	0.926	0.938	0.671	0.339

Source: IMF staff estimates.

[a]Dependent variable: private investment-to-GDP ratio. Arellano–Bond estimation technique used. Robust standard errors in parentheses. ***, **, and * indicate significance at 1, 5, and 10 percent levels, respectively.

[b]Arellano–Bond test of no second-order autocorrelation in first-differenced errors.

by structural changes following the Asian crisis (Table 3.1). The regression framework used is an Arellano-Bond GMM estimation, which allows for the inclusion of lagged values of investment spending and a set of controls—GDP growth as a proxy for the aggregate return on investment, the standard deviation of GDP growth over rolling four-year windows to capture macroeconomic uncertainty, the real interest rate, the manufacturing share of value added, an index of financial market development, and a measure of the ease of doing business (or the perceived investment climate)—along with country-specific, time-invariant fixed effects.[8] Across a large cross-country panel of emerging and advanced economies, the approach identifies the following key determinants:

- *The aggregate return on investment (average growth) is positively associated with investment spending.* Following the Asian crisis, average real GDP growth in emerging Asia (excluding China and India) slowed appreciably. The slowdown in real GDP growth relative to the precrisis period reduced investment spending by 2½ percentage points of GDP on average.

[8]The index of financial development (Abiad, Detragiache, and Tressel, 2008) is a normalized average across seven indicators (banking supervision, privatization, entry barriers, directed credit, credit ceilings, interest rate controls, and securities market reform). The measure of ease of doing business is based on an index compiled by the *International Country Risk Guide* (www.prsgroup.com/ICRG.aspx) and largely reflects perceptions of corruption in the private and public sectors.

- *Macroeconomic uncertainty (volatility) is negatively correlated with investment spending.* As uncertainty rises, firms hold back on costly and potentially irreversible investment since they prefer the option value of waiting until the uncertainty clears. Growth in emerging Asia has been relatively more volatile as the recovery from the 1997–98 downturn gave way to the tech boom-and-bust cycle, which was then followed by a period of solid growth that, in turn, ended sharply with the current crisis. This higher volatility over the past decade has depressed investment spending in the region by approximately 1 percentage point of GDP relative to the early 1990s.
- *A surprising deterioration in investors' perceptions of the business climate has also dampened investment.* The altered perceptions are associated with a further decline in investment spending of three-quarters of a percentage point of GDP compared with the early 1990s.

In addition, infrastructure weaknesses may be constraining investment in emerging Asia. Increases in the stock of infrastructure can boost investment through several channels. Improved connectivity (better roads, bridges, and telecommunications) will reduce transport and communication costs, facilitate internal specialization, and allow for an improved division of labor within the country. Furthermore, the decline in transportation costs can support clustering of industries, with attendant gains in productivity that raise the return on investment through knowledge spillovers and agglomeration effects (Krugman, 1991, and Venables, 2006). This is particularly important for countries such as India, Indonesia, and China, where vast distances separate potential producers and end users. Power and energy infrastructure that minimizes work stoppages and disruptions in production and distribution can also augment returns on investment by raising productivity. Better roads, electricity, and water supply will also enhance health and education investments, reducing inequality and raising the human capital of the work force.[9]

Empirically, improvements in infrastructure appear to have a powerful impact on private investment spending in the region. Across four commonly used indicators of infrastructure (electricity generation, telephone lines, cell phone subscribers, and road length), there is strong evidence of a positive association with private investment spending.[10] Estimates from a simple regression framework as outlined above suggest that electricity and roads have the strongest impact on private

[9]Calderon and Serven (2004a, 2004b) point out that improvements in infrastructure are associated with reduced inequality and higher growth. But there may still be an equity-efficiency trade-off in the short term when current needs in the education and health sectors must be weighed against the requirements for infrastructure.

[10]These physical stocks of infrastructure do not adjust for quality differences across countries, but are preferable as indicators of infrastructure services to expenditure-based measures, which often capture other categories of spending (Pritchett, 1996).

TABLE 3.2

Effect of Infrastructure on Private Investment spending[a]

Lagged private investment	0.701 ***	0.741 ***	0.673 ***	0.422 ***
	(0.050)	(0.054)	(0.046)	(0.081)
Real interest rate	−0.026	0.006	0.018	−0.038
	(0.024)	(0.026)	(0.021)	(0.027)
Growth Tate of GDP	0.244 ***	0.285 ***	0.228 ***	0.153 **
	(0.049)	(0.050)	(0.042)	(0.077)
Volatility	−0.104 *	-0.164 ***	−0.032	−0.345 ***
	(0.057)	(0.048)	(0.044)	(0.108)
Electricity	2.204 **			
	(1.122)			
Telephones		1.420 **		
		(0.592)		
Cell phones			0.689 ***	
			(0.186)	
Roads				4.015 ***
				(1.236)
Observations	316	325	325	120
Number of countries	41	42	42	32
Autocorrelation in first-differenced errors (p-value)[b]	0.347	0.758	0.72	0.267

Source: IMF staff estimates.

[a]Dependent variable: private investment-to-GDP ratio. Arellano–Bond estimation technique used. Robust standard errors in parentheses. ***, **, and * indicate significance at 1, 5, and 10 percent levels, respectively.

[b]Arellano–Bond test of no second-order autocorrelation in first-differenced errors.

investment, while increases in the number of telephone lines and cell phone subscribers are also positively associated with higher private investment (Table 3.2).[11]

Why Has the Composition of Investment Changed?

What explains the shift in investment away from services and small firms in more developed parts of the region since the Asian crisis? Firm-level panel data is used to estimate the standard neoclassical investment model, which relates current investment to expectations of future profitability through Tobin's *Q* ratio, defined as the ratio of the stock market valuation of the firm to the replacement cost of its capital stock.[12] The model is estimated using a first-differenced GMM approach and augmented by additional regressors, including (1) cash flow, which measures the internal funds available to finance investment projects and is typically used in the literature as a proxy for financing constraints; (2) leverage, measured by the debt-to-assets ratio, as a proxy for the effect of financial restructuring

[11]Greater use of telephones (particularly mobile phones) is increasingly seen as an important facilitator of business activities. For an example of how the spread of mobile telephones has enhanced price discovery, eliminated waste, and enhanced efficiency in a specific industry, see Jensen (2007) on the impact of cell phones on the fisheries industry in Kerala, India.

[12]See Appendix (below) for details. Table 3A.1 provides summary statistics. Regression results are reported in Tables 3A.2 and 3A.3.

TABLE 3.3

How Would an Improvement in Fundamentals Affect Investment in Asia?

Drivers	Region	Type of firm	Effect on investment
10 percent increase in profitability	NIEs	Small firms	3 percent
	ASEAN-4	Large firms	2 percent
10 percent increase in external finance	NIEs	Domestically oriented; labor-intensive	2 percent
	Japan, ASEAN-4	Small firms; domestically oriented; service sector	2 percent
10 percent decrease in leverage	NIEs	Service sector	3 percent
	Japan	Small firms; domestically oriented; labor-intensive; service sector	2–5 percent
	ASEAN-4	Large firms; export oriented; manufacturing sector	4–6 percent
10 percent decrease in risk	NIEs	Service sector	4 percent
	Japan	Labor-intensive firms	3 percent
	ASEAN-4	Export oriented; manufacturing sector; capital-intensive firms	3–5 percent

Source: IMF staff estimates.

on investment; and (3) the standard deviation of returns on the weekly stock price index to capture the potential negative impact of uncertainty on investment.

In recent years, several factors appear to have been inhibiting investment by domestically oriented firms. In the period before the Asian crisis, the firm-level relationship between investment and fundamentals was relatively weak, lending support to the hypothesis of overinvestment. In the postcrisis period, however, a much stronger link has emerged, with the relative importance of different factors varying based on firm characteristics (Table 3.3).

Expectations of future profitability are significant drivers of investment spending for most firms in the NIEs and, to a lesser extent, in Japan. In these economies, relatively lower returns on investment by small firms and in the service sector may be contributing to the unbalanced composition of investment.

In the NIEs and in Japan, inadequate access to external finance is a binding constraint on investment for small and domestically oriented firms. Despite significant progress in financial restructuring since the Asian crisis, a legacy of excess leverage and dependence on debt financing continues to hold back investment for some firms (Figure 3.10). By necessitating repayments regardless of profitability, excessive debt financing can retard investment, particularly in longer-term and more risky projects. In the NIEs, such effects seem to be evident in the services sector. In Japan, they inhibit investment by smaller firms, nonexporters, and those using labor-intensive technology. The results suggest that greater reliance on equity could promote investment by such firms.

Uncertainty also has powerful dampening effects on investment in the services sector in the NIEs and labor-intensive firms in Japan. In part, the effect of uncertainty may reflect the close integration of these economies with global markets

Figure 3.10
Corporate Sector Leverage, 2000–08
(In percent)

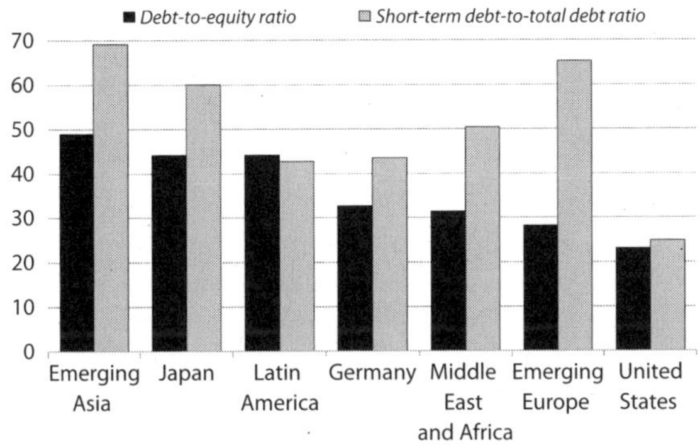

Source: IMF, Corporate Vulnerability Utility Database.

Figure 3.11
Uncertainty: Stock Price Deviation, 2000–08
(Standard deviation of weekly stock price index)

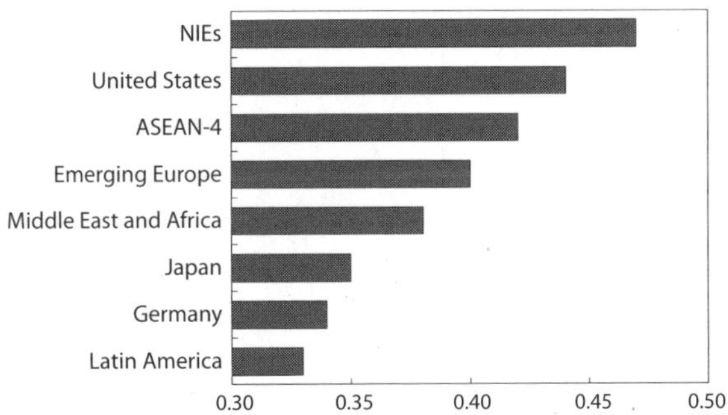

Source: IMF staff calculation.

and their associated susceptibility to global shocks (Figure 3.11). In addition, with greater competition at each step of the supply chain, firms might be less able to adjust markups procyclically and use them as buffers against external shocks. This may have made them more cautious in their investment decisions than they would have been previously.[13]

[13]Linden, Kraemer, and Dedrick (2009) illustrate the supply chain of the iPod and demonstrate how Asian firms capture very little of the value added at each stage compared with the share garnered by the U.S.-based providers of the intellectual capital behind the product, suggesting limited profit margins in the Asian segments of the chain.

Overall, smaller, more domestically oriented, labor-intensive, and service sector firms in the NIEs and in Japan have faced stronger headwinds to their investment compared with larger, exporting, capital-intensive, and manufacturing firms. These headwinds are reflected in the greater sensitivity of their investment to profitability, internal funding, leverage and risk, as well as the generally lower improvement in these indicators since the Asian crisis relative to larger, exporting, capital-intensive, and manufacturing firms (Table 3.4).[14]

Moreover, these headwinds appear to be specific to the region and do not affect firms in other emerging and advanced economies to the same extent.

- In other emerging economies, investment is less affected by risk or capital structure. The detrimental effects of uncertainty and the overhang of debt were less pronounced than in Asia reflecting, respectively, the relatively more open nature of Asian economies, and the relatively heavier reliance of Asian firms on short-term funding.
- Outside the region, financing constraints and leverage do not have as dominant a role in advanced economies with well-developed capital markets. German firms, which operate in a similar bank-oriented financing environment as firms in the NIEs and Japan, display the same cross-sectional pattern in financing constraints. However, there is less evidence in recent years of financing constraints or detrimental effects of debt financing in the case of firms in the United States and United Kingdom, partly reflecting more diverse sources of funding for small companies, including bond markets, equity funding, and venture capital.

POLICY IMPLICATIONS: HOW CAN ASIA FACILITATE REBALANCING THROUGH INVESTMENT?

To help rebalance Asia's economies, private investment needs to be raised in some cases, such as the ASEAN-4, while in other economies, such as Japan and the NIEs, it needs to be reconfigured toward domestically oriented sectors. At the same time, the region's pressing infrastructure needs are a constraint on private investment and growth and will have to be addressed urgently. This section discusses potential policy responses to meet these challenges suggested by the econometric results and best practices for funding infrastructure investments based on cross-country evidence.

Policies Suggested by Empirical Results

The empirical results presented in this chapter suggest that policies to boost private investment could focus on four broad areas: (1) increasing the returns on investment; (2) improving access to external financing to reduce the cost of capital, especially for smaller and domestically oriented firms; (3) reducing excess leverage and promoting

[14]In the case of the ASEAN-4, financing constraints are found to be even more binding and to apply across a broader range of firms, while the detrimental effects of leverage and risk were mostly concentrated in larger firms and the export sector.

TABLE 3.4

NIEs and Japan: Changes in Fundamentals, 1990–97 versus 2000–07 by Firm and Type
(Median)

	NIEs			Japan		
	1990–97	2000–07	Percent change	1990–97	2000–07	Percent change
Small						
Tobin's *Q*	2.9	2.1	–28.0	3.2	1.5	–52.7
Cash flow-to-capital stock	0.2	0.2	11.9	0.1	0.1	2.9
Debt-to-assets	18.4	18.8	2.2	28.6	19.9	–30.1
Uncertainty	0.3	0.5	42.1	0.3	0.4	8.3
Large						
Tobin's *Q*	2.5	1.9	–24.6	2.5	1.7	–30.7
Cash flow-to-capital stock	0.1	0.2	94.0	0.1	0.1	4.1
Debt-to-assets	41.8	26.4	–36.9	36.1	22.4	–37.8
Uncertainty	0.4	0.4	22.5	0.3	0.3	13.3
Services						
Tobin's *Q*	2.8	1.9	–30.1	4.5	1.7	–62.7
Cash flow-to-capital stock	0.1	0.2	36.0	0.1	0.1	4.3
Debt-to-assets	24.8	21.4	–13.8	30.8	20.3	–34.0
Uncertainty	0.3	0.5	36.7	0.3	0.3	10.7
Manufacturing						
Tobin's *Q*	2.6	1.9	–27.9	2.6	1.6	–39.4
Cash flow-to-capital stock	0.1	0.2	34.7	0.1	0.1	4.2
Debt-to-assets	32.7	23.9	–26.9	35.0	22.0	–37.1
Uncertainty	0.4	0.4	25.6	0.3	0.3	3.7
Domestic						
Tobin's *Q*	3.1	1.9	–39.2	3.4	1.5	–56.0
Cash flow-to-capital stock	0.2	0.2	–18.4	0.1	0.1	2.1
Debt-to-assets	19.8	23.6	19.4	30.2	20.4	–32.4
Uncertainty	0.3	0.5	48.0	0.3	0.3	7.8
Exporters						
Tobin's *Q*	2.6	2.1	–19.5	2.7	1.8	–36.1
Cash flow-to-capital stock	0.1	0.2	46.6	0.1	0.2	3.9
Debt-to-assets	31.3	22.2	–29.0	34.4	22.4	–34.9
Uncertainty	0.4	0.5	30.7	0.3	0.3	10.6
Labor-intensive						
Tobin's *Q*	3.4	2.5	–27.2	3.5	1.8	–48.6
Cash flow-to-capital stock	0.2	0.2	9.2	0.2	0.2	10.4
Debt-to-assets	22.2	18.5	–16.9	27.9	19.3	–30.9
Uncertainty	0.3	0.5	39.3	0.3	0.3	15.2
Capital-intensive						
Tobin's *Q*	2.4	1.7	–27.1	2.5	1.5	–40.9
Cash flow-to-capital stock	0.1	0.2	51.0	0.1	0.1	3.3
Debt-to-assets	32.5	26.5	–18.6	38.6	24.1	–37.7
Uncertainty	0.4	0.5	30.8	0.3	0.3	2.3

Source: IMF staff estimates.

SME restructuring to create space for new investment; and (4) strengthening risk management and bolstering the business climate to reduce uncertainty.

First, raising the rate of return on investment will be important, suggesting these strategies:

Figure 3.12
Effective Corporate Tax Rates in OECD
(In percent; 2005)

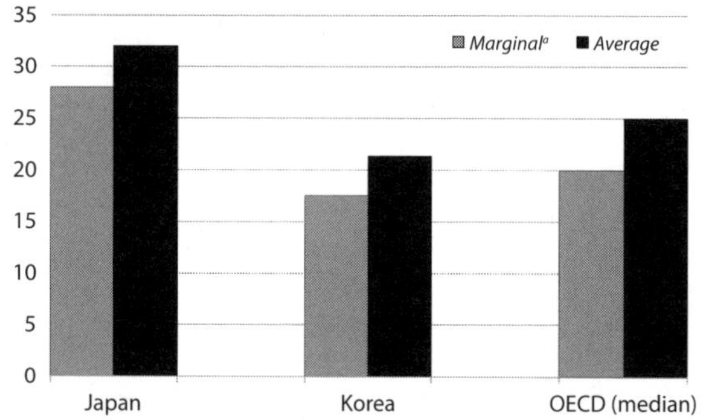

Sources: Institute for Fiscal Studies; and IMF staff estimates.
[a]Plant and machinery, and equity financed.

- *In some parts of the region, the tax code is an obvious candidate,* since taxes raise the bar for investment to be profitable and fall especially hard on capital-intensive industries. Japan, for instance, has among the highest average and marginal effective corporate tax rates (AER and MER) in the OECD (Figure 3.12).[15] Lowering the corporate tax rate may be an effective strategy for reducing distortions and boosting domestic and foreign investment. Accelerating depreciation allowances for industrial buildings, which are the lowest among the G-7, and extending corporate tax-loss carry-forwards to allow firms to recoup some of the losses incurred in the early years of large investments may also help (IMF, 2010a).[16] Elsewhere, such as in Korea where effective tax rates are already low by OECD standards due to generous tax exemptions, changes in taxation are likely to have a more modest impact.[17]
- *On the other hand, tax incentives are unlikely to be cost-effective.*[18] Their key weaknesses include costliness, scope for abuse by taxpayers, lack of transparency, introducing distortions into business decisions, and

[15]The average effective rate (AER) is the proportion of lifetime pretax profit that is taken in tax and is an important determinant of the location of investment. The marginal effective tax rate (MER) is the difference between the before- and after-tax returns on a project that an investor finds just worthwhile; it affects the desired level of investment.

[16]Buildings are subject to straight-line depreciation only, with a much longer useful tax life than elsewhere (50 years against, for example, 39 years in the United States). Japan currently allows for a seven-year carry-forward period, compared with 20 years in the United States.

[17]A wide range of incentives are currently provided under the special tax treatment and control law of 1999. Moreover, the literature suggests that tax effects on investment may be secondary if other factors, such as the quality of governance, regulatory framework, infrastructure, macropolitical stability, and labor market conditions, are problematic. See Norregaard and Khan (2007) for a review.

[18]Among others, see Zee, Stotsky, and Ley (2002) for a survey of the evidence.

ineffectiveness, relative to other measures, in reaching intended goals. Instead, international evidence suggests that establishing a simple, credible, broad-based and transparent corporate tax regime may be a better strategy for creating an environment conducive to investment (Botman, Klemm, and Baqir, 2008).

Second, improving access to external financing would lower the cost of capital for smaller businesses and firms in the nontradable sectors. Problems faced by SMEs in accessing financing typically reflect an incomplete range of financial products, regulatory rigidities, gaps in the legal framework, and information asymmetries between financiers and firms. Possible strategies to mitigate these effects include:

- *Deepening and broadening financial systems.* Only Korea and Malaysia have sizable corporate bond markets among emerging economies in the region, while the rest rely on relationship-based financing through banks (Figure 3.13). Encouraging corporate bond market development would help open up additional channels for funding (IMF, 2007).
- *Improving the financial infrastructure for smaller and more service-oriented firms* by encouraging more lending on risk-based terms; reforming collateral laws to allow a wider range of securitization (beyond real estate and other fixed assets), as is being done in Japan through a program accepting inventories and accounts receivables as collateral; and deepening credit information and extending the coverage of credit registries. The latter was initiated in the Philippines through the establishment of the Credit Information Corporation in 2008.

Figure 3.13
Size of the Corporate Bond Market: Selected Asian Economies, 2009
(In percent of GDP)

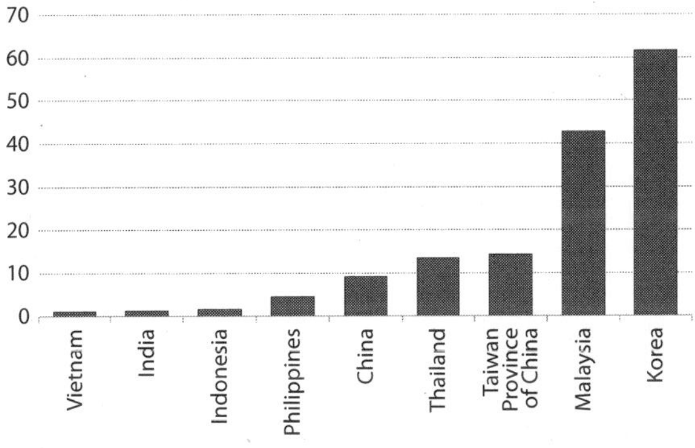

Sources: Asian Development Bank; and Bank for International Settelements.

Figure 3.14
Venture Capital Investment: Selected Advanced Economies, 2006
(In percent of GDP)

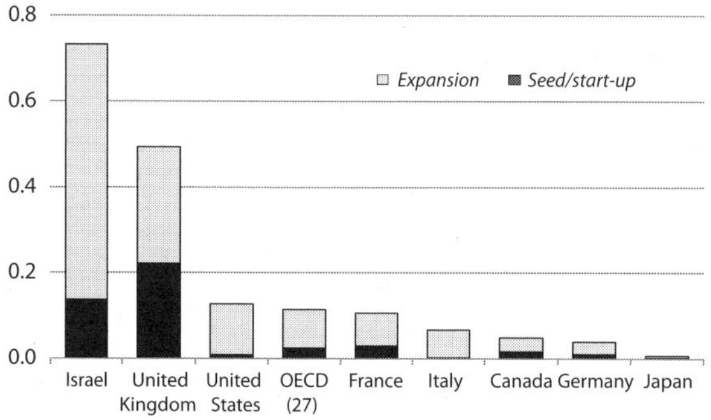

Source: OECD, 2008.

- *Widening the pool of venture capital funding available for start-ups in new emerging sectors.* Targeted tax breaks or allocations of a larger share of public pension funds to venture capital investments could support the industry, which is relatively underdeveloped, even in advanced parts of Asia (Figure 3.14).[19] More funding could also be drawn in by providing information on venture capital investment performance and developing performance benchmarks on emerging equity exchanges (such as JASDAQ in Japan).[20]

Third, reducing leverage and improving incentives for corporate restructuring will help create space for new investment.

- *As the global recovery firms up, restructuring could be promoted by phasing out credit guarantees.* Significant progress has been made on corporate and financial restructuring over the last decade, but smaller companies have tended to fall behind (IMF, 2006a, 2006b). This partly reflects the still-sizable credit guarantees for SMEs, which can limit their incentives for restructuring and create an entry barrier by making it difficult for many newer firms to access bank credit (McKinsey and Company, 2000).[21] In Korea, for instance,

[19]In Japan, for instance, the Government Pension Investment Fund does not undertake any alternative investments such as venture capital, real estate, and private equity. By contrast, a number of OECD countries allocate some share of their assets to such investments, including California Public Employees' Retirement System (14 percent) and New Zealand Superannuation Fund (11 percent). See also IMF (2010b).

[20]In the United States and Europe, VentureOne and Thomson Financial store information on start-ups—including profitability and investment flows—regularly used by venture capitalists and institutional investors.

[21]Uesugi, Sakai, and Yamashiro, 2006, suggest that credit guarantees can lead to a significant increase in leverage and do not translate into efficiency gains in the case of high-risk firms.

banks tend to direct loans to existing and well-established SMEs that have secured credit guarantees, since most of the associated default risk is borne by the government. While these guarantees declined from 8 percent of GDP in 2001 to about 6 percent in 2005, they remained almost 30 times larger than in the United States.[22] Over the longer term, attention should shift away from relying on guarantees to addressing the root cause of SMEs' limited access to credit. Improvements in the financial infrastructure can improve credit availability, including by expanding credit information sharing, allowing the securitization of movable assets, and developing venture capital markets for SMEs (Beck and Demirguç-Künt, 2006).

- *Assisting the exit of nonviable companies would also help,* including through out-of-court workouts and further reforms to streamline bankruptcy procedures. Combined with reforms to the public support system, these measures could jumpstart a market for private-led restructuring of distressed SMEs, similar to what took place for large enterprises after the Japanese banking crisis in the 1990s. In the same vein, after the Asian crisis, the Korea Asset Management Corporation successfully created a market for distressed Korean corporate debt by purchasing nonperforming loans (NPLs) from banks and repackaging them for eventual sale to investors.[23] A similar restructuring and consolidation of the SME sector might be accomplished by promoting asset management companies that specialize in repackaging distressed debt of small firms.

Fourth, reducing uncertainty would help lower the risks associated with long-term investment decisions. The empirical results suggest that investment decisions can be affected by uncertainty about many aspects of the operating environment, such as demand, prices, costs, and exchange rates. In addition, risk related to policies, notably the tax code and other business regulations, could deter private investment. Options to address this include:

- *Promoting the use of financial instruments to manage risks.* Even in relatively advanced parts of the region, international comparisons suggest that large exporters tend to underinsure against credit, commodity, and marketable security price risk. SMEs undertake much less hedging in general (Heaney and others, 1999).
- *Further improvements to the perceptions of the ease of doing business.* While the structural reforms implemented since the Asian crisis have potentially made a substantive difference in the region's investment climate, it appears that perceptions have not yet caught up with the new reality. Surveys suggest that a streamlined process for business creation, greater labor market flexibility, an improved legal and regulatory framework for entrepreneurs and bankruptcy, and a more transparent tax system could help reduce investor

[22]More recently, credit guarantees have increased significantly across the region as part of the policy response to the crisis (see Box 1.7 in IMF, 2009).

[23]See Kang and Kim (2006).

perceptions of risk in many parts of the region (Guimaraes and Unteroberdoerster, 2006; and IMF, 2008b). Ongoing efforts in these areas—the adoption of a competition law in Hong Kong SAR, the lowering of restrictions on foreign investment in the services sector in Malaysia, the establishment of one-stop shops to reduce administrative delays in Indonesia and Malaysia—could make it more attractive for companies to expand operations domestically rather than overseas.

Meeting Infrastructure Needs

Government financing and provision of infrastructure may not be sufficient to meet the growing needs of the region. Over the next decade, emerging Asia's total infrastructure needs are estimated to be in the vicinity of US$7.5 trillion (AsDB, 2009). While several governments across the region have stepped up their allocation to infrastructure as part of crisis-induced stimulus packages, their ability to sustain elevated levels of investment in roads, telecommunications, and electricity in the years ahead may be limited by other demands on their budgets, shrinkages in fiscal space, and diminishing tolerance of bond investors for rising sovereign expenditure.[24]

Public-private partnerships offer an alternative provision mechanism, but effective design of these vehicles calls for coordinated action on many fronts. Historically, the provision of infrastructure has been almost entirely in the public domain in Asia and elsewhere, including in advanced economies. As pressures on government budgets have intensified worldwide, more attention has been paid to hybrid public-private forms of provision. The projects initiated under this organizational form offer some important lessons for the design of future public-private partnerships:

- The Theun Hinboun hydropower project, implemented jointly by Thailand and Lao PDR between 1994 and 1998, has turned out to be highly profitable (AsDB, 2009). Potential time inconsistency and hold-up problems (which may arise in instances where firms are asked to sink capital into a multiyear project but then are subsequently exposed to midcourse changes in tariff or tax policies) were solved by the Lao PDR government committing to meet its obligations under a 30-year license, backed up by the establishment of an offshore escrow account pledged to the investors in the project.
- The new international airport terminals at Delhi and Mumbai have been financed through a joint venture with 74 percent private consortium equity. Construction began in 2006 and is nearing completion in both cities. Regulatory uncertainty has been mitigated by having a dedicated regulator with sole legal jurisdiction over the projects. The new Airports Economic Regulatory Authority is focused entirely on monitoring services

[24]The disconnect between infrastructure finance needs and government ability to raise funding through general tax revenue is already acute in developing and emerging market contexts. Because the tax base tends to be narrower than in advanced economies, the marginal cost of generating additional revenue is likely to be relatively high (Swaroop, 1994).

at the airports and has laid out clear *ex ante* guidelines on pricing and cost pass-through and the quality of services.

A general principle in public-private partnerships is that optimal risk sharing involves allocating the burden of a particular risk to the entity best placed to bear it. Construction and operating risks are best borne by the private concessionary while the government entity bears the political and regulatory risks (Akitoby, Hemming, and Schwartz, 2007). A transparent sharing of risks along these lines can minimize delays, cost overruns, and funding disruptions. At the same time, the delineation of risks may be blurred if, for example, the government guarantees the debt raised by the private entity. In such instances, a clear accounting of the contingent fiscal risk will help anchor expectations and align sovereign borrowing costs more closely with fundamentals.

Measures to unlock saving and channel it into targeted infrastructure investment funds may help meet some of the funding shortfall. An innovation under consideration in India is the establishment of dedicated funding intermediaries with well-defined capital adequacy norms that can issue tax-free infrastructure bonds and tap into pension and insurance fund holdings. This will help overcome the problems of a bank-heavy funding structure where banks typically encounter an asset-liability mismatch when they lend long-term to infrastructure projects but rely largely on short-term wholesale funding and retail deposits.

SUMMARY

Looking ahead, a strategy for rebalancing growth in Asia will have many dimensions. One such dimension is the level and composition of investment. In some economies, such as the ASEAN-4, investment appears to be low relative to the level of development. In other parts of the region, such as Japan and the NIEs, the composition of investment is skewed toward export-oriented, capital-intensive firms in the manufacturing sector to the detriment of domestically oriented, labor-intensive firms in the services sector.

The pattern of investment could be influenced by financial reforms and improvements in infrastructure. In Japan and the NIEs, increasing investment by smaller, domestically oriented firms would help rotate the composition of investment toward nontradable sectors and promote rebalancing. Policies likely to advance this objective include promoting risk-based financing, SME restructuring through the reform of bankruptcy laws, and streamlining tax codes and regulations. In the ASEAN-4 economies, where the main concern is the overall level of investment, improvements in infrastructure could also help crowd in private investment and lift potential growth. How Asia adjusts to the postcrisis world of reduced external demand depends crucially on whether the region's economies create conditions conducive to investment-led rebalancing.

APPENDIX. FIRM-LEVEL ANALYSIS

The data used in the empirical analysis include all listed nonfinancial firms in our selected jurisdictions covered in the *Worldscope* database during the period 1989–2008. The *Worldscope* database is well known for its standardized presentation of global investment portfolios and its good coverage of historical data. The database covers more than 96 percent of the world's market value represented by it. One important advantage of using the database is that it provides standardized data for countries with different reporting practices, yielding relatively more reliable cross-country comparisons. Several firms entered the data set after 1995, implying somewhat shorter series for them. Outliers were excluded from the analysis based on standard criteria.

The company-specific variables included are those that potentially affect firm-level investment decisions, as suggested by the standard model of investment outlined in this chapter. These variables are obtained primarily from cash flow statements and include expected future profitability (Tobin's Q), cash flow, sales growth, leverage (defined as total debt to total assets), and uncertainty (measured as the standard deviation of returns on the weekly stock price index for the firm). The capital stock measure was estimated using the standard perpetual inventory method, with the net book value of plant, property, and equipment treated as the starting value and subsequent values determined using data on investment, disposals, and acquisitions.

Incorporating the standard adjustments for debt, Tobin's Q is defined as:

$$Q_{it} = \left[\frac{V_{it} + B_{it} - C_{it}}{p_t(1-\delta)K_{i,t-1}} \right], \tag{1}$$

where V is the firm's fundamental value or the expected present discounted value of future payments to shareholders; B is the book value of its outstanding debt; C is current assets; p is the price of the investment good; δ is the capital depreciation rate (assumed to equal 8 percent); and K is the replacement value of the firm's capital stock.

Model

The firm-level panel data were used to estimate the standard neoclassical investment model, which relates current investment to expectations of future profitability through Tobin's Q ratio, augmented by additional factors. The model estimated can be expressed as follows:

$$\Delta\left(\frac{I}{K}\right)_{it} = c_t + b\Delta Q_{it} + c\Delta Z_{i,t} + \Delta\varepsilon_{it}, \tag{2}$$

where I/K is the investment rate, Q is Tobin's Q,[25] and Z is a vector of additional variables.

[25]Defined as the ratio of the stock market valuation of the firm to the replacement cost of its capital stock.

TABLE 3A.1

Selected Financial Indicators for Firms, 1990–97 and 2000–07 *(Median)*

	Selected Asia			Nonregional comparators[a]					
	ASEAN4	NEs	Japan	United States	United Kingdom	Germany	Emerging Europe	Middle East and Africa	Latin America
Investment Rate									
1990–97	0.19	0.17	0.14	0.15	0.14	0.18	...	...	...
2000–07	0.10	0.11	0.09	0.12	0.11	0.11	0.16	0.15	0.12
Profitability (in percent)									
Operating margins[b]									
1990–97	11.14	7.14	4.16	7.17	6.56	0.33	...	...	...
2000–07	6.23	5.05	4.42	5.63	5.29	1.95	5.07	7.66	10.54
Valuation									
Tobin's *Q*									
1990–97	3.35	2.76	2.98	3.11	2.38	2.06	...	...	...
2000–07	2.00	2.07	1.73	3.35	2.39	1.82	2.67	2.39	1.94
Liquidity									
Current ratio[c]									
1990–97	1.25	1.27	1.36	1.93	1.35	1.75	...	...	...
2000–07	1.55	1.54	1.44	1.86	1.27	1.59	1.42	1.37	1.40
Capital intensity									
Capital-labor ratio									
1990–97	43.63	94.52	163.09	38.23	20.55	42.23	...	...	...
2000–07	31.66	68.16	113.38	57.88	32.46	58.53	46.23	24.98	76.48
Leverage (in percent)									
Debt to equity									
1990–97	66.63	63.13	88.57	49.49	38.46	55.60	...	...	...
2000–07	43.59	41.13	42.49	41.02	39.85	51.14	29.67	42.08	50.72
Short-term debt to total debt									
1990–97	68.48	56.73	47.52	14.96	48.41	48.33	...	...	...
2000–07	65.05	68.00	59.02	13.88	35.21	41.07	63.58	45.85	38.59

Sources: Worldscope; and IMF staff calculations.
[a]Emerging Europe includes Czech Republic, Hungary, Poland, Russia, and Turkey. Middle East and Africa includes Israel, Egypt, Morocco, Pakistan, and South Africa. Latin America includes Argentina, Brazil, Chile,
[b]Operating earnings (EBIT) in percent of sales.
[c]Current assets to current liabilities.

The models were estimated using a GMM approach to allow for endogeneity and measurement error in the dependent variables. Estimation was in first-differences and included year dummies to control for firm- and time-specific effects. This approach yields consistent estimates provided there is no higher-order serial correlation in the residuals and the instruments are valid.[26] Diagnostic tests were used to verify these conditions.[27]

[26]The instruments reported are lagged values of the dependent variable and our regressors, but results were robust to using alternative instrument sets.
[27]The models were assessed based on tests for serial correlation (m1 and m2) and instrument validity (Hansen).

TABLE 3A.2

Investment Equations, Full Sample (1991–2008)[a,b]

	ASEAN-4	NIEs	China	India	Emerging Europe	Middle East and Africa	Latin America	Japan
Tobin's Q	0.010	0.012**	–0.011	–0.000	0.010	0.015**	0.004	0.007**
	(0.01)	(0.00)	(0.01)	(0.01)	(0.01)	(0.01)	(0.01)	(0.00)
Liquidity[c]	0.150**	0.006	–0.009	0.205**	0.119**	0.051*	0.247**	0.012
	(0.07)	(0.03)	(0.10)	(0.08)	(0.05)	(0.03)	(0.06)	(0.04)
Leverage[d]	0.000	–0.001	0.001	0.001	–0.000	0.000	–0.001	–0.002**
	(0.00)	(0.00)	(0.00)	(0.00)	(0.00)	(0.00)	(0.00)	(0.00)
Uncertainty[e]	–0.127**	–0.119**	–0.044	–0.065	0.111	–0.048	–0.050	–0.062**
	(0.06)	(0.05)	(0.15)	(0.14)	(0.11)	(0.07)	(0.06)	(0.03)
p-value of specification tests								
m1	0.000	0.000	0.071	0.000	0.001	0.000	0.000	0.000
m2	0.283	0.407	0.329	0.804	0.488	0.186	0.156	0.196
Hansen-test	0.280	0.291	0.256	0.787	0.814	0.278	0.196	0.189
Number of firms	1505	3223	1066	513	410	451	566	2695
Number of observations	7481	14784	3527	2375	1610	2404	3528	10649

Sources: Worldscope; and IMF staff estimates.

[a]Dependent variable is investment rate. First-differenced GMM specifications, with lagged dependent variable and year dummies. Instruments are lagged values of regressors.

[b]Robust standard errors in parentheses, with * indicating significance at 10 percent and ** at 5 percent level.

[c]Cash flow-to-capital ratio.

[d]Debt-to-assets ratio.

[e]Standard deviation of return on weekly price index (annualized).

TABLE 3A.3

Asia: Investment Equations, Sub-Sample Analysis[a,b]

	Time period		Size		Market exposure		Capital intensity		Sector	
ASEAN-4	**Precrisis**	**Postcrisis**	**Big**	**Small**	**Foreign**	**Domestic**	**High**	**Low**	**Manufacturing**	**Services**
Tobin's *Q*	0.027**	0.004	0.011**	0.002	0.006	0.015	0.013**	0.019**	0.006	0.010
	(0.01)	(0.01)	(0.01)	(0.02)	(0.01)	(0.01)	(0.01)	(0.01)	(0.01)	(0.01)
Liquidity[c]	−0.093	0.161**	−0.003	0.169**	−0.019	0.103*	0.077**	−0.033	−0.052	0.115**
	(0.09)	(0.08)	(0.05)	(0.08)	(0.03)	(0.06)	(0.04)	(0.09)	(0.05)	(0.05)
Leverage[d]	0.002	−0.000	−0.003**	0.001	−0.002**	−0.001	−0.000	−0.000	−0.002**	0.000
	(0.00)	(0.00)	(0.00)	(0.00)	(0.00)	(0.00)	(0.00)	(0.00)	(0.00)	(0.00)
Uncertainty[e]	0.203	−0.139**	−0.034	0.065	−0.119**	−0.050	−0.138**	0.081	−0.083*	0.022
	(0.13)	(0.07)	(0.07)	(0.08)	(0.04)	(0.07)	(0.06)	(0.06)	(0.05)	(0.07)
					p-value of specification tests					
m1	0.032	0.000	0.000	0.001	0.000	0.000	0.000	0.005	0.000	0.000
m2	0.269	0.199	0.836	0.454	0.839	0.995	0.708	0.895	0.548	0.633
Hansen-test	0.116	0.735	0.112	0.409	0.077	0.120	0.297	0.540	0.201	0.385
Number of firms	389	1375	753	809	654	851	1129	556	901	604
Number of observations	1040	6441	3572	3447	3884	3597	3838	1740	4590	2891
	Time period		**Size**		**Market exposure**		**Capital intensity**		**Sector**	
NIEs	**Precrisis**	**Postcrisis**	**Big**	**Small**	**Foreign**	**Domestic**	**High**	**Low**	**Manufacturing**	**Services**
Tobin's *Q*	0.005	0.010**	0.018**	0.010**	0.015**	0.007	0.017**	0.008*	0.019**	0.010
	(0.01)	(0.01)	(0.01)	(0.00)	(0.00)	(0.01)	(0.01)	(0.01)	(0.00)	(0.00)
Liquidity[c]	0.171	−0.008	0.029	−0.000	0.039	0.140**	0.054	0.097**	0.046	−0.012
	(0.14)	(0.04)	(0.05)	(0.03)	(0.05)	(0.05)	(0.04)	(0.03)	(0.03)	(0.03)
Leverage[d]	0.009	−0.002	0.000	−0.000	−0.003**	0.000	−0.001	0.002	−0.002	−0.002*
	(0.01)	(0.00)	(0.00)	(0.00)	(0.00)	(0.00)	(0.00)	(0.00)	(0.00)	(0.00)
Uncertainty[e]	−0.049	−0.108*	−0.129*	−0.055	−0.156**	−0.013	−0.038	−0.072	−0.085*	−0.103*
	(0.11)	(0.06)	(0.07)	(0.05)	(0.07)	(0.04)	(0.05)	(0.08)	(0.05)	(0.05)
					p-value of specification tests					
m1	0.074	0.000	0.001	0.000	0.000	0.000	0.005	0.015	0.000	0.001
m2	0.526	0.757	0.376	0.187	0.083	0.694	0.087	0.200	0.088	0.558
Hansen-test	0.505	0.512	0.161	0.259	0.173	0.550	0.272	0.396	0.275	0.873
Number of firms	607	3085	1622	1703	1695	1528	2182	1445	2137	1086
Number of observations	1634	13150	7110	6685	9531	5253	7657	4461	9966	4818
	Time period		**Size**		**Market exposure**		**Capital intensity**		**Sector**	
Japan	**Precrisis**	**Postcrisis**	**Big**	**Small**	**Foreign**	**Domestic**	**High**	**Low**	**Manufacturing**	**Services**
Tobin's *Q*	0.017 **	0.005*	0.005*	0.004	0.008**	0.005	0.010**	0.004	0.012**	0.002
	(0.01)	(0.00)	(0.00)	(0.00)	(0.00)	(0.00)	(0.00)	(0.00)	(0.00)	(0.00)
Liquidity[c]	−0.179	0.045	0.012	0.089*	−0.012	0.103*	−0.019	0.103**	0.038	0.092*
	(0.13)	(0.04)	(0.05)	(0.06)	(0.04)	(0.06)	(0.06)	(0.05)	(0.05)	(0.06)
Leverage[d]	0.000	−0.002**	−0.002**	−0.002**	−0.002**	−0.001*	−0.002**	−0.002**	−0.002**	−0.002**
	(0.00)	(0.00)	(0.00)	(0.00)	(0.00)	(0.00)	(0.00)	(0.00)	(0.00)	(0.00)
Uncertainty[e]	−0.033	−0.063**	−0.072**	−0.057	−0.054*	−0.011	−0.088**	−0.064**	−0.042	−0.024
	(0.09)	(0.03)	(0.03)	(0.04)	(0.03)	(0.03)	(0.03)	(0.03)	(0.03)	(0.04)
					p-value of specification tests					
m1	0.000	0.000	0.000	0.000	0.000	0.000	0.000	0.000	0.000	0.000
m2	0.52	0.150	0.211	0.220	0.120	0.165	0.734	0.207	0.856	0.201
Hansen-test	0.344	0.267	0.185	0.625	0.131	0.852	0.322	0.271	0.253	0.916
Number of firms	356	2529	1244	1553	1014	1681	1371	1395	1635	1060
Number of observations	1256	9393	5298	4590	5102	5547	4869	4465	7029	3620

Sources: Worldscope; and IMF staff estimates.

[a]First-differenced GMM specifications, with lagged dependent variable and year dummies. Instruments are lagged values of regressors.

[b]Robust standard errors in parentheses, with * indicating significance at 10 percent and ** at 5 percent level.

[c]Cash flow-to-capital ratio.

[d]Debt-to-assets ratio.

[e]Standard deviation of return on weekly price index (annualized).

REFERENCES

Abiad, A., E. Detragiache, and T. Tressel, 2008, "A New Database of Financial Reforms," IMF Working Paper No. 08/266 (Washington: International Monetary Fund).

Abiad, A., D. Leigh, and M. Terrones, 2010, "Getting the Balance Right: Transitioning Out of Sustained Current Account Surpluses," *World Economic Outlook* (Washington: International Monetary Fund), April.

Akitoby, B., R. Hemming, and G. Schwartz, 2007, "Public Investment and Public-Private Partnerships," *Economic Issues*, Vol. 40 (Washington: International Monetary Fund).

Asian Development Bank (AsDB), 2009, "Infrastructure for a Seamless Asia" (Manila).

Barclays Capital, 2009, "Correcting Global Imbalances: A Policy Prescription for Emerging Asia" (unpublished; London: Barclays Emerging Markets Research).

Beck, T., and A. Demirguç-Künt, 2006, "Small- and Medium-Size Enterprises: Access to Finance as a Growth Constraint," *Journal of Banking and Finance*, Vol. 30, pp. 2931–43.

Blanchard, O., and G. M. Milesi-Ferretti, 2009, "Global Imbalances: In Midstream," IMF Staff Position Note No. 09/29 (Washington: International Monetary Fund).

Botman, D., A. Klemm, and R. Baqir, 2008, "Investment Incentives and Effective Tax Rates in the Philippines: A Comparison with Neighboring Countries," IMF Working Paper No. 08/207 (Washington: International Monetary Fund).

Calderon, C., and L. Serven, 2004a, "The Effects of Infrastructure Development on Growth and Income Distribution," Policy Research Working Paper No. 3400 (Washington: World Bank).

———, 2004b, "Trends in Infrastructure in Latin America, 1980–2001," Policy Research Working Paper No. 3401 (Washington: World Bank).

Cardarelli, R., and A. Rebucci, 2007, "Exchange Rates and the Adjustment of External Imbalances," *World Economic Outlook* (Washington: International Monetary Fund), April.

———, and M. Terrones, 2005, "Global Imbalances: A Saving and Investment Perspective," *World Economic Outlook* (Washington: International Monetary Fund), September.

DeLong, J. B., 2002, "Productivity Growth in the 2000s," in *NBER Macroeconomics Annual*, Vol. 17, ed. by M. Gertler and K. Rogoff (Cambridge, Massachusetts: National Bureau of Economic Research).

Devarajan, S., V. Swaroop, and H. Zhou, 1996, "The Composition of Public Expenditure and Economic Growth," *Journal of Monetary Economics,* Vol. 37, pp. 313–44.

Guimaraes, R., and O. Unteroberdoerster, 2006, "What's Driving Private Investment in Malaysia? Aggregate Trends and Firm-Level Evidence," IMF Working Paper No. 06/190 (Washington: International Monetary Fund).

Heaney, R., C. Koga, B. Oliver, and A. Tran, 1999, "The Size Effect and Derivative Usage in Japan," Working Paper Series in Finance 99-02 (The Australian National University: Canberra).

Hori, M., 2008, "Investment Recovery from Financial Crises," in IMF Country Report No. 08/194 (Washington: International Monetary Fund, June).

Hsieh, C. T., and P. Klenow, 2007, "Relative Prices and Relative Prosperity," *American Economic Review*, Vol. 97, No. 3, pp. 562–85.

International Monetary Fund, 2006a, "Asia's Investment Decline," in *Regional Economic Outlook: Asia and Pacific* (Washington: International Monetary Fund, May).

———, 2006b. "Savings and Investment: An Emerging Asian and Singaporean Perspective," IMF Country Report No. 06/151 (Washington, May).

———, 2007. "Investment Recovery from Financial Crises: A View from Cross-Country Experiences," IMF Country Report No. 07/231 (Washington, July).

———, 2008a, "What Determines Investment in Korea?" in *Republic of Korea: Selected Issues,* IMF Country Report No. 08/296 (Washington, September).

———, 2008b, *Regional Economic Outlook: Asia and Pacific* (Washington: November).

———, 2009, *Regional Economic Outlook: Asia and Pacific* (Washington: October).

———, 2010a, "Raising Medium-Term Growth: What Role Can Investment Play?" in *Japan: Selected Issues*, IMF Country Report No. 10/212 (Washington).

———, 2010b. *Japan: 2010 Article IV Consultation Staff Report,* IMF Country Report No. 10/211 (Washington).

Jensen, R., 2007, "The Digital Provide: Information (Technology), Market Performance, and Welfare in the South Indian Fisheries Sector," *Quarterly Journal of Economics*, Vol. 122, No. 3, pp. 879–924.

Kang, K., and S. Y. Kim, 2006, "A Strategy for Restructuring the SME Sector in Korea," IMF Country Report No. 06/381 (Washington: International Monetary Fund, October).

Krugman, P., 1991, "Increasing Returns and Economic Geography," *The Journal of Political Economy*, Vol. 99, No. 3, pp. 483–99.

Linden, G., K. Kraemer, and J. Dedrick, 2009, "Who Captures Value in a Global Innovation Network? The Case of Apple's iPod," *Communications of the Association for Computing Machinery*, Vol. 52, No. 3, pp 140–44.

Lueth, E., C. Steinberg, and M. Syed, 2009, "Exit from SME Support Measures," in *Regional Economic Outlook: Asia and Pacific* (Washington: International Monetary Fund), October.

McKinsey and Company, 2010, "Asian Financial Sector—The Changing Landscape," presented at Asia Banking and Finance Conference, Federal Reserve Bank of San Francisco (June).

Mercereau, B., 2005, "FDI Flows to Asia: Did the Dragon Crowd-Out the Tigers?" IMF Working Paper No. 05/189 (Washington: International Monetary Fund).

Mohommad, A., P. N'Diaye, and O. Unteroberdoerster, 2010, "Does Asia Need Rebalancing?" in *Regional Economic Outlook: Asia and Pacific* (Washington: International Monetary Fund, April).

Norregaard, J. and T. Khan, 2007, "Tax Policy: Recent Trends," IMF Working Paper No. 07/274 (Washington: International Monetary Fund).

Pritchett, L., 1996, "Mind Your Ps and Qs: The Cost of Public Investment is Not the Value of Public Capital," Policy Research Working Paper No. 1660 (Washington: World Bank).

Rangarajan, C., 2010, "Economic Outlook for 2010/11" (New Delhi: Prime Minister's Economic Advisory Council), available via the Internet at http://eac.gov.in/.

Straub, S., 2008, "Infrastructure and Growth in Developing Countries: Recent Advances and Research Challenges," Policy Research Working Paper No. 4460 (Washington: World Bank).

———, C. Vellutini, and M. Walters, 2008, "Infrastructure and Economic Growth in East Asia," Policy Research Working Paper 4589 (Washington: World Bank).

Swaroop, V., 1994, "The Public Financing of Infrastructure: Options and Issues," Policy Research Working Paper No. 1288 (Washington: World Bank).

Uesugi, I., K. Sakai, and G. Yamashiro, 2006, "Effectiveness of Credit Guarantees in the Japanese Loan Market," RIETI Discussion Paper No. 06-E-004 (Tokyo: Research Institute of Economy, Trade and Industry).

Venables, A., 2006, "Shifts in Economic Geography and Their Causes," paper presented at the Federal Reserve Bank of Kansas City Symposium, The New Economic Geography: Effects and Policy Implications, August (Available via the Internet at http://KansasCityFed.org).

World Bank, 1994, "Infrastructure for Development," in *World Development Report* (Washington).

Young, A., 1995, "The Tyranny of Numbers: Confronting the Statistical Realities of the East Asian Growth Experience," *Quarterly Journal of Economics*, Vol. 110, No. 3, pp. 641–80.

Zee, H. H., J. G. Stotsky, and E. Ley, 2002, "Tax Incentives for Business Investment: A Primer for Policy Makers in Developing Countries," *World Development*, Vol. 3, No. 9, pp. 1497–1516.

PART II

Rebalancing Growth in China: Relying Less on Exports and More on Consumption

CHAPTER 4

Is China's Export-Oriented Growth Sustainable?

KAI GUO AND PAPA N'DIAYE

INTRODUCTION

The global financial crisis interrupted China's rapid growth of the past three decades. Indeed, after an average growth rate of around 10 percent during 1980–2008, China's GDP growth fell to 6½ percent in the first quarter of 2009 before bouncing back in response to substantial fiscal and monetary stimuli. The sharp slowdown reflected China's dependence on exports, particularly to advanced economies—the culmination of years of reforms to open up and become more market-oriented. Looking ahead, a natural question is whether this export-oriented growth is tenable over the medium to long term. This question is all the more relevant given the reduction in global demand following the Great Recession. The authorities in China are well aware of such risks and are taking measures to rebalance growth toward domestic demand, particularly private consumption. They are also taking measures to increase needed infrastructure investment and reduce households' precautionary savings.

Against this backdrop, this chapter assesses the sustainability of China's export-oriented growth over the medium to long term. First, it takes stock of the historical experience of other economies to gain insights into the tenability of and limits to an export-oriented growth model. Second, it looks at the implications of this export-oriented model for China's growth composition, from both the expenditure and the production side. The chapter then analyzes these implications from a global perspective by looking at the expansion of key export industries that would be required and the potential constraints placed on China by the absorption capacity of global markets. Finally, the chapter discusses alternative growth patterns that could prove more tenable over the medium term.

The main conclusions are the following:

- For China, maintaining the current export-oriented growth would require a rapid increase in exports and significant gains in market share. Both these requirements will likely be challenging in light of the sluggish recovery in global demand and possibly lower global growth potential.

- An illustrative analysis of what the current export-oriented growth would imply for China's key export industries, such as steel, shipbuilding, and machine tools, suggests that China would have to accept substantial reductions in prices for these products over the medium term in order to gain greater market share. These price cuts could be achieved through some combination of the three following channels: (1) increases in relative productivity that keep costs below those of competitors, (2) a squeeze in corporate profits, and (3) greater implicit or explicit subsidies through continued price distortions. While perhaps feasible, the evidence suggests that even a combination of all these factors would likely be insufficient to achieve the scale of export expansion needed in the coming years.
- Room for further export expansion could be provided by moving up the value-added chain, entering new industries, shifting the composition of exports, diversifying the export base, and increasing domestic value added of exports (by relying less on imported inputs), as well as increased globalization. Indeed, the leading export sectors of today were minor industries in China as recently as five years ago. However, the experiences of other Asian economies that had similar export-oriented growth, such as Japan and Korea, suggest that such changes may not be sufficient to support permanent gains in market share on a scale that China may need in order to sustain export-oriented growth.
- Raising private consumption over the longer term through structural reforms that lower precautionary savings would provide a large impetus to output growth and reduce the need for gaining further market share. It could allow productive capacity in tradable sectors to be directed to the internal market and new capacity to be built in sectors that serve domestic consumers. As such, it would avoid the limits to overreliance on export-oriented growth that were seen in other major exporters, such as Japan and Korea.

CHINA'S RECENT GROWTH PATTERN

China's growth relies heavily on external demand and investment, with much of that investment concentrated in manufacturing, and this dependence has increased in recent years. During 2001–08, net exports and investment, which are predominantly linked to building capacity in tradable sectors, have accounted for about 60 percent of China's growth, up from 40 percent in the 1990s (Figure 4.1). This is much larger than the 2001–08 average of the G7 (16 percent), Euro area (30 percent), and the rest of Asia (35 percent).

From the production side, current exports are estimated to contribute about 30 percent in terms of value added to output growth—a striking figure for an economy of the size of China's—up from 15 percent in the 1990s

Figure 4.1
China: Contribution to Growth, 1990–2008
(In percent of total growth)

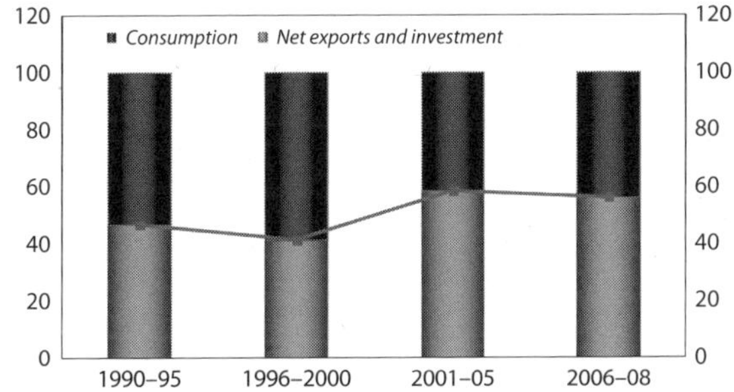

Sources: CEIC Data Co. Ltd; and IMF staff estimates.

Figure 4.2
Estimated Contribution of Exports to GDP Growth
(In percent of total GDP growth)

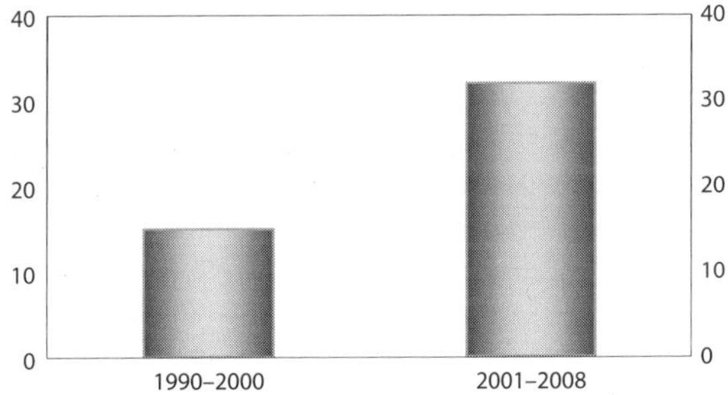

Source: CEIC Data Co. Ltd.; and IMF staff estimates.

(Figure 4.2).[1] This large contribution reflects a rapid growth in exports (on average by 18½ percent since the end of the 1990s before the crisis hit) and also an increase in the domestic content of these exports. This, in turn, has led to a substantial expansion of China's global market share, reaching 9¾ percent of world goods exports in 2009 (up from 3½ percent in 1999). On current trends, we expect China's exports to account for about 15 percent of world trade by 2015.

[1]These estimates, which reflect both the direct and indirect value added of exports (through consumption and investment), have been derived using the Koopman, Wang, and Wei (2008) estimates of the domestic value added of processing and nonprocessing trade and their shares in exports. There is, however, a large uncertainty over these figures. Studies by Hummels, Ishii, and Yi (2001) find even larger domestic value added in China's exports, while He and Zhang (2008) finds it to be relatively small. Cui, Shu, and Su (2009) estimate that for every 10 percent growth in exports, GDP expands by 2½ percentage points, which in our metric would mean that exports contribute 45 percent of GDP growth.

Figure 4.3
Investment-to-GDP Ratio, 2004–08

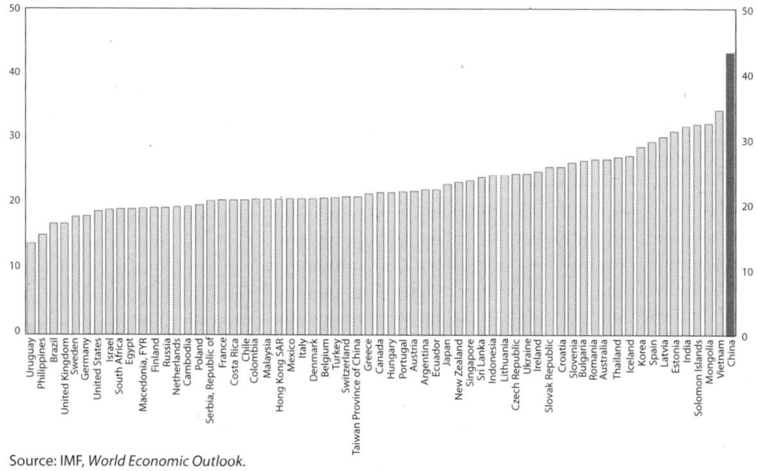

Source: IMF, *World Economic Outlook.*

At around 40 percent of GDP, China has one of the highest investment rates in the world (Figure 4.3). Investment goes predominantly into manufacturing (30 percent), real estate sector (23 percent), and infrastructure (18 percent). It is financed primarily through retained earnings and bank loans. Therefore, around one-third of investment is ultimately connected to the tradable sector's expansion.

Exports and investment have been encouraged by significant cost advantages from the low cost of capital, the low costs of utilities, pollution, energy, and land, tax incentives, and a substantial undervaluation of the exchange rate. However, there have also been rapid gains in relative productivity in the manufacturing sector, and we estimate that total factor productivity (TFP) growth averaged 6½ percent annually during 2002–07. For the economy as a whole, we estimate productivity growth at an average of 3⅓ percent during the same period, which is about three times the OECD average.[2]

WHAT CAN WE LEARN FROM OTHER ECONOMIES' EXPERIENCE?

China's export-oriented growth is not unprecedented; Korea, Japan, and the newly industrialized economies (NIEs) of Asia have all maintained rapid

[2]Young (2003) claimed that TFP growth in China may have been as low as 1.4 percent per year between 1978 and 1998, after adjusting official GDP growth numbers and more careful measurements of labor force and human capital. More studies, however, seem to suggest the TFP growth should range between 2 percent and 4 percent per year in the post-reform era, depending on the methodology and data used (Maddison, 1998; Zheng and Hu, 2006; Chow and Li, 2002; and Kuijs and Wang, 2006). For OECD average TFP growth, the data are from OECD Factbook; and 2008 Economic, Environmental, and Social Statistics.

export growth and increased market shares over a sustained period of time (Figure 4.4). On the face of it, it even seems that China may still have some way to go when compared with the experience of these economies. However, there seem to be clear limits to how much market share can expand. Few economies have managed to maintain high export growth rates once their market share has risen above a certain level. Japan stands out as being the only economy across Asia that has achieved similar growth rates and a global market share of around 10 percent, but its export expansion ended in a prolonged period of declining market share (Figure 4.5).

Focusing on the expansion period, there has been a clear shift in the composition of exports, with economies like Japan and Korea exporting more higher-value-added products over time. In Japan, for example, in the 1960s

Figure 4.4
Pattern of Exports of Goods in Selected Countries Since Their Growth Take-Off

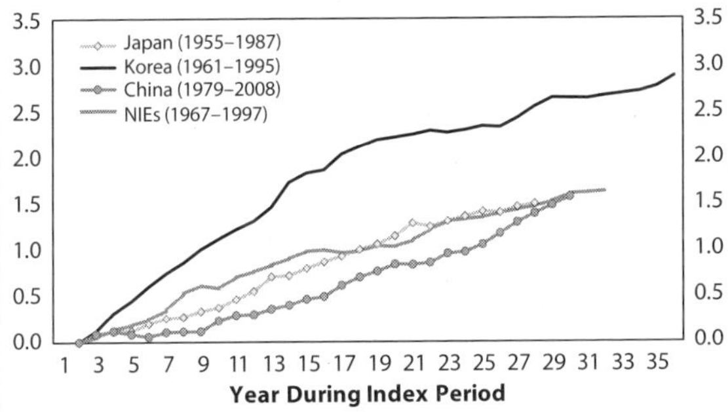

Sources: CEIC Data Co. Ltd.; and IMF staff estimates.

Figure 4.5
Market Share in Selected Economies Since Their Growth Take-Off

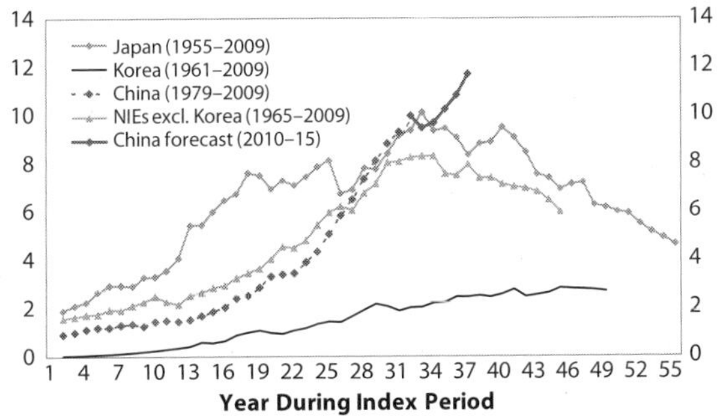

Sources: CEIC Data Co. Ltd.; and IMF staff estimates.

Figure 4.6
Changing Composition of Exports, China, Japan, and Korea

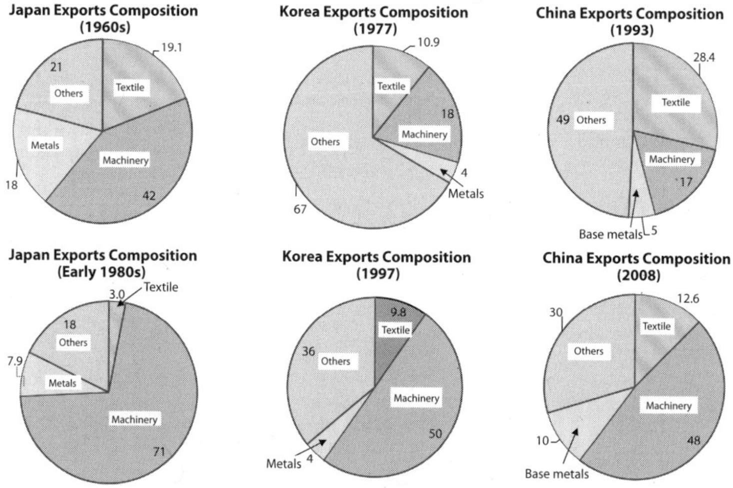

Sources: CEIC Data Co., Ltd.; Statistics Bureau of Japan; and IMF staff estimates.

low-value-added goods such as textiles represented around 25 percent of total exports, while machinery (including transportation equipment and precision instruments) accounted for about 40 percent. By the end of Japan's longest expansion period in the 1980s, textiles represented less than 4 percent of total exports, while the share of machinery had increased to more than 70 percent (Figure 4.6).

China's composition of trade has also changed in recent years, alongside the vertical specialization of production within Asia. China is at the end of a supply chain in the manufacturing sector in East Asia, importing primarily raw materials, intermediary goods, and finished capital goods that are either assembled or go into the production of final consumption goods destined for exports to third economies. Processing trade represents around one-half of China's exports and one-third of its imports. While limited in its early stages, the domestic value-added content of exports has increased steadily, with import substitution and trade in high technology goods. Over time, China's exports are becoming more sophisticated, including a rising share of machinery and electronics, and China produces domestically a greater share of the component inputs further down the supply chain. However, in the past other export-oriented economies also experienced similar shifts in the composition of their exports but found that these shifts proved insufficient to support permanent gains in market share.

Admittedly, multiple ancillary factors may have stalled the expansion in global markets of other economies that pursued export-oriented growth. In Japan, these factors included inflated asset prices, rapid credit growth to the property market, and gaps in the financial regulatory and supervisory system. Today, these problems are less likely to disrupt China's growth, since the authorities have carefully avoided bubbles in construction-related sectors, equity markets, and real estate. As a result, China could be more successful than other economies have been in pursuing such a growth pattern for a longer period. However, in some export-related sectors that are frothy, a much smaller return on investment than envisaged runs the risks of worsening credit quality in the banking system, which would ultimately lower growth and have quasi-fiscal implications.

CAN CHINA MAINTAIN ITS EXPORT-ORIENTED GROWTH GOING FORWARD?

To answer the question of whether China is likely to be able to maintain export-oriented growth over a sustained period of time, we performed an illustrative scenario that envisages a continuation of China's current growth pattern over the medium term, assuming that global trade growth will average 6½ percent annually during 2010–15 and 7 percent afterwards. Our illustrative scenario involves (1) deriving a medium-term path for China's exports, (2) comparing that path with the absorption capacity of the global economy, and (3) at a more disaggregated level, obtaining a path for the exports of key industries (notably steel, shipbuilding, and machinery) by assuming that all other export industries maintain their current market share.

An Illustrative Medium-Term Path for Exports

Step 1. First, we assume China's real GDP will grow at about 10 percent during 2010–15. Beyond 2015, we assume that China will follow a similar pace as Korea in closing the gap in income per capita relative to the United States. China's income per capita (PPP basis) in 2009 was about 14 percent that of the United States, roughly the same relative level as that of Korea at the beginning of its expansion. Korea raised its income per capita to around 50 percent of the U.S. level during its 30 years of expansion. Using the United Nations' forecasts for China's population and the income gap path of Korea, and assuming a 2½ percent growth rate for U.S. GDP, we derive a path for China's GDP growth based on the assumption that the China-U.S. income gap closes at a pace that is similar to Korea's (Figures 4.7 and 4.8).

The envisaged output growth path shows an average growth rate of 8¼ percent between 2010–20 and about 5 percent thereafter. Overall, output growth decelerates gradually as China becomes richer and the labor force shrinks. Under this scenario, China's level of real GDP will grow nearly sevenfold between 2010 and 2040, making China's share in the world economy 17 percent (over twice that of the United States) by 2040.

Step 2. Second, we assume that during 2016–40, consumption will grow in line with output. This assumption seems reasonable in the absence of additional structural reforms, such as reforms in healthcare, pensions, and education that would lower households' high precautionary saving rate. In comparison,

Figure 4.7
Convergence Process of Per-Capita GDP, China, Japan, and Korea
(PPP, relative to United States)

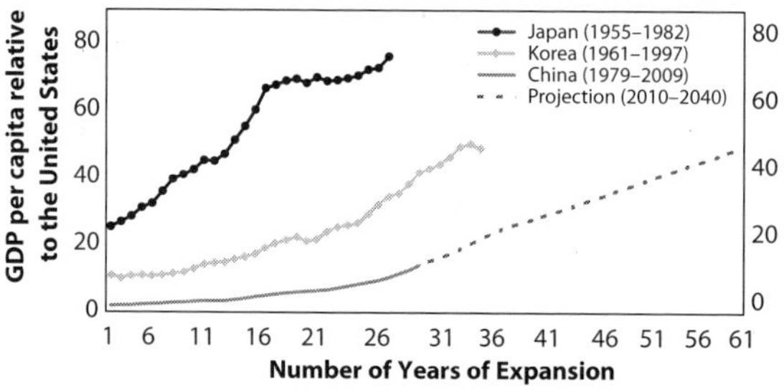

Source: IMF staff estimates.

Figure 4.8
China: Real GDP Growth (1980–2010) and Forecast Growth

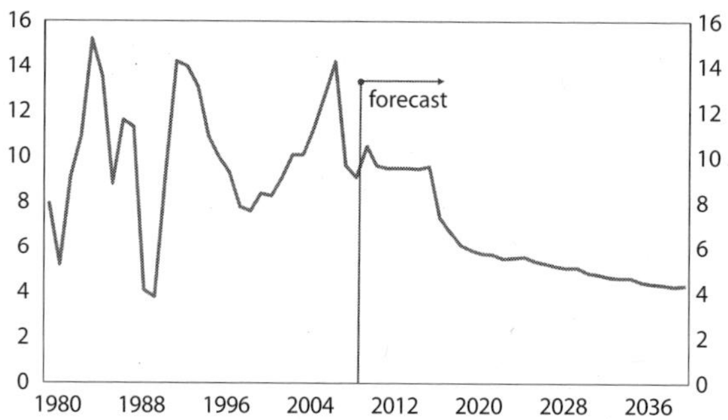

Sources: CEIC Data Co. Ltd.; and IMF staff estimates.

consumption grew on average much more slowly than output between 1990 and 2009. Moreover, recent data on the structure by age of Chinese households' saving rates show that saving rates are higher for older people—so that population aging would not necessarily lower saving rates (Figure 4.9).

Step 3. Third, we determine investment by calculating the capital stock consistent with the growth path obtained in step 1, assuming an average TFP growth of 3 percent (equal to the average of the past 10 years) and using the UN population forecasts. The capital stock is derived from a standard growth accounting framework. Investment is then constructed using the perpetual inventory method.

Step 4. Fourth, we compute net exports and their components. Net exports are obtained by netting out of GDP (step 1) consumption and investment (steps 2

Figure 4.9
China: Average Saving Rate by Age of Head of Household, 1990 and 2005

Source: Chamon and Prasad (2010).

and 3). Assuming a constant elasticity of import demand for ordinary trade (total trade excluding processing trade) of around 1.7 (average of 2001–08), we derive a path for ordinary imports. We assume that processing imports grow at the same rate as ordinary imports. This assumption implies that the share of domestic value-added of exports rises over time. Exports are then residual from net exports and imports.

Estimated import and export growth under this scenario is shown in Figures 4.10 and 4.11. While both export growth and import growth are expected to moderate, they would still be elevated in the next several decades. To sustain the growth needed for convergence to U.S. income levels under the current export-oriented growth model, real exports would need to grow by around 14 percent annually during 2011–20, while imports would need to grow modestly below that level (with the current account balance reaching about 15 percent of GDP). With such trends, Chinese exports would stabilize at around 23 percent of world exports by 2040, more than twice their current share (Figure 4.12).

Prospects for Key Export Industries and Implications for Prices

Is it plausible for China to obtain more than 20 percent of global exports in the next 30 years? To answer this question, we look at some of the key industries that should provide the growth potential to achieve this goal. Our industry analysis focuses on steel, shipbuilding, and machine tools (which belongs to the broader category of machinery), industries where China is either a major player or has significant growth potential. Steel, shipbuilding, and machinery account for over 50 percent of China's exports. The medium-term path for the industries is obtained by assuming, for simplicity, that China maintains its market share in all other export industries, with growth in those industries being the same as growth

Figure 4.10
China: Growth of Real Exports of Goods and Services, 1980–2010 and Forecast

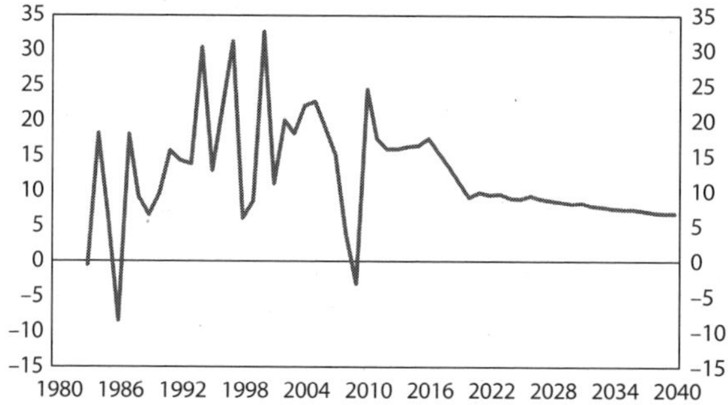

Figure 4.11
China: Growth of Real Imports of Goods and Services, 1980–2010 and Forecast

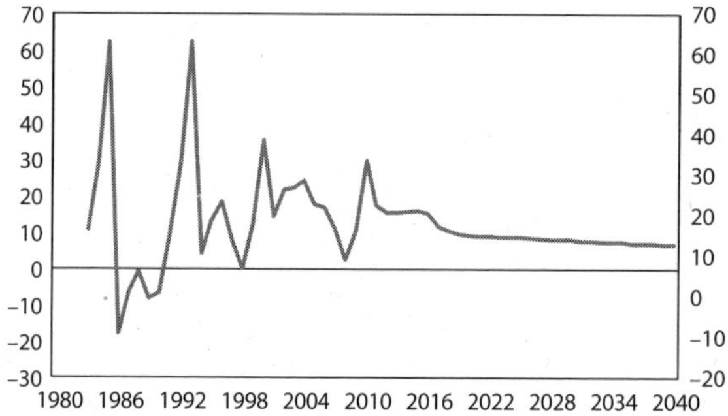

Sources: IMF, WEO database and staff estimates.

Figure 4.12
China: Market Share in World Trade, 1980–2010 and Forecast

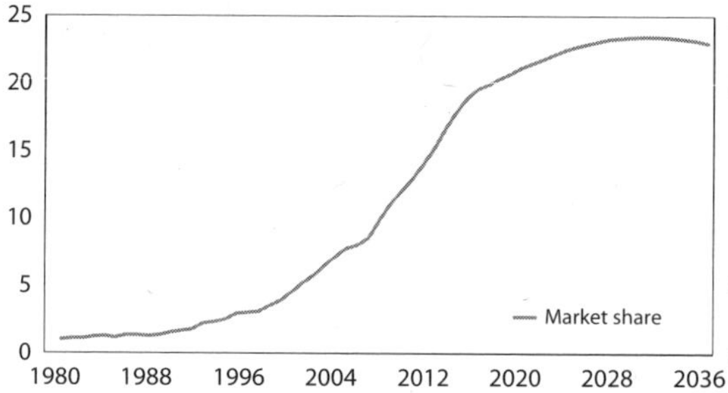

Source: IMF, WEO database and staff estimates.

in global trade.[3] These three industries provide the growth in market share to achieve the average 14 percent real growth in exports—growing by an average of 17½ percent between 2011 and 2020. The price implications are then obtained through estimated export demand functions, assumptions about world demand for each of these commodities, and the price elasticity of world demand. This scenario is, of course, intended to be illustrative. China might not see such growth in these sectors but instead rely on other alternatives and industries such as green energy, biotechnology, or even products not yet widely commercialized. Nonetheless, the idea is to indicate the scale of the challenge presented by a rapid increase in global market share of tradable goods and the risks, particularly those related to overcapacity and rising nonperforming loans.

Steel Industry

China's steel industry drives the global market. In 2008, China accounted for just under 40 percent of world crude steel production (about 500 million tons), up from 5 percent in the early 1980s (Figure 4.13). According to the World Steel Association, China's capacity is estimated at about 600 million tons, accounting for about 40 percent of global capacity in 2008. The steel industry may benefit from further domestic demand associated with China's urbanization and continued development, and its production is destined primarily for the domestic market. Nevertheless, China's role in global markets has increased markedly in recent years as it has become the world's largest exporter, accounting for 14 percent of world steel exports as of 2006.

Our industry analysis entails a few assumptions about the export demand and price elasticities (Table 4.1). We set the export price elasticity to the value estimated by Aziz and Li (2007) for total exports because of limited data availability.

Figure 4.13
China's Share in World Production, 1980–2007

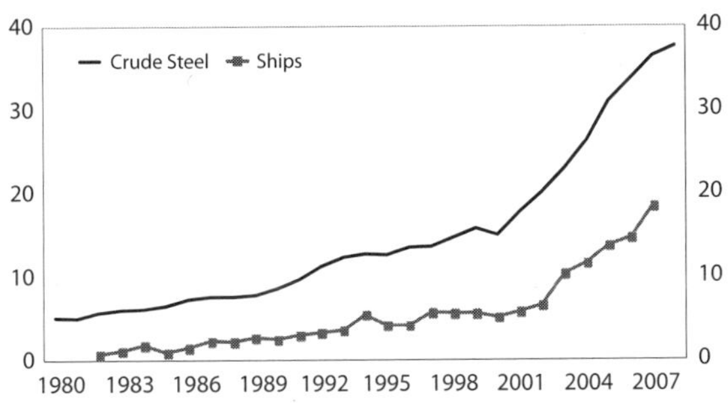

Sources: World Steel Association; Lloyd's Register of Shipping; and IMF staff estimates.

[3]Sensitivity analyses of this exercise's main assumptions are carried out in the next section.

TABLE 4.1

Baseline Elasticity Assumptions

	Demand	Price
Steel		
Export	2.0	–1.6
World demand		–0.3
Ship building		
Export	2.0	–0.4
World demand		–1.0
Machine tools		
Export	2.0	–1.6
World demand		–1.0

Source: IMF staff estimates.

For the demand elasticity, we set it at one-half of Aziz and Li's estimate given China's size in the global steel market. This assumption still appears conservative (that is, on the high side) given that the elasticity could be expected to decline as China gains market share.[4] The price elasticity of world demand for steel is set at -⅓, the value estimated by Winters (1995). For the growth of world steel demand, we used the medium-term forecast of the World Steel Association (around 3 percent growth a year) before taking into account any price effects. The investment needs in the steel industry are obtained by assuming a constant capital-output ratio and applying the perpetual inventory method.

Under our assumptions, of the 17½ percent required export growth, about 9 percentage points could be absorbed by higher external demand and the remaining amount would have to come from a reduction in steel prices and an increase in market share. World prices would have to fall by a cumulative 43 percent during 2011–20 to accommodate additional exports from China (Table 4.2), with China's production accounting for around 50 percent of world output by 2020. In addition, there would likely be a need to increase investment to expand production capacity by about 90 percent over the same horizon. Given that current profit margins in the steel industry are about 5½ percent, without either productivity gains or cost reductions profit margins would be eliminated within two years. This means that achieving the required growth in steel exports could become very difficult as early as 2012.

Shipbuilding

In terms of tonnage, China is the world's third largest producer of ships behind Korea and Japan. In 2008, China's production was 13.9 million gross tonnage (GT) compared with 26.4 GT for Korea and 18.7 GT for Japan. Its production is expanding very rapidly, with its order book representing about one-third of world orders,

[4]In the limit, demand elasticity should not exceed 1 when the market share of Chinese steel approaches 100 percent.

TABLE 4.2

Illustrative Conditions to Sustain China's Growth Strategy
(In percent)

	2008	Baseline 2011–20
Production volume (in percent of world production)		
Steel	36.1	54.1[a]
Shipbuilding	18.4	47.2[a]
Machine tools	17.0	44.6
Excess capacity utilization rate		
Steel	16.6	–68.9
Shipbuilding		
Machine tools		
Annual investment growth		
Steel	12.3[b]	8.8
Shipbuilding		9.3
Machine tools	34.7	15.0
Annual average profit margin		
Steel	3.5	
Shipbuilding	9.6	
Machine tools	6.4	
Scenario: Annual average export growth		
Steel	48.6[b]	17.6
Of which:		
Annual average world demand		5.8
Cumulative required price change		–54.7
Shipbuilding	31.5	17.6
Of which:		
Annual average world demand		11.8
Cumulative required price change		–79.9
Machinery	14.7	17.6
Of which:		
Annual average world demand		12.3
Cumulative required price change		–28.7

Source: IMF Staff estimates.
[a]End of period.
[b]Average 2005–08.

second after Korea (37½ percent of world orders) at the end of 2008, according to data compiled by Lloyd's Register. China has moved quickly up the value-added chain, producing sophisticated vessels, such as very large crude carriers, liquefied natural gas carriers, and high-speed container ships, in addition to bulk carriers and crude oil tankers. The authorities expect China to become an even more important player in shipbuilding by 2015, and recent data support this expectation.

For the industry analysis, the demand and price elasticities (2 and –0.4, respectively—see Table 4.1) have been estimated using data on China's exports, world fleet production, and a price index for ships.[5] With regard to the growth of world demand for ships, we obtained the global demand (7½ percent) by first regressing the size of the world fleet on the volume of world trade to get the stock of ships and then deriving from the estimated stock of ships the annual flow of new ships.[6] The investment needs in the ship industry have been obtained in a similar manner as for the steel industry.

Under such assumptions, of the 17½ percent required export growth, about 16½ percentage points could be absorbed through higher external demand and the remaining amount would have to come from a reduction in ship prices and an increase in China's market share. World prices would have to fall by a cumulative 21 percent during 2011–20 to accommodate additional exports from China (Table 4.2), with China's production accounting for around 40 percent of world output by 2020 (up from 20½ percent in 2008). In addition, there will likely be a need to increase investment by 9 percent a year to expand production capacity over the same horizon. Unlike in steel, in shipbuilding profit margins are relatively high and allow such an expansion to be feasible for the next five to seven years without either productivity gains or cost reductions.

Machine Tools

Machinery is the largest export industry in China (over 40 percent of total exports), but because it includes a wide range of products we focus on machine tools. China's machine tool industry accounted for 17 percent of world production in 2008. China's production increased 7 percent in 2008 after 43 percent growth in 2007. More recent data suggest that China might have surpassed Germany and Japan to become the world's largest machine tool producer in 2009. While China remains by far the world's largest consumer of machine tools, absorbing one-fourth of the value of all new installations around the globe, it has started to play an increasingly important role in export markets. China accounted for around 4¾ percent of world machine tool exports in 2008 and has substantial growth potential going forward.

For the industry analysis, we assume that the demand elasticity for machine tools is similar to that for shipbuilding, but because China plays a smaller role in the market we assume a higher price elasticity (equal to the aggregate price elasticity estimated by Aziz and Li, 2007). Here again, our assumptions regarding demand elasticities appear high. The projected growth in demand for machine tools (6¼ percent) is based on expected world growth (4¾ percent per year) and an estimated elasticity with respect to world growth of 1 (see Table 4.1). The investment needs in the machine tools industry are obtained in a similar manner as for the steel industry.

Under such assumptions, of the 17½ percent required export growth, about 15 percentage points could be absorbed through higher external demand. World prices would have to fall by nearly 14 percent during 2011–20 to accommodate additional export from China (Table 4.2), with China's production accounting

---

[5]Oil prices have also been added to the equation to control for the effects of energy prices on the demand for ships. The estimated coefficient of oil prices is positive (0.3), that is, rising energy cost increases the demand for ships, but it is not statistically significant at standard levels.

[6]This is based on an estimated annual depreciation rate of 2 percent using data from 1989–2007.

for around 37½ percent of world output by 2020. In addition, investment would need to increase by 15 percent a year to expand production capacity over the same horizon. Profit margins (about 6½ percent) are around the same magnitude as in the steel industry, providing little room for price reductions without productivity gains and cost reductions, and they could cover around four years of expansion.

Sensitivity Analysis

This section explores the sensitivity of the conclusions of the illustrative scenario presented above to assumptions about the behavior of China's competitors, price elasticities, world growth, the composition of exports, the domestic value-added of exports, and the current account surplus (Table 4.3).

Increased Production Capacity from Competitors

The baseline scenario assumes that other producers would respond passively to China's expansion and simply occupy the residual world demand. However, if China's competitors were to expand their capacity at a pace consistent with the underlying world demand for steel, ships, and machine tools (3 percent, 7½ percent, and 4¾ percent, respectively), prices would fall even further. In such a case, it would be more challenging for China to achieve the required export growth.

Price Elasticities

The conclusions also remain qualitatively unchanged under alternative assumptions about the price elasticity of world demand. Under the assumption of totally inelastic world demand, prices would naturally have to be reduced even further in all three cases. Under another scenario of more elastic world demand (twice as high as in the baseline scenario), the price cuts would be smaller, but such an assumption might be unrealistic for the selected industries, since the exported commodities are capital goods, which generally have low price elasticities.

World Growth

Another scenario envisages growth rates of world demand 20 percent above and below that in the baseline. With stronger demand than in the baseline, prices for steel and machine tools would still have to fall substantially to accommodate China's exports (particularly for steel), while the pressure on ship prices to decline would be lower. However, the pressure on ship prices could remain significant if other producers scaled up their production. Alternatively, lower demand would increase the need for prices to decline by more relative to baseline, particularly for shipbuilding.

Export Diversification

A more diversified export structure could be a relatively more sustainable strategy. Indeed, if the required medium-term aggregate export growth were achieved by expansion in all export industries (with all of them growing on average by 9 percent a year), the downward pressure on prices in China's key industries

TABLE 4.3

Illustrative Conditions to Sustain China's Growth Strategy
(In percent)

		2011–20							
	2007	Additional Supply	Low Price Elasticity of World Demand	High Price Elasticity of World Demand	High World Growth	Low World Growth	Export Diversification	Increased Domestic Value Added	Constant Current Account Surplus
Scenario: Annual average export growth									
Steel	66.6[a]	17.6	17.6	17.6	17.6	17.6	14.9	15.8	13.6
Of which:									
Annual average world demand		9.7	5.8	10.9	9.9	8.2	8.3	8.6	8.0
Cumulative required price change		–48.8	–54.7	–35.5	–39.8	–46.3	–35.1	–38.0	–44.8
Shipbuilding	31.5	17.6	17.6	17.6	17.6	17.6	14.9	15.8	13.6
Of which:									
Annual average world demand		18.3	11.8	17.0	17.0	16.2	14.4	15.1	13.3
Cumulative required price change		–27.7	–79.9	–12.2	–13.1	–28.9	–11.9	–15.3	–20.9
Machinery	14.7	17.6	17.6	17.6	17.6	17.6	14.9	15.8	13.6
Of which:									
Annual average world demand		16.6	12.3	16.0	16.3	14.1	13.7	14.2	13.0
Cumulative required price change		–19.6	–28.7	–9.0	–7.6	–19.5	–7.0	–9.4	–9.9

Source: IMF staff estimates.
[a]Average 2005–07.

would be much smaller, particularly in machinery. Prices could even rise in industries with strong world demand, such as shipbuilding. For the steel industry, however, deep price cuts appear to be unavoidable. Such price cuts would of course be unnecessary if China responded to demands for new products, a scenario that is not covered in this exercise.

Increased Domestic Value Added

Raising the domestic value added of China's exports could provide some breathing room to China's export-oriented growth, but it would likely remain untenable. Assuming that the share of processing imports falls to one-fifth of total imports by 2020, down from just over one-third in 2008, China's total exports could grow by 1½ percentage points less than under the baseline, and hence its key industries would need to expand by less (about 1¾ percentage points). Nevertheless, prices would still have to be reduced markedly to gain the needed market share in global markets.

Steady Current Account Surplus

A final scenario maintains the current account surplus at 10 percent of GDP between 2016 and 2020 (compared to an increase to about 15 percent of GDP in the baseline) and assumes the same GDP and consumption as in the baseline. As expected, export growth is lower than under the baseline. The results suggest that even under such a scenario, prices would have to fall by a substantial amount to build market share, particularly for steel.

Maintain Growth Without Hitting the Global Absorption Constraint

As shown in the illustrative scenario, maintaining export-oriented growth going forward would require a continued rapid expansion of exports that could be achieved only through some combination of the following three channels: (1) larger increases in relative productivity in key export sectors in order to lower costs below those of competitors, (2) a further squeeze in profits, and (3) greater subsidies (implicit or explicit) through continued price distortions. Each of those strategies will prove increasingly difficult to realize, for the following reasons:

- Productivity growth and the marginal return to investment have been slowing in recent years, possibly signaling overinvestment in some key sectors of the economy (particularly in manufacturing) as well as China's moving further up the production frontier.
- Reducing profit margins in key export sectors provides some scope for expansion, since profits are at relatively healthy levels. However, such margins would be exhausted well before the required expansion in market share could be achieved, and in many industries that would happen in just a few years.
- Further price distortions and subsidies to lower the cost of capital and make tradable sectors more competitive run several risks: of fueling more

overinvestment in the manufacturing sector, of raising nonperforming loans, of increasing trade tensions, and ultimately of lowering growth.[7]

The task ahead could prove even more daunting if the recovery in demand among China's main trading partners turned out to be slower than we assume and remained well below its precrisis levels for some time. Slower import demand from those economies would naturally lower the feasible pace of China's export expansion. In such a case, China's exports would have to gain an even bigger share in world markets than we assume above.

Instead, implementing policies to lower precautionary savings, such as reforming the health care, education, and pension systems, would raise private consumption and support growth in a more sustainable manner. As an illustration, were private consumption to substitute in part for net exports in order to make the contribution of net exports to growth zero during 2011–20, the need to build market share would fall noticeably and imply much smaller reductions in global prices, a reduced risk of corporate losses, and lower exposure to worsening credit quality (Table 4.4). In some instances, the required growth in exports could be even smaller if GDP growth were to decline as a result of rebalancing the economy away from the highly productive tradable sectors toward the less productive nontradable sectors. But such a scenario might not necessarily prevail if the rebalancing were brought about by structural reforms, while factors like increased

TABLE 4.4

Higher Consumption and Zero Net Exports Contribution to Growth

	2007	Average 2011–20 Scenario	Average 2011–20 Baseline
Annual average export growth			
Steel	66.6[a]	15.0	18.3
Of which:			
Annual average world demand		8.4	9.3
Cumulative required price change		−35.5	−45.1
Shipbuilding	31.5	15.0	18.3
Of which:			
Annual average world demand		15.0	17.8
Cumulative required price change		0.0	−12.8
Machinery	14.7	15.0	18.3
Of which:			
Annual average world demand		14.0	15.8
Cumulative required price change		−6.3	−14.5

Source: IMF staff estimates.
[a]Average 2005–07.

[7]In its eleventh five-year economic plan, the Chinese government has vowed to make the ship industry one of the world's largest by 2020. The government plans to achieve this goal through further financial support to the industry, expansion of capacity, consolidation of the industry, investment in and support for research and development, and greater openness (including through cooperation with foreign firms and foreign direct investment).

diffusion of information and communication technology (ICT) could also lift productivity in both the nontradable and the tradable sectors (N'Diaye, 2010).

REFERENCES

Aziz, J., and X. Li, 2007, "China's Changing Trade Elasticities," IMF Working Paper No. 07/266 (Washington: International Monetary Fund).

Bosworth, B., and S. Collins, 2007, "Accounting for Growth: Comparing China and India," NBER Working Paper No. 12943 (Cambridge, Massachusetts: National Bureau of Economic Research).

Chamon, M., and E. Prasad, 2010, "Why Are Saving Rates of Urban Households in China Rising?" *American Economic Journal: Macroeconomic*, Vol. 2, No. 1, pp. 93–130.

China Machine Tool and Tool Builders Association, *Annual Report on the Machine Tool Industry*, (Beijing, various issues).

Chow, G. C., and K. Li, 2002, "China's Economic Growth: 1952–2010," *Economic Development and Cultural Change*, Vol. 15, Issue 1, pp. 247-56.

COSTIND, *Annual Report on National Shipbuilding Industry*, (Beijing, various issues).

Cui, L., C. Shu, and X. Su, 2009, "How Much Do Exports Matter for China's Growth?" Hong Kong Monetary Authority *China Economic Issues*, No. 1/09, March.

He, D., and W. Zhang, 2008, "How Dependent Is the Chinese Economy on Exports and In What Sense Has Its Growth Been Export-Led?" Working Paper No. 814 (Hong Kong: Hong Kong Monetary Authority).

Hummels, D., J. Ishii, and K. Yi, 2001. "The Nature and Growth of Vertical Specialization in World Trade," *Journal of International Economics*, Vol. 54, pp. 75–96.

International Monetary Fund (IMF), 2009, *World Economic Outlook* (Washington, October).

Koopman, R., Z. Wang, and S. Wei, 2008, "How Much of Chinese Exports Is Really Made In China? Assessing Domestic Value-Added When Processing Trade Is Pervasive," NBER Working Paper No. 14109 (Cambridge, Massachusetts: National Bureau of Economic Research).

Kuijs, L., and T. Wang, 2006, "China's Pattern of Growth: Moving to Sustainability and Reducing Inequality," *China and the World Economy*, Vol. 14, Issue 1, pp. 1-14.

Lloyd's Register of Shipping, *World Fleet Statistics*, various issues.

Maddison, A., 1998, "Chinese Economic Performance in the Long-Run" (Paris: Organisation for Economic Co-operation and Development).

N'Diaye, P., P. Zhang, and W. Zhang, 2010, "Structural Reform, Intra-Regional Trade, and Medium-Term Growth Prospects of East Asia and the Pacific—Perspectives from a New Multi-Region Model," *Journal of Asian Economics*, Vol. 21, No. 1, pp. 20–36.

Organisation for Economic Co-operation and Development (OECD), 2008, "The Shipbuilding Industry in China," Working Party on Shipbuilding Report C, Working Paper No. 6 /Rev. 1 (Paris).

———, 2005, *Economic Survey of China 2005* (Paris).

Prasad, E., 2004, "China's Growth and Integration into the World Economy: Prospects and Challenges," IMF Occasional Paper No. 232 (Washington: International Monetary Fund).

United Nations, 2008, *World Population Prospects: The 2008 Revision* (New York).

Winters, L. Alan, 1995, "Liberalizing European Steel Trade," *European Economic Review*, Vol. 39, Issues 3-4, pp. 611–21 (April).

World Machine Tool Output and Consumption Survey, 2009, World Steel Association, 2008, *World Steel in Figures 2008* (Brussels) (Cincinnati: Gardner Publications, Inc.).

Young, A., 2003, "Gold into Base Metals: Productivity Growth in the People's Republic of China during the Reform Period," *Journal of Political Economy*, Vol. 111, No. 6 (December), pp. 1220–61.

Zheng, J., and A. Hu, 2006, "An Empirical Analysis of Provincial Productivity in China (1979–2001)," *Journal of Chinese Economic and Business Studies*, Vol. 4, No. 3, pp. 221–39.

CHAPTER 5

Employment Effects of Growth Rebalancing in China

KAI GUO AND PAPA N'DIAYE

INTRODUCTION

There is a growing sense, as noted in Chapter 4, that China's export-oriented growth will be difficult to sustain over the medium to longer term and that shifting toward a more consumption-based economy, where the nontradable sector plays a larger role than it does now, could be a more viable alternative. Achieving a successful rebalancing of China's growth will require action on several fronts, including structural reforms to level the playing field between the tradable and nontradable sectors, development of the domestic financial market, and improvement in the public provision of services like health and education (Blanchard and Giavazzi, 2005; and N'Diaye, Zhang, and Zhang, 2010). Such actions are considered by many, including the Chinese government, as being necessary to lift private consumption and transfer resources from the externally oriented tradable industries to sectors oriented toward the domestic market.

Shifting to private consumption-led growth would likely mean more demand for both existing and new services and reorienting the production of tradable goods toward domestic markets. In China's case, this would also imply moving a large number of less skilled workers from the tradable to the nontradable sector. This process of rebalancing growth would likely present both opportunities and challenges, and while the longer-term benefits (particularly in sustainability) of rebalancing growth are now widely recognized, there could be short-term costs, especially in employment. Mitigating these costs will require labor market policies to cushion the employment impact during the transition, particularly in meeting the skills gap associated with the transition.

This chapter gauges the potential effects on employment of rebalancing China's economic growth. The first section presents some key features of the labor market in China. The second section evaluates China's sectoral allocation of employment against a panel of economies and uses model-based simulations to gauge the likely effects on employment of rebalancing growth.

The conclusions are as follows:

- In the longer term, rebalancing China's growth toward domestic demand would likely raise aggregate employment.

- In the shorter term, however, there could be employment losses as the economy moves away from the tradable sector toward the nontradable sector. In the tradable sector, reduced profit opportunities would prompt firms initially to shed labor and adapt to the more challenging environment. These job losses would be offset in part by job creation in the nontradable sector, where firms would see more opportunities and new businesses would likely be created. However, given time-to-build constraints, the process of new job creation is likely to be slower and may evolve only with a lag.
- The short-term employment costs of rebalancing China's growth could be mitigated, both in magnitude and in duration, by measures to retrain workers, reduce skills mismatches, further promote labor mobility across sectors and regions, and raise productivity in all sectors.
- The short-term employment costs could also be substantially reduced if the shift from tradables to nontradables were part of a broader strategy that aimed to lower private savings and develop the domestic financial system.

SECTORAL EMPLOYMENT ALLOCATION

This section presents some stylized facts on employment by sector and region using employment data from the National Bureau of Statistics (NBS). Employment data in China suffers from significant gaps. There are two main sources of data on employment: the labor force survey and the establishment survey. In both the labor force and the establishment surveys, employed persons are defined as active individuals age 16 or older. The labor force survey is done on a biannual basis and covers one million people. The establishment survey covers over two million units (enterprises) in urban areas, excluding the private sector. Data from the labor force survey are published annually, while those from the establishment survey are published quarterly.

Sectoral Distribution of Employment

The primary, secondary, and tertiary industries accounted for 40¾ percent, 26¾ percent, and 32⅓ percent of employment, respectively, at end-2007.[1] With the construction industry employing about 15 percent of workers in the secondary sector, the nontradable sector (which we define as the sum of tertiary and construction) accounted for around 36 percent of employment. This share had risen from about 30 percent in the mid-1990s, reflecting rapid growth in the sector (Figure 5.1).

The nontradable sector expanded rapidly in the aftermath of the restructuring of state-owned enterprises at the end of the 1990s, which led to the layoff of over 40 million workers.[2] An event study that looks at the state-owned enterprises

[1]Available industry data are from the labor force survey.

[2]See Garnaut and others (2005) for details about the impact on labor of the restructuring of state-owned enterprises.

Figure 5.1
China: Employment Share of Tradable and Nontradable, 1996–2007

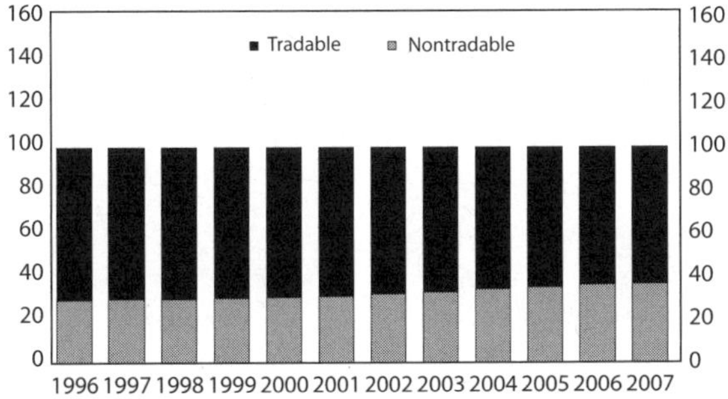

Sources: CEIC Data Co. Ltd.; and IMF staff estimates.

Figure 5.2
China: Employment Creation Before and After End-SOE Restructuring

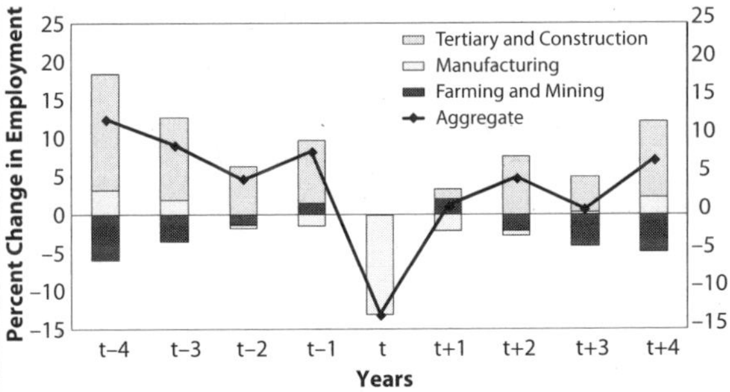

Sources: CEIC Data Co. Ltd.; and IMF staff estimates.

restructuring of the late 1990s confirms that the nontradable sector has been responsible for most job creation in recent years (Figure 5.2). This outcome owes to the government's commitment to provide alternative employment to laid-off workers. State-owned enterprises were obliged to set up reemployment centers that provided subsistence and training to workers. In overall labor market flexibility, China performs better than the OECD average, according to the World Bank *Doing Business 2008* survey, but performs relatively poorly in the "cost of firing workers" category.[3] China's relatively elevated cost of firing could somewhat slow down a potential shift of labor from the tradable to the nontradable sector, if market forces were allowed to play.

[3]On a scale of 0 to 100 (with higher scores indicating a poor performance), China scores 27 in overall labor market rigidity (compared with 31.4 for the OECD average).

Figure 5.3
China: Employment by Industry, 2007

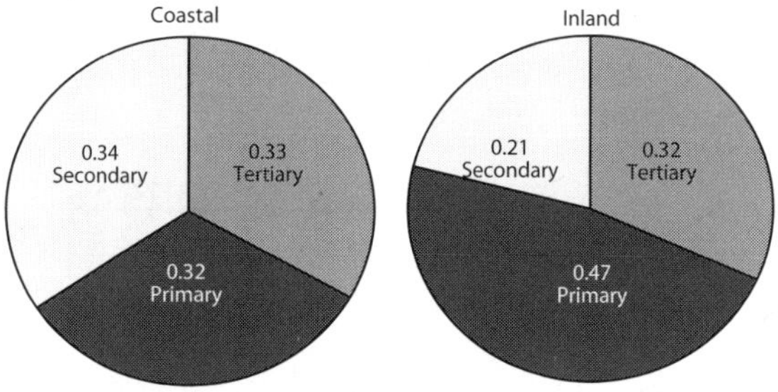

Sources: CEIC Data Co. Ltd.; and IMF staff estimates.

Regional Distribution of Employment

Employment is more evenly distributed across industries in coastal areas than inland, where the primary sector, generally agriculture, takes up the lion's share (Figure 5.3). Coastal areas have seen faster job growth than inland areas, particularly in services, reflecting the creation of special economic zones and strong growth as well as structural reforms to increase competition, open up the economy, and improve access to credit (Brooks and Tao, 2003). However, looking ahead, uncertainty over the portability of pensions and restrictions on the flow of labor between rural and urban areas could limit labor mobility across regions.

Skills Intensity of Employment by Sector

In terms of skills, about 80 percent of the workforce has attained no higher than a junior school level. This proportion is higher for female than for male workers. The manufacturing sector employs fewer skilled people than the services sector; over 70 percent of the manufacturing workforce has no more than a junior school education, compared with around 35–50 percent in the services sector (Table 5.1). This difference in skill intensity suggests that there could be some skill mismatches that hinder the shift of labor from the tradable to the nontradable sector. In this context, female workers may be more affected than male workers. Nevertheless, such skill mismatches could be reduced through job retraining programs and job centers, consistent with the experience after the state-owned enterprise reform in the 1990s.

Labor Intensity by Sector

The tertiary sector is more labor intensive than the secondary sector. Labor productivity in the tertiary sector is about 60 percent lower than that it is in the secondary sector (which includes manufacturing). Therefore, for a given level of output, a shift from the manufacturing sector toward the tertiary sector would

TABLE 5.1

China: Sectoral Education Attainment, 2006

	Total	Manufacturing	Services: Weighted Average[a]	Services: Weighted Average[b]	Services: Simple Average
Total	100.0	100.0	100.0	100.0	100.0
Illiterate	6.7	1.3	0.7	1.0	0.8
Primary school	29.9	15.1	7.3	11.1	7.7
Junior school	44.9	55.0	27.9	40.6	31.8
Senior school	11.8	21.0	25.4	24.5	27.0
College	4.3	5.2	23.3	13.9	19.6
University	2.1	2.2	13.7	7.9	11.6
Graduate	0.2	0.2	1.7	0.9	1.6

Source: *China Labor Statistical Yearbook.*
[a]Weighted using sectoral employment data in urban areas.
[b]Weighted using 2002 sectoral national employment data.

increase employment. However, within the manufacturing sector there is great heterogeneity, with some industries being as labor intensive as the tertiary industry (e.g., textile and garment industry), suggesting that there could also be net job losses in the transition from these industries to services.[4]

EMPLOYMENT EFFECTS OF REBALANCING

This section presents two simulation exercises. The first is based on a cross-country model of the determinants of the sectoral allocation of labor. The second uses the IMF Global Integrated Monetary and Fiscal model (GIMF) to illustrate the potential effects on employment of rebalancing China's growth toward the nontradable sector.[5]

Determinants of the Sectoral Allocation of Employment From Cross-Country Experience

Several factors can influence the sectoral allocation of labor, including the ability and willingness of labor to move, income per capita, relative productivity of the different sectors, demographics, and urbanization. Of all these factors, income per capita has been found, empirically, to be the most robust determinant of the sectoral allocation of labor across economies and over time. It explains the shift of labor from agriculture or the primary sector toward services, with the share of employment in the services sector growing as economies get richer. Relative productivity between sectors captures the concept of the "Baumol disease" (Baumol,

[4]Sectoral employment and output data suggest that labor productivity in textile, garment, culture, and education and sports is 45 percent, 60 percent, and 65 percent, respectively, below the average of the manufacturing sector.

[5]The GIMF was developed by Michael Kumhof and Douglas Laxton. For details see Kumhof and Laxton (2007) and N'Diaye, Zhang, and Zhang (2010).

1967)—that is, the tendency for an increasing share of employment to be channeled through the services sector as an economy develops, despite that sector's lower productivity.[6] Demographic factors, such as the labor participation of women, have been found to be important determinants of the share of employment in services. Institutional specificities, such as union density, the extent of wage centralization, employment protection laws, and product market regulations, which affect the ability and willingness of labor and capital to move—that is, the flexibility of labor and product markets—could also play a key role.[7] However, the empirical evidence that institutions have a statistically significant impact on the sectoral allocation of labor is relatively limited.

To evaluate the employment structure of China's economy, we use cross-country data and regress the share of employment in services, agriculture, and manufacturing on per capita GDP, relative productivity between the tradable and the nontradable sector, the deviation of the real effective exchange rate (REER) from its long-run value, and government consumption in relation to GDP. Formally, the model takes the following form:[8]

$$SH = 1 - \exp\left(\alpha_1 Y^{\alpha_2} + \alpha_3 \frac{A^T}{A^N} + \alpha_4 REERGAP + \alpha_5 G\right), \tag{1}$$

where *SH* is alternatively the share of employment in services, agriculture, and manufacturing, *Y* is GDP per capita on a PPP basis, and A^T and A^N are indices of total factor productivity in the tradable and nontradable sectors, respectively. *REERGAP* is the deviation of the REER from its long-run value. A positive gap represents an overvaluation. The long-run value of the REER is defined as the fitted value of an estimated cointegration relationship between the REER and a set of fundamentals, including (relative) productivity growth in the tradable and nontradable sectors (Balassa-Samuelson effect), the net foreign assets position, terms of trade, openness, and the fiscal balance. *G* is the ratio of government consumption to GDP.

The model is estimated using the Generalized Method of Moments estimator with an unbalanced sample of 29 economies for a total of 575 observations.[9] The set of instruments includes per capita income, lagged relative

---

[6]With labor productivity in the services sector lower than in the manufacturing sector, a rise in total factor productivity would lead to higher wages across sectors. Unit labor costs would eventually fall in the manufacturing sector but rise in the services sector and hence lead to higher prices in the services sector.

[7]See D'Agostino, Serafini, and Ward-Warmedinger (2006) for an analysis of the role of institutions in the sectoral allocation of employment.

[8]This model is an extension of Fuchs (1980).

[9]Selected economies include 21 OECD members (Australia, Austria, Belgium, Canada, Czech Republic, Denmark, Finland, Germany, Ireland, Italy, Japan, Korea, New Zealand, Norway, Portugal, Slovak Republic, Spain, Sweden, Switzerland, United Kingdom, and United States), six Executives' Meeting of East Asia-Pacific Central Banks (EMEAP) members (China, Hong Kong SAR, Indonesia, Malaysia, Singapore, and Thailand), and Taiwan Province of China.

TABLE 5.2

China: Determinants of the Share of Employment in the Service Sector[a]
(In percent)

	Equation (1)
GDP per capita ($ thousands, ppp)	
intercept (b1)	−0.29 [0.00] ***
curvature (b2)	0.43 [0.00] ***
Relative productivity (percent)	0.04 [0.07] *
Deviation in REER (percentage point)	−1 10e-3 [0.03] **
Government consumption/GDP (percentage point)	−0.07 [0.56]

Source: IMF staff estimates.
[a]Figures in brackets are p-values. *, **, and *** denote the 10 percent, 5 percent, and 1 percent significance levels, respectively.

productivity, lagged REER gap, lagged change in REER, lagged government consumption, and country dummies. The data on the share of employment in the agriculture, manufacturing, and services sectors are from the OECD main economic indicators and CEIC databases. The per capita GDP and government consumption data are from the IMF World Economic Outlook database. The relative productivity data are from the Consultative Group on Exchange Rates database.

Share of Employment in Services

Table 5.2 shows the estimation results for the share of employment in the services sector. A negative sign indicates a positive effect on employment in the services sector.

- Per capita income, relative productivity, and the REER gap have a statistically significant impact on the share of employment in the services sector. As typically found in the literature, the share of employment in services rises as economies get richer.
- A rise in productivity in the tradable sector relative to the nontradable sector lowers the share of employment in the services sector, contrary to the Baumol disease effect. This could reflect relative price effects on demand, with lower productivity in the nontradable sector increasing the relative price of services and reducing the demand for nontradable goods. On the supply side, such an effect could be consistent with cases where higher wages in the tradable sector attract more labor to that sector.
- The share of employment in services increases as the exchange rate rises above its long-run value (a positive exchange rate gap), reflecting the increased purchasing power of households, which spills into greater demand for imported goods (which become more attractive) and the larger profitability of the nontradable sector. The role of the REER gap in explaining employment in the services sector, although significant, appears small, the

share of employment in the services sector rising by 1 percentage point for every 10 percent increase of the exchange rate above its long-run value.

- Government consumption increases the share of employment in the services sector, albeit this effect does not seem statistically significant. This latter result might be due to the heterogeneity in the paneled economies, which include both economies with large spending on or subsidies for social services, such as E.U. economies, and some with less spending, such as Korea.

Figure 5.4 plots China's actual and fitted values of the share of employment in the services sector against income per capita. China appears to have a low share of employment given its level of income per capita, and this gap has been rising in recent years. Given that services are relatively labor intensive, this has translated into relatively low employment-intensive growth compared with other economies (Figure 5.5). The fact that services tend to be relatively labor intensive suggests that

Figure 5.4
China: Services Share of Employment, Model's Prediction vs. Actual

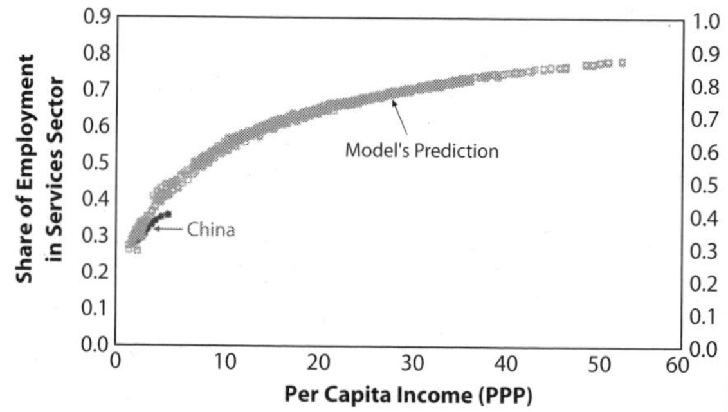

Figure 5.5
Employment Intensity of Growth, Selected Economies
(Average 2003–07)

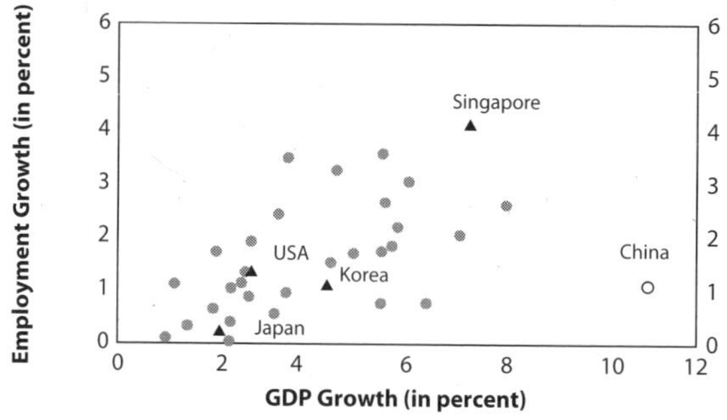

Source: IMF staff estimates.

there is scope for employment to increase as the economy reorients from manufacturing toward services.

Share of Employment in Agriculture

Equation (1) was also estimated for the share of employment in agriculture and in manufacturing. The results are displayed in Table 5.3 and Figures 5.6 and 5.7. Again, a negative sign represents a positive effect on the employment share. Per capita income, relative productivity, and government consumption have a statistically significant impact on the share of employment in agriculture and in manufacturing. The REER gap is significant only for the share of employment in agriculture.

- For agriculture: The share of employment in agriculture declines as economies get richer and as the exchange rate rises above its long-run value, reflecting the lower demand for tradable goods. Government consumption reduces the share of employment in agriculture, probably reflecting its larger services-related content.
- For manufacturing: The effect of per capita GDP on the share of employment in manufacturing is positive but small. Faster productivity in the tradable sector relative to the nontradable sector lowers the share of employment in manufacturing, as does a positive REER gap, reflecting lower competitiveness, but the impact is small (smaller than for the services and agriculture sectors). Government consumption increases the share of employment in manufacturing.

Figures 5.6 and 5.7 plot China's actual and fitted values of the shares of employment in agriculture and in manufacturing against income per capita. China appears to have a high share of employment in agriculture, given its level of income per capita, despite a rapid pace of urbanization in recent years. However, this large share of employment in agriculture is undesirable given low productivity and income elasticity for agricultural goods. For manufacturing, China appears to have a share of employment consistent with its level of per capita income after controlling for relative productivity, the REER gap, and government

TABLE 5.3

China: Determinants of the Share of Employment in the Agriculture Sector[a]
(In percent)

	Equation (1)
GDP per capita ($ thousands, ppp)	
intercept (b1)	−1.43 [0.00] ***
curvature (b2)	−0.92 [0.00] ***
Relative productivity (percent)	−0.02 [0.00] ***
Deviation in REER (percentage point)	1.02 10e-3 [0.00] ***
Government consumption/GDP (percentage point)	0.26 [0.00] ***

Source: IMF staff estimates.
[a]Figures in brackets are p-values. *, **, and *** denote the 10 percent, 5 percent, and 1 percent significance levels, respectively.

Figure 5.6
China: Agriculture Share of Employment, Model's Prediction vs. Actual

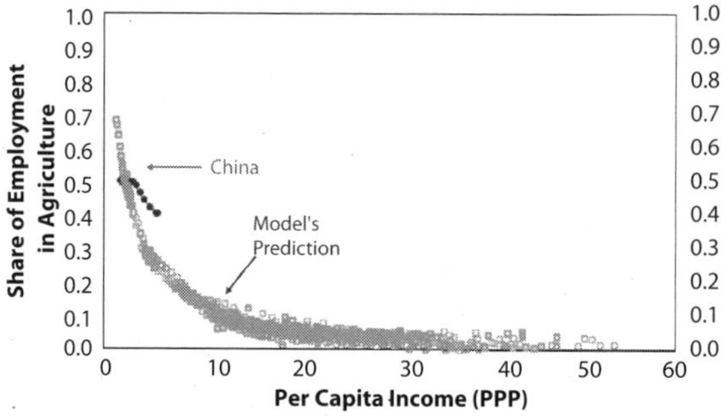

Figure 5.7
China: Manufacturing Share of Employment, Model's Prediction vs. Actual

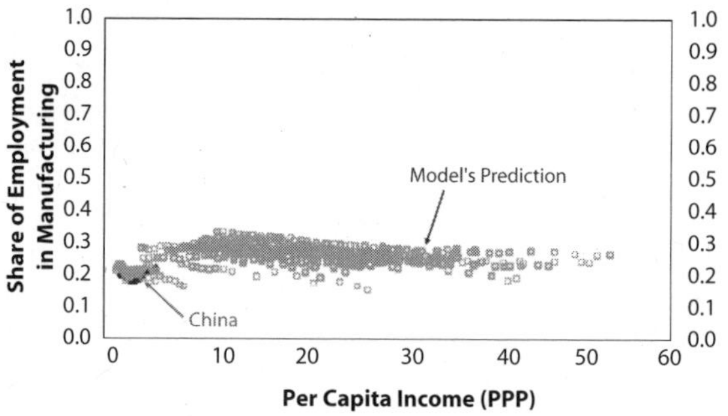

Source: IMF staff estimates.

consumption. Overall, the estimation results of equation (1) suggest that there is room for more labor in the services sector and that the labor could come from the agriculture sector (rather than the manufacturing sector).

Other economies in the region that had a similar reliance on exports in the past, such as Japan and Korea, have in fact experienced significant transfers of labor to the services sector. In Japan, the share of employment in services rose to nearly 60 percent in 1987 (the end of its longest expansion period) from around 38 percent in 1955. In Korea, the shift was even larger, with the share of employment in services rising to around 65 percent in 1995, from around 30 percent in 1961 (Figure 5.8).

The factors that contributed to such shifts in the sectoral allocation of employment in Japan and Korea could include those mentioned in equation 1, namely GDP per capita, the REER, relative productivity, and (to a lesser extent) government consumption. However, there are some differences between the Japanese

Figure 5.8
Services Share of Employment,
Model's Prediction vs. Actual for Selected Countries

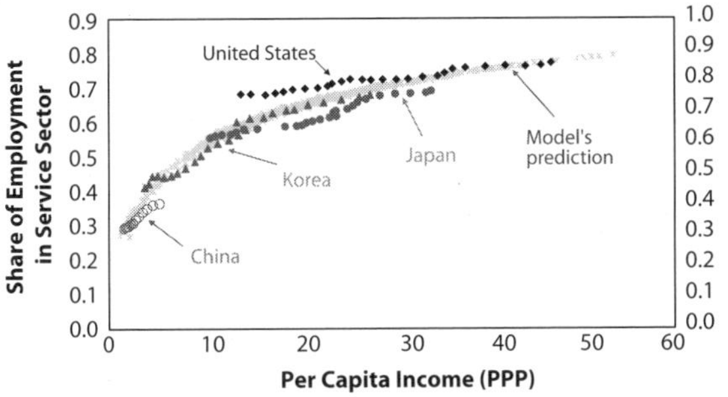

Source: IMF staff estimates.

Figure 5.9
Share of Employment in Primary Industry, China, Japan, and Korea
(In percent, index beginning period = 1)

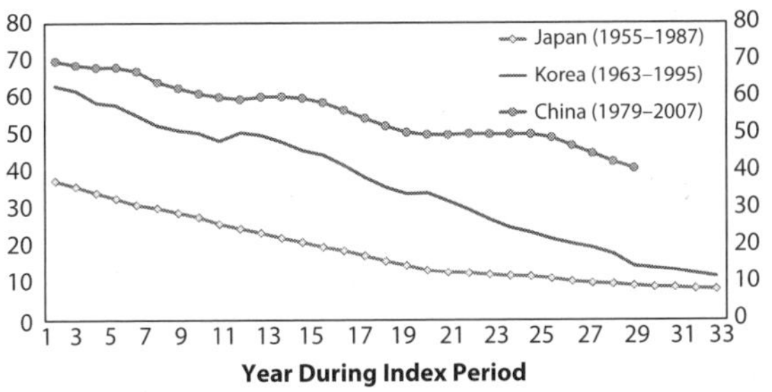

Sources: Statistics Bureau of Japan; National Statistics Office of China; and Ministry of Labor and Social Services of China.

and Korean experiences in the evolution of the REER. The labor shift was accompanied by a trend in REER appreciation in Japan, while in Korea the REER depreciated, contrary to standard economic theory. Interestingly, the difference between China and these economies in the evolution of the share of employment seems to lie in the role played by the agriculture sector: China has reduced its share of employment in agriculture at a slower pace than Japan and Korea (Figure 5.9).

At its current per capita income level, relative productivity between the nontradable and the tradable sector, REER, and government consumption, China could absorb 70 million more workers (about 9 percent of total employment) into the services sector. Policies that could facilitate such a move include tax deductions for setting up service businesses, subsidies, transfers, urbanization, and job training programs. The shift to the services sector would be facilitated by structural reforms to improve productivity in the nontradable sector (across sectors with larger gains in the nontradable sector) and by allowing the exchange rate to appreciate.

Model-Based Simulations of the Potential Impact on Employment of Rebalancing Growth

This section complements the analysis in the previous section by carrying out alternative simulation scenarios of shifts from the tradable to the nontradable sector and higher private consumption. Two scenarios are considered: (1) structural reforms that raise productivity in the nontradable sector, accompanied by a shift in households' preference toward nontradable goods, and (2) in addition to raising productivity in the nontradable sector and shifting preferences, reforms that lower households' saving rate.

The first scenario assumes that structural reforms raise productivity in the nontradable sector, and at the same time, that improvements in the quality of goods and services increase Chinese households' preferences for those nontradable goods. The structural reforms could include measures that level the playing field between the tradable and nontradable sector and increase contestability in markets, for example through further opening up the economy and liberalizing the services sector.[10]

The second scenario adds to the assumptions made in the first scenario by including, for example, reforms of the pension, health care, and education systems as well as the domestic financial market that result in an increase in households' consumption by about 3 percent of GDP.

The model simulations are based on the GIMF model.[11] The rich structure of the GIMF allows a detailed exploration of the interaction between different sectors of an economy and the transmission of shocks. There are wide-ranging nominal and real rigidities at the sectoral level that generate realistic inertial dynamics for the key macroeconomic aggregates.

The simulation results suggest that under these alternative scenarios, rebalancing China's growth toward domestic demand could raise aggregate employment in the long run (Figures 5.10 and 5.11, respectively). Higher productivity in the nontradable sector and an increase in domestic demand create incentives for higher employment in nontradable industries that compensate for short-term employment losses in the exporting sector. Those employment effects are larger when private consumption is promoted than when it is not.[12]

---

[10]Arguably, such measures could also raise productivity in the tradable sector (see N'Diaye, Zhang, and Zhang (2010) for more details).

[11]All scenarios assume a constant exchange rate for China and a floating exchange rate.

[12]The results reported are deviations from a steady state. Assuming that the simulations are done from a situation of disequilibrium could alter the dynamics of the variables and hence the conclusions.

Figure 5.10
China: Illustrative Employment Effects From Shift Toward Nontradable Sector

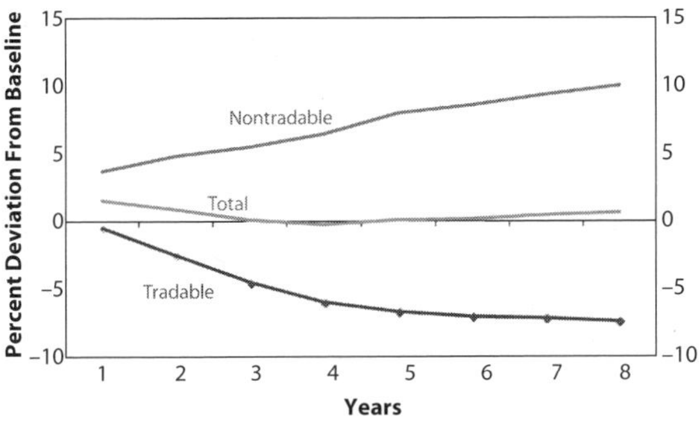

Figure 5.11
China: Illustrative Employment Effects From Shift Toward Nontradable Sector and Lower Saving Rate

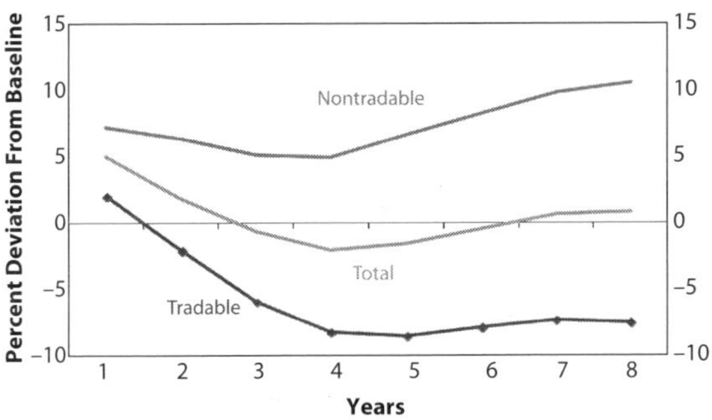

Sources: GIMF; and IMF staff estimates.

In the shorter term, however, it is likely that employment growth would be compromised as the economy moves away from the tradable sector and toward the nontradable sector, notwithstanding some short-lived initial employment gains as stronger consumption increases demand for both tradable and nontradable goods.

Reduced opportunities for profits in export-related industries would prompt firms to shed labor as they adapted to the more challenging environment. These job losses would be offset in part by job creation in the nontradable sector where firms would see more opportunities for profits and new businesses would be created. Higher wages and stronger demand for labor in the nontradable sector would lead to higher employment in nontradable industries. However, time-to-build and other adjustment costs could create delays in new job creation that fully compensates for job losses in the export-oriented industries. In this context, increasing the flexibility of the labor market, providing training and information, and increasing transfers to displaced workers from the tradable sector would facilitate the transition to the nontradable sector and probably reduce the short-term employment losses.

To summarize, China's employment share in services appears to be significantly below the level suggested by international experiences, after taking into account China's stage of development and other fundamentals. This indicates that there is significant scope for China to create employment in the nontradable sector. Therefore, in the long run, rebalancing China's growth toward domestic demand will increase aggregate employment, particularly in the nontradable sector. However, the transition from the tradable to the nontradable sector could generate short-term employment losses, since the tradable sector may shed more workers than new jobs created in the nontradable sector initially. Policies such as training and promotion of labor mobility should be deployed to mitigate the short-term employment cost. A broader strategy that lowers private saving and develops the financial system would also help to substantially reduce the transition cost.

REFERENCES

Baumol, W., 1967, "Macroeconomics of Unbalanced Growth: The Anatomy of Urban Crisis," *American Economic Review,* Vol. 57, No. 3, pp. 415–26.

Blanchard, O., and F. Giavazzi, 2005, "Rebalancing Growth in China: A Three-Handed Approach," MIT Department of Economics Working Paper No. 05–32 (Cambridge, Massachusetts: Massachusetts Institute of Technology).

Brooks, R., and R. Tao, 2003, "China's Labor Market Performance and Challenges," IMF Working Paper No. 03/210 (Washington: International Monetary Fund).

D'Agostino, A., R. Serafini, and M. Ward-Warmedinger, 2006, "Sectoral Explanations of Employment in Europe: The Role of Services," ECB Working Paper No. 625 (Frankfurt: European Central Bank).

Fuchs, V., 1980, "Economic Growth and the Rise of Service Employment," NBER Working Paper No. 486 (Cambridge, Massachusetts: National Bureau of Economic Research).

Garnaut, R., L. Song, S. Tenev, and Y. Yao, 2005, "Ownership Transformation in China" (Washington: World Bank).

Guo, K., and P. N'Diaye, 2009, "Is China's Export-Oriented Growth Strategy Sustainable?" IMF Working Paper No. 09/169 (Washington: International Monetary Fund).

Kumhof, M., and D. Laxton, 2007, "A Party Without a Hangover? On the Effects of U.S. Government Deficits," IMF Working Paper No. 07/202 (Washington: International Monetary Fund).

N'Diaye, P., P. Zhang, and W. Zhang, 2010, "Structural Reform, Intra-Regional Trade, and Medium-Term Growth Prospects of East Asia and the Pacific: Perspectives From a New Multi-Region Model," *Journal of Asian Economics*, Vol. 21, No. 1, pp. 20–36.

CHAPTER 6

Determinants of China's Private Consumption: An International Perspective

KAI GUO AND PAPA N'DIAYE

INTRODUCTION

China's private consumption as a share of GDP has declined from around 55 percent in the early 1980s to around 37 percent in 2008. The decline in a country's share of private consumption during the early development stages is not in itself a surprise—savings naturally rise at early stages of development as households move away from subsistence levels of income and greater capital accumulation is needed to finance investment and growth. However, the size of the fall in China's private consumption share certainly stands out when compared with other countries.

Reasons put forward to explain this downward trend in private consumption relate both to households' saving rates and income as well as to purely statistical factors. Studies by Blanchard and Giavazzi (2005), Kuijs (2005), and Modigliani and Cao (2004) attribute the decline in private consumption to a rise in household saving rates, particularly precautionary saving and particularly by elderly households, in the face of limited health care, pension, and education benefits. Indeed, Chamon and Prasad (2010) find that it is the elderly who save the most in China, contrary to typical lifecycle patterns. Wei and Zhang (2009), on the other hand, attribute about half the increase in household saving rates during 1990–2007 to growing gender imbalances as the shrinking number of women relative to men fosters a more competitive marriage environment, one that requires higher and higher saving in households where the one child is a male. Aziz and Cui (2007) find that, rather than a higher saving *rate*, the fall in the share of private consumption is due to a decline in households' income as a share of GDP and that this decline is broad-based, reflecting income from wages, returns on saving, and government transfers. In this connection, Bai and Qian (2009) explain the decline in the labor share of income as mainly a statistical artifact resulting from changes in the way labor income is compiled.[1]

[1]The authors indicate that, after 2004, individual business owners' income was reclassified from labor income to capital income. This change explains 58 percent of the decline in the labor share of income during 1995-2004.

This chapter gauges the key determinants of China's private consumption in relation to GDP using data on the Chinese economy and evidence from other countries. The empirical framework relates the share of private consumption to that of household income in GDP as well as to other factors that could influence the household saving rate (including the old-age dependency ratio, the level of financial development, per capita GDP, the share of employment in the services sector, changes in the real exchange rate, and the real interest rate).

The model fits the historical profile of China's private consumption quite well and explains most of its evolution over the selected sample. The results show that around one-third of the fall in private consumption from 2000 to 2007 can be directly attributed to a fall in household income, while the remaining two-thirds are due to other factors that may affect, directly or indirectly, household saving rates and incomes. In addition, we find that the fit of the model is not enhanced by including a China-specific dummy variable.

The results suggest that efforts to further raise household income and the share of employment in the services sector, as well as to develop capital markets through liberalizing interest rates and creating alternative savings instruments, are likely to have the largest impact on consumption. However, there is also a role for other mechanisms to raise household income and mitigate household-specific risk, such as improving the health care and pension systems. In addition, the lack of any China-specific factor suggests that a small set of economic and social variables can adequately explain the behavior of Chinese consumers. In this sense, there is nothing "special" about China. Rather, the challenge is to explain why the conditioning variables—notably a low level of services sector employment, the level of financial sector development, and low real interest rates—are so different in China relative to other countries' historical experience.

The chapter is organized as follows. The next section provides an overview of the empirical framework. This is followed by an exploration of the role of the income share in explaining China's share of private consumption. The role of the saving rate in explaining China's share of private consumption is explored last.

EMPIRICAL FRAMEWORK

To explain the dynamics of private consumption in China, we use cross-country panel data and regress private consumption as a share of GDP on household income and public consumption (both as a share of GDP), the level of per capita GDP (to capture the level of development), real GDP growth, real interest rates, CPI inflation, the change in the terms of trade, the old-age dependency ratio, the change in the real effective exchange rate, the share of employment in the services sector, a measure of past foreign financing, and a measure of financial development. The goal is to use this panel data framework to assess the relative contributions to the dynamics of private consumption made by changes in income and other factors that affect the saving rate in China and, as well, to relate those factors to the broader international experience.

To capture the potential for a nonlinear relationship between the regressors and private consumption, the reduced form of the consumption equation can be written as follows:

$$\frac{C}{Y} = 1 - \exp\left[\alpha_1\left(\frac{Y}{N}\right)^{\alpha_2} + \alpha_3\left(\frac{G}{Y}\right) + \alpha_4\frac{\dot{Y}}{Y} + \alpha_5 r + \alpha_6 \pi + \alpha_7 \tau \right.$$
$$\left. + \alpha_8 D + \alpha_9 s^* + \alpha_{10} f + \alpha_{11}\frac{L^s}{L} + \alpha_{12} e + \alpha_{13}\frac{Y^h}{Y}\right] + \varepsilon^c \qquad (1)$$

where Y^h is household income and Y is real GDP. Per capita GDP $\left(\frac{Y}{N}\right)$ and real GDP growth $\left(\frac{Y}{N}\right)$ capture saving behaviors at different stages of development (Modigliani, 1966) and the real interest rate (r) reflects the substitution or income effect from higher interest rates. Inflation (π) may increase consumption through the Pigou effect or lower it through its impact on interest rates and measured household income. Changes in the terms of trade (τ) through their impact on income could lower consumption if they are temporary, while the impact of permanent terms of trade shocks on private consumption is ambiguous. The old-age dependency ratio (D) captures the effects of demographics, with private consumption generally expected to increase as the dependency ratio rises. Public consumption (G) embeds Barro's (1981) idea that what matters to consumers is their effective consumption, which includes both public and private spending, and that consumers take into account public spending when they make their private spending decisions. Public spending could hence complement private spending. Public consumption could also entail some crowding-out effects, with higher deficit-financed expenditure dampening private spending. Changes in the real effective exchange rate (e) affect households' income and purchasing power and hence influence their spending decisions. A higher share of employment in the services sector (L^s) raises both labor income and the availability of services, both of which can raise private consumption. Foreign savings (s^*) capture the possibility that the availability of foreign financing could affect households' spending decisions. Financial development could increase private consumption by increasing the availability of financing sources and providing alternative instruments for saving with higher returns.

The model is estimated using the Generalized Method of Moments estimator with an unbalanced panel of 39 economies for a total of 515 observations.[2] To handle simultaneity, lagged values of the regressors are used as instruments. The real interest rates, changes in the terms of trade, the old-age dependency ratio, and the share of employment in the services sector are considered as exogenous

[2]The 39 economies are Argentina, Australia, Austria, Belgium, Brazil, Canada, Hong Kong SAR, Chile, Colombia, Denmark, Egypt, Finland, France, Germany, Greece, Iceland, India, Indonesia, Ireland, Israel, Italy, Japan, South Korea, Malaysia, Netherlands, New Zealand, Norway, Peru, Philippines, Portugal, Singapore, South Africa, Spain, Sweden, Switzerland, Taiwan Province of China, United Kingdom, United States, and China. The longest sample in the unbalanced panel starts in 1980 and ends in 2008.

TABLE 6.1

Determinants of Private Consumption for 39-Country Panel
(In percent of GDP)

Explanatory variables[a]	Coefficients[b]
GDP per capita[c]	
Intercept (b1)	0.1972 [.001] ***
Curvature (b2)	0.2372 [.000] ***
Public consumption/GDP	0.0093 [.000] ***
Real GDP growth	0.0067 [.001] ***
Real interest rate	–0.0023 [.088] *
Inflation	0.0031 [.138]
Change in terms of trade	0.0027 [.002] ***
Old-age dependency ratio	–0.0031 [.003] ***
Financial development[d]	–0.0106 [.034] **
Share of employment in service sector	–0.0094 [.000] ***
Change in real effective exchange rate	–0.0055 [.000] ***
External financing	0.0125 [.000] ***
Household disposable income/GDP	–0.0126 [.000] ***

Source: IMF staff estimates.
[a]In percentage point unless otherwise specified.
[b]Figures in brackets are p-values. *,**,*** denote the 10 percent, 5 percent, and 1 percent significance levels, respectively.
[c]In thousands of US dollar (ppp).
[d]Measured by stock market total value traded/GDP.

variables. The instrument set also includes country dummies, but no country dummies are included in the regression itself.

Table 6.1 shows the estimation result for the share of private consumption with positive (negative) coefficients indicating a negative (positive) impact of the associated explanatory variable. The results indicate that all the main regressors—except for inflation—have a significant impact on private consumption. The two sections following this one will discuss these factors in more detail.

Figure 6.1 shows that, even without accounting for China-specific factors beyond those captured by the various regressors, the trend decline in Chinese consumption over the last decade or so can be reasonably estimated by the model, even though the model is fitted on a cross-section of 39 economies, and so there is no guarantee in advance that there will be a good fit for any particular country. This suggests that the unexplained component behind China's declining consumption share may be relatively small. As such, rather than "culture" or "history," a larger part of the explanation for China's low household saving lies in more conventional economic forces, such as China's rapid economic growth, declining labor share of income, relatively low level of financial development, relatively capital-intensive means of production, and low level of service employment.

One can decompose the estimate into how much of the change in consumption over a particular period has been due to changes in household

Figure 6.1
China: Private Consumption, Predicted vs. Actual, 1992–2007
(In percent of GDP)

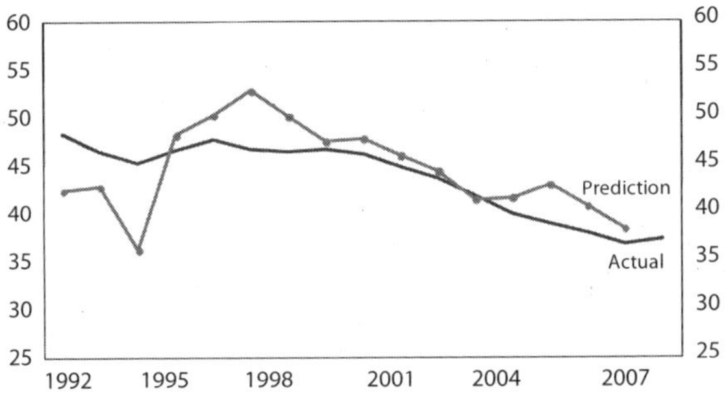

Source: IMF staff estimates.

Figure 6.2
Cumulative Change in Private Consumption to GDP Ratio 2000–07: Estimated Contribution of Disposable Income and Saving Rate
(In percent)

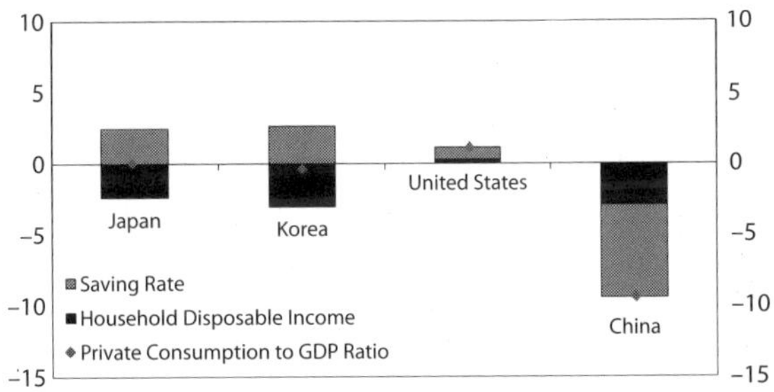

Source: IMF staff estimates.

income versus other factors that may affect the saving rate. For China, around one-third of the change in consumption behavior from 2000–07 can be directly attributed to a decline in household income (Figure 6.2).[3] This contrasts with developments in other countries in the region (e.g., Japan and Korea) where falling household income (as a share of GDP) was largely offset by a fall in the saving rate. In contrast, in the United States, the increase in private consumption can largely be attributed to a lower saving rate (with household income changing little as a share of GDP).

[3]A similar calculation for the 1992–2007 period would raise the contribution of households' income to the decline in private consumption to around 45 percent, a figure consistent with findings by Aziz and Cui (2007).

THE ROLE OF THE HOUSEHOLD SHARE OF INCOME

The share of household disposable income in GDP has declined in China from about 59 percent in 1992 to 53 percent in 2007. Not only is China's share of household income low relative to international comparators, but it seems also to have fallen faster than that of other economies. The decline in China's disposable income share reflects falling real wages, investment income, and transfers (Aziz and Cui, 2007). Looking at each of these factors in turn suggests the following:

- *Labor income.* The labor share of income fell to less than 49 percent in 2008 from around 54 percent in 1997 (based on flow of funds data). The fall is nearly twice as large when provincial data are used (from 51 percent to 40 percent). The fall reflects mostly sluggish employment growth, as wages have generally outpaced productivity over the past 10 years. China's rapid GDP growth has generated relatively little employment compared with other countries (Figure 6.3) and this, in turn, has suppressed household income.

The low employment intensity of growth results from China's export-oriented growth which, combined with a low cost of capital, favors more capital-intensive means of production. As shown in Chapter 5, China has a far lower share of employment in the services sector than one would expect from other economies' experience and China's fundamentals (Figure 6.4). On a sectoral basis, the primary, secondary, and tertiary sectors account for 41 percent, 27 percent, and 32 percent of employment, respectively, as of 2008.[4] With the services sector typically being more labor intensive, China's export-oriented growth has naturally

Figure 6.3
Employment Intensity of Growth
(Average 2003–07)

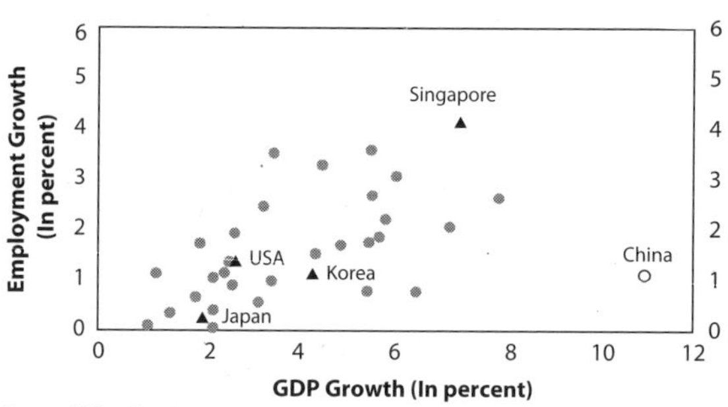

Source: IMF staff estimates.

[4]Preliminary estimates from the second economic census indicate that the size of the services sector was underestimated. Nevertheless, that underestimate is unlikely to change the fact that the share of employment in the services sector in China is far lower than international experiences and China's fundamentals would suggest.

Figure 6.4
Service Sector Share of Employment, China, Japan, Korea, and the United States

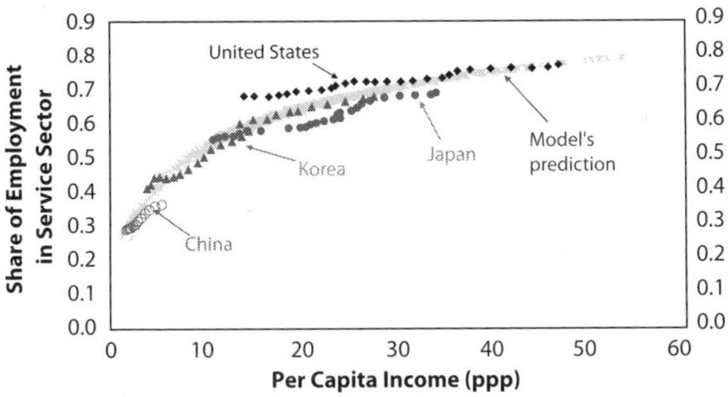

Source: IMF staff estimates.

Figure 6.5
Agriculture Sector Share of Employment, China vs. Model Prediction

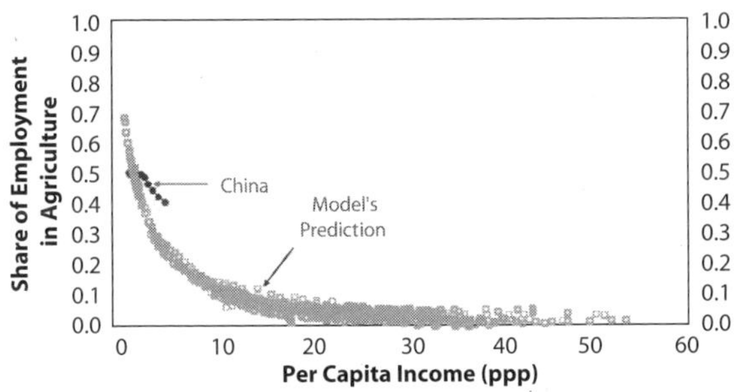

Source: IMF staff estimates.

translated into relatively low employment growth compared with other economies.

As a corollary to the relatively low share of employment in its services sector, China has a larger share of employment in agriculture than one would expect from international comparators (Figure 6.5). This feature implies that shifting labor out of agriculture toward services, including labor intensive services, could raise the aggregate labor share. The above arguments suggest that greater employment creation, especially in the services sector, could raise the household share of income and hence boost private consumption. Other Asian economies that have also relied heavily on exports in the past, such as Japan and Korea, experienced a significant transfer of labor to the services sector during the course of their development, something that is not being seen in China. In Japan, for example, the share of employment in services rose to around 60 percent by the end of Japan's longest expansion period (in 1987) from around 38 percent in 1955. In Korea, the transfer of labor to the services sector was even larger, with the share of employment in services rising to around 65 percent in 1995 from around 30 percent in 1961.

- *Investment Income.* Households' investment income has also fallen as a share of GDP since the early 1990s. It represents 2⅓ percent of GDP, down from about 5 percent in the early 1990s (Figure 6.6). The share of investment income is also low in China compared to the levels in other countries (Figure 6.7). Households' investment income mainly consists of interest income, which accounts for around 80 percent of investment income. Dividends and other sources of property income play a minor role, since the underdeveloped financial system has limited alternative investment instruments. The decline in interest income seems to have been mostly driven by

Figure 6.6
China: Share of Investment Income in GDP, 1992–2007

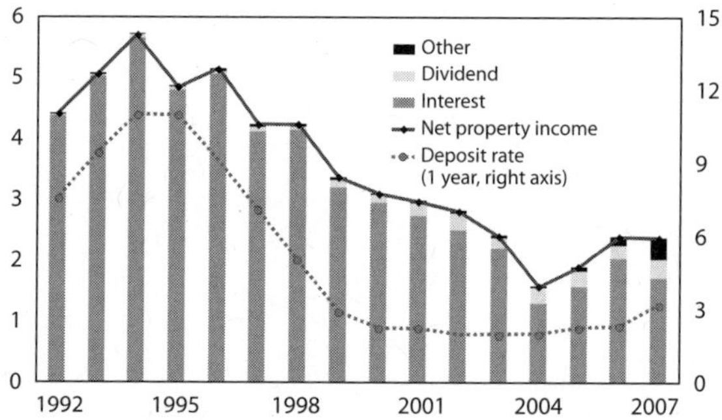

Sources: CEIC Data Co. Ltd.; and UN statistics.

Figure 6.7
China: Share of Net Property Income in Disposable Income
(Average 2000–06)

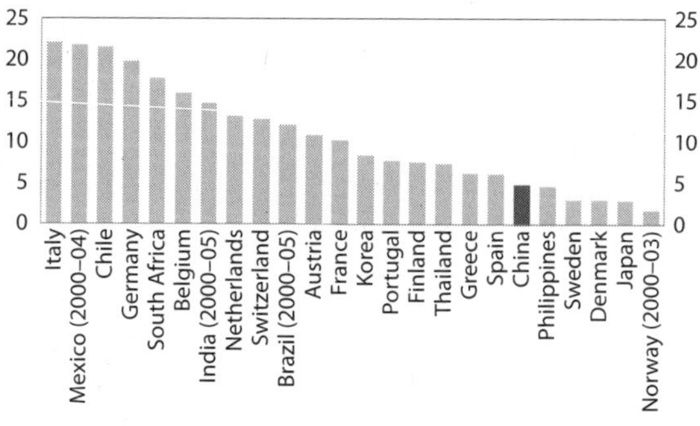

Source: CEIC Data Co. Ltd.; and UN statistics.

the fall in deposit rates. Deposit rates, like lending rates, are administered: deposit rates are subject to a ceiling, while lending rates are subject to a floor. Lending and deposit rates are kept low, while ensuring that banks benefit from comfortable interest margins. This favors investment at the expense of consumption, with households effectively subsidizing borrowers. Higher deposit rates could be best achieved within the context of a broader strategy of interest rate liberalization. Indeed, Porter and others (2009) show that interest rate liberalization in China would likely result in higher interest rates, which would discourage marginal investment, improve the effectiveness of intermediation and monetary transmission, and enhance access to financial services by underserved sectors. China's low share of property income in GDP (by international standards) suggests some room for further expansion, which could be achieved by providing alternative instruments for saving.

- *Transfers.* Net transfers to households have fallen to ⅓ percent of GDP, down from 2½ percent of GDP in 1992. Gross transfers also stand well below international comparators (Figure 6.8). The low share of transfers results in large part from the state-owned enterprise reform of the late 1990s, which created a void in social safety nets that the government has been able to fill only gradually.

In sum, the falling shares of labor income, investment income, and transfers have held back household disposable income and private consumption. However, the decline in the share of household income does not fully explain why China's share of private consumption is smaller than that of international comparators. China's share falls outside the range of estimates based on equation (1) (highlighted area in Figure 6.9), and the gap has been widening over time, indicating that the household saving rate has also been rising.

Figure 6.8
Share of Current Transfer in Disposable Income
(Average 2000–06)

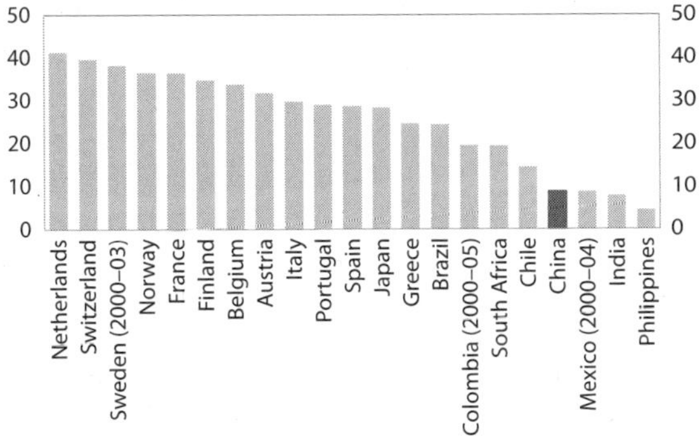

Sources: CEIC Data Co. Ltd.; and UN statistics.

Figure 6.9
Share of Private Consumption and Disposable Income
(Growth periods)

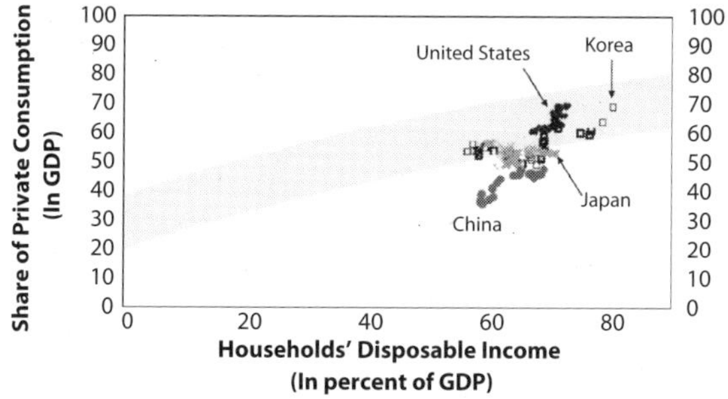

Source: IMF staff estimates.

THE ROLE OF THE SAVING RATE

A stylized fact from the behavior of other countries is that the consumption share in GDP falls as per capita GDP rises at the lowest levels of per capita income. The consumption share declines in part because, at lower levels of income, household income is generally at subsistence level, leaving little room for saving. In this regard, China is no different from other countries. A large part of the decline in China's private consumption has been a natural result of China's rapid pace of economic development. Indeed, on average across countries, the consumption share declines steadily as countries get richer, and it eventually stabilizes when per capita GDP is around \$2,500 to \$3,000 on a PPP basis. Looking back to 1980, China's share of private consumption in GDP was on the low side, but nevertheless it was broadly consistent with other international comparators at similar levels of development. However, the consumption share in China then fell at a faster pace than would be suggested by the cross-country model, and by 2008 it was substantially below the level in other countries (Figure 6.10). This rate of decline of consumption is not unprecedented. Indeed, Korea, Japan, and the United States saw similar rapid reductions in consumption as a share of GDP when their income per capita rose, although their starting points were at initial levels of consumption that were much higher than China's was in 1980.

What are the main factors, then, after controlling for the level of per capita income, that have led to this rapid fall in consumption? There are six factors, as follows:

- *Employment in services.* The empirical results suggest that the consumption share could increase by 3½ percentage points for every 10 percentage point increase in the share of employment in the services sector. Employment in the services sector increases the labor share of income since the services sector is, in general, more labor-intensive than other industries. The higher share of income raises aggregate consumption. This effect of a rise in the

Figure 6.10
Share of Private Consumption and Per Capita GDP
(Growth periods)

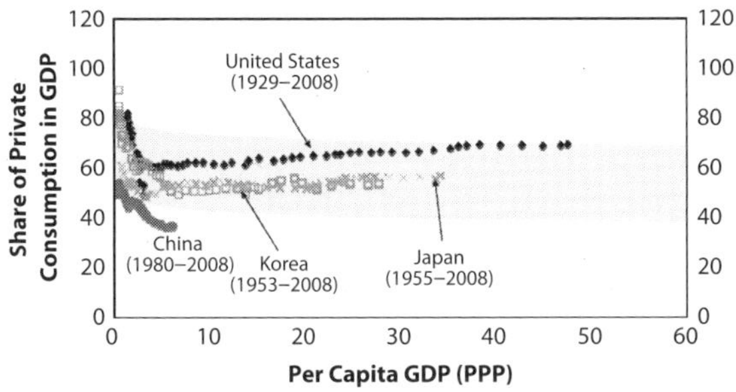

Source: IMF staff estimates.

employment share of services is even larger when the increase in the services sector is accompanied by higher wages brought about by structural reforms that raise productivity. In addition to this demand effect, the employment in services variable captures supply-side effects related to the increased availability of services, with households increasing their consumption as new and better services become available. Overall, structural reforms that level the playing field between the tradable and nontradable sectors, increase contestability in markets, and improve access to financing could raise productivity in the services sector and at the same time enhance the quality of services.

- *Real exchange rate.* An appreciating exchange rate increases the share of private consumption, even after controlling for the effect it would have on household income. The independent effect of the exchange rate is significant, with the share of consumption increasing by around 2 percentage points for every 10 percent appreciation in the real effective exchange rate.
- *Financial development and real interest rates.* Greater financial development tends to increase consumption, perhaps highlighting the impact that alternative investment instruments have on reducing precautionary savings or that greater access to financing can have on consumption itself, particularly for people who are credit constrained. China's financial system is large but not very developed, and it is dominated by banks. The dominance of state-owned banks suggests that savings are not efficiently used, with the banking sector assets lent primarily to state-owned enterprises (Arora, 2009, and Feyzioğlu, 2009). Efforts have been made toward liberalization (for example, interbank repo lending rates and bond market yields were liberalized in the late 1990s). Despite the large market capitalization of stock markets in China ($3.5 trillion on average in 2008), only one company was listed for every million persons, as compared with around 40 (on average) for the sampled economies. Bond markets also remain relatively underdeveloped. Developing capital markets through corporate bond markets, mutual funds,

and broader equity ownership could broaden the range of saving instruments for households' saving and offer a variety of insurance products to help pool risks. That, in turn, would facilitate higher consumption. Moreover, since the real interest rate is estimated to have a positive impact on the share of private consumption, a liberalization of interest rates would further promote private consumption, since it likely would lead to higher deposit rates (Porter and others, 2009).

- *Public consumption.* The share of private consumption is found to decline with increases in public consumption. The reason could be that to some extent public consumption substitutes for private consumption across the selected economies. An alternative explanation could be that public consumption captures crowding-out behavior, with households reducing their spending in the face of higher deficit-financed spending. However, for China this result is inconsistent with alternative evidence from provincial data, which suggests that government spending on health (but not on education) reduces urban household saving (discussed further in Chapter 7).
- *Demographics.* The evidence in Table 6.1 suggests that the consumption share rises with the dependency ratio across economies as older people draw down their lifetime savings. China's lower dependency ratio versus that of other countries has a depressing effect on its relative private consumption share (Figure 6.11). However, despite the expectation of a rising dependency ratio in China in the coming years, it is unclear that this will translate into higher consumption. Indeed, contrary to theory and the behavior in other countries, the evidence suggests that average urban household saving rates in China are in fact highest among both the youngest and the oldest households (Chamon and Prasad, 2010). Therefore, the aging of the population in China and the increase in the dependency ratio may not necessarily lead

Figure 6.11
Old-Age Dependency Ratios

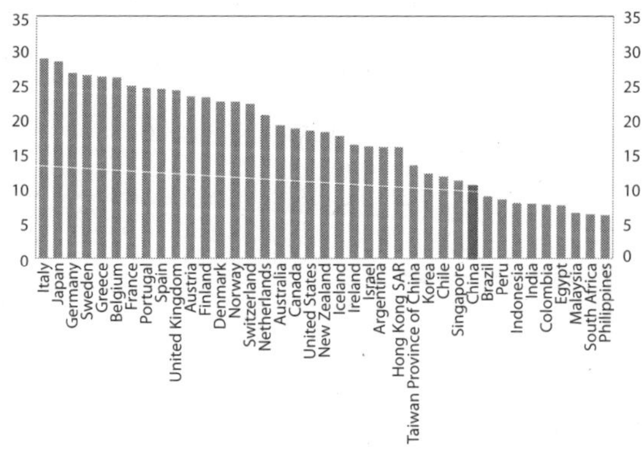

Source: World Bank, World Development Indicator database.

to an increase in consumption. This highlights the importance of implementing measures to reduce precautionary saving among the elderly, such as pension and health care reform, so that the rising dependency ratio could help increase consumption over time.

- *Pensions.* Available information on the sampled economies suggests that most of them introduced pension systems after World War II and have undertaken major reforms to their systems, particularly with regard to the replacement rates (Table 6.2). However, because of data limitations (especially on the time dimension of pension data), we have not included in equation (1) a variable to control for the role pensions play in households' consumption. Nevertheless, Figures 6.12 and 6.13 show a positive relationship between the residual in equation (1) and key features of pension systems, such as coverage ratios and replacement rates. The effect of pension coverage appears to die out as economies get close to full coverage, but

Figure 6.12
Pension System Replacement Ratios

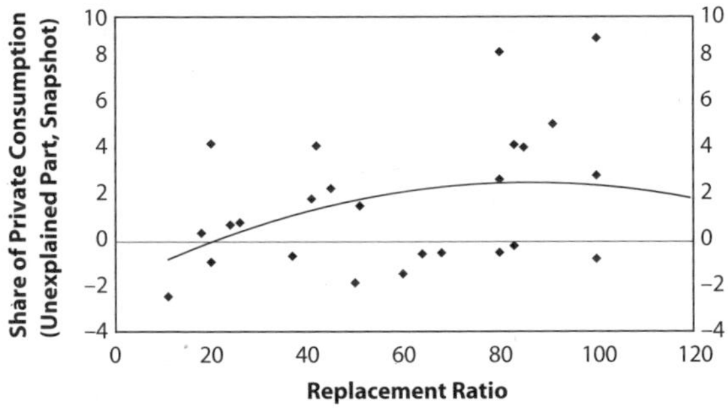

Source: IMF staff estimates.

Figure 6.13
Pension System Coverage

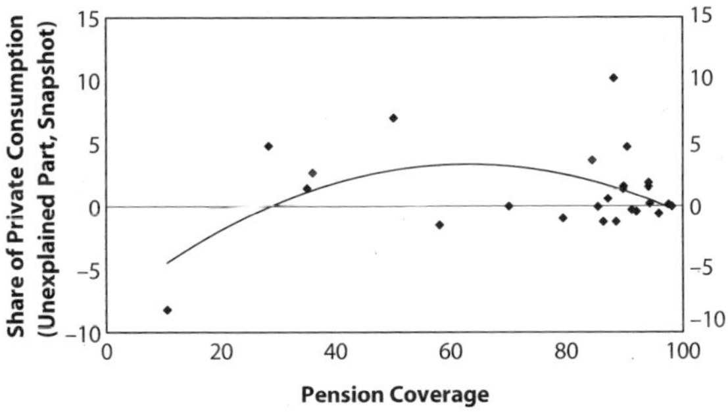

Source: IMF staff estimates.

TABLE 6.2

International Pension Comparison

	Pension introduced[a]	Most recent major reform[a]	Contributors / Labor Force[b]
Argentina	1946	2008	53.0
Australia	1908	1991	
Austria	1906	1955	95.8
Belgium	1900	1967	86.2
Brazil	1936	1991	36.0
Canada	1927	1952	91.9
China, P.R.: Hong Kong	1973	2000	
Chile	1924	1980	70.0
Colombia	1965	1993	35.0
Denmark	1891		89.6
Egypt	1950	1975	50.0
Finland	1937	1956	90.3
France	1910	1945	88.4
Germany	1889	2002	94.2
Greece	1934	1951	88.0
Iceland	1909	2007	92.0
India	1952	1995	10.6
Indonesia	1977	1992	8.0
Ireland	1908		79.3
Israel	1957	1974	
Italy	1919	1995	87.0
Japan	1941	1959	97.5
Korea, Republic of	1973	2007	58.0
Malaysia	1951	1991	48.7
Netherlands	1901	1957	91.7
New Zealand	1898	2001	
Norway	1936	1997	94.0
Peru	1936	1992	20.0
Philippines	1954		28.3
Portugal	1935	2007	84.3
Singapore	1955	2001	73.0
South Africa	1928	2004	
Spain	1919	1994	85.3
Sweden	1913	1998	91.1
Switzerland	1946		98.1
Taiwan Province of China	1950	2008	
United Kingdom	1908	1995	89.7
United States	1935		94.0

[a]Social Security Administration, 2009.
[b]Palacios and Pallares-Miralles, 2000.

non-negligible gains could be made during the transition (with coverage explaining about 20 percent of the residual). The relationship between the residual and the replacement rate is also non-negligible. This result suggests that government efforts to expand the coverage of the pension system to include rural and urban workers could help lift private consumption (Dunaway and Arora, 2007).

CONCLUSION

The analysis presented in this chapter finds that China's share of private consumption in GDP is low when compared with benchmarks derived from international comparators. China's low share of private consumption in GDP can be largely explained by its relatively low share of household income and by other factors that influence household saving rates, including the level of development, the share of employment in the services sector, the level of financial development, and changes in the real exchange rate.

The analysis also suggests that the current level of consumption is not preordained and somehow special to China due to its historical or cultural background. Instead, policy efforts in a range of areas can yield results in bringing China back to a level of household consumption that is more consistent with countries that are or were at similar levels of development. In particular, efforts to further increase household income, develop capital markets—including liberalizing interest rates and creating alternative saving instruments—and raise the share of employment in the services sector can generate tangible results.

REFERENCES

Arora, V., 2009, "China's Financial Sector Policies," in *Innovation for Development and the Role of Government: A Perspective from the East Asia and Pacific Region*, pp. 71–90, ed. by Yang Dong, Q. Fan, K. Li, R. Peng, and D. Zhihua Zeng (Washington: World Bank).

Aziz, J., and L. Cui, 2007, "Explaining China's Low Consumption: The Neglected Role of Household Income," IMF Working Paper No. 07/181 (Washington: International Monetary Fund).

Bai, C., and Z. Qian, 2009, "Factor Income Share in China: The Story Behind the Statistics," *China Economic Journal*, Vol. 2.

Barnett, S. and R. Brooks, 2009, "China: Does Government Health and Education Spending Boost Consumption?" IMF Working Paper No. 10/16 (Washington: International Monetary Fund).

Barro, R., 1981, "Output Effects of Government Purchases," *Journal of Political Economy*, Vol. 89, No. 6, pp. 1086-121.

Blanchard, O., and F. Giavazzi, 2005, "Rebalancing Growth in China: A Three-Handed Approach," MIT Department of Economics Working Paper No. 05–32 (Cambridge, Massachusetts: Massachusetts Institute of Technology).

Chamon, M., and E. Prasad, 2010, "Why are Saving Rates of Urban Households in China Rising?" *American Economic Journal: Macroeconomic*, Vol. 2, No. 1, pp. 93–130.

Dean, A., M. Durand, J. Fallon, and P. Hoeller, 1989, "Saving Trends and Behaviour in OECD Countries," OECD Economics Department Working Paper No. 67 (Paris: Organisation for Economic Co-operation and Development).

Dunaway, S., and V. Arora, 2007, "Pension Reform in China: The Need for a New Approach," IMF Working Paper No. 07/109.

Feyzioğlu, T., 2009, "Does Good Financial Performance Mean Good Financial Intermediation in China?" IMF Working Paper No. 09/170 (Washington: International Monetary Fund).

Guo, K., and P. N'Diaye, 2009, "Employment Effects of Growth Rebalancing in China," IMF Working Paper No. 09/169 (Washington: International Monetary Fund).

Kuijs, L., 2005, "Investment and Saving in China," Policy Research Working Paper No. 3633 (Washington: World Bank).

Masson, P., T. Bayoumi, and H. Samiei, 1998, "International Evidence on the Determinants of Private Saving," *World Bank Economic Review*, Vol. 12, No. 3, pp. 483–501.

Modigliani, F., 1966, "The Life Cycle Hypothesis of Saving, the Demand for Wealth and the Supply of Capital," *Social Research,* Vol. 33 (summer), pp. 160–217.

Modigliani, F., and S. L. Cao, 2004, "The Chinese Saving Puzzle and the Life-Cycle Hypothesis," *Journal of Economic Literature*, Vol. 42, No. 1, pp. 145–170.

Palacios, R., and J. Pallares–Miralles, 2000, "International Patterns of Pension Provision," Pension Reform Primer Series, Social Protection Discussion Paper No. 0009 (Washington; world bank).

Porter, N., E. Takáts, and T. Feyzioglu, 2009, "Interest Rate Liberalization in China," IMF Working Paper No. 09/171 (Washington: International Monetary Fund).

Social Security Administration, 2009, "Social Security Programs Throughout the World," (available via Internet at http://www.socialsecurity.gov/policy/docs/progdesc/ssptw/).

Wei, S., and X. Zhang, 2009, "The Competitive Saving Motive: Evidence from Rising Sex Ratios and Savings Rates in China," NBER Working Paper No. 15093 (Cambridge, Massachusetts: National Bureau of Economic Research).

CHAPTER 7

Does Government Spending on Health and Education Raise Consumption?

STEVEN BARNETT AND RAY BROOKS

INTRODUCTION

The previous chapter noted that consumption in China is unusually low as a share of GDP and has declined over the past decade. A key policy question is how to reverse this trend and rebalance growth away from reliance on exports and investment and toward consumption. China's low household consumption, or equivalently high saving, is often linked to precautionary motives. Government health, education, and pension systems are underdeveloped, leaving individuals to bear a large share of the costs. As a result, households build up saving to cover these expenses as well as to self-insure against uncertainty, especially regarding future health and pension needs. Of course, to explain the low and declining consumption rate, precautionary motives must be large and also rising over time. Indeed, Chamon and Prasad (2010) argue that this is the case, because the breaking of the "iron rice bowl" by the reforms in the 1990s—especially the reform of state-owned enterprises—led to a breakdown of existing systems and increased household uncertainty.

An obvious channel for boosting consumption, therefore, is a reduction in precautionary saving. Indeed, this has become a consistent view in the literature. For example, IMF (2007) and Blanchard and Giavazzi (2005) both emphasize reducing precautionary saving as one of the key requirements for rebalancing growth. The goal of this chapter is to explore the empirical relationship between government spending on health and education and household saving.

The main conclusion from this analysis is that government spending on health, but not on education, reduces urban household saving in China. Moreover, the impact is large. A 1-yuan increase in government health spending was associated with a 2-yuan increase in household consumption. Total (household plus government) consumption could thus increase by as much as 3 yuan, depending on the extent to which government health spending takes the form of consumption instead of transfers. For rural households, on the other hand, the evidence is more mixed. Increased government health spending in rural areas appears only to have an impact on savings in the higher-income provinces.

We focus narrowly on the impact on household consumption of government spending, and not on the broader question of what is driving consumption behavior, which is covered in the previous chapter. Household income, as the previous chapter notes, may be an even more important driver of consumption's falling GDP share than the saving rate. This would suggest that policies to boost household income would also bear fruit, particularly if they were combined with policies that were effective in reducing the household saving rate, such as improving the health care system.

The remainder of this chapter proceeds as follows. In the next section, we describe some stylized facts about consumption and saving in China. In the subsequent section, we use provincial household data to examine, econometrically, the relationship between household saving and government spending on health and education. The last section reviews the main findings.

CONSUMPTION AND SAVING IN CHINA: STYLIZED FACTS

Consumption Is Falling

As a share of GDP, consumption in China has steadily declined and is low relative to other countries. This is clearly illustrated in Figure 7.1, where the top panel shows *total* consumption as a share of GDP for a cross-section of countries. Since there is some substitutability between public and private consumption—government provision of free education, for example, means less need for household education spending—it is useful to look at total consumption. The second panel shows how the share of *household* consumption in China had been falling over time but stabilized in 2009.

Saving rates have risen, which helps to explain the decline in the consumption ratio (Figure 7.2). From the household survey data it is clear that rural and urban households have followed quite different paths. The urban saving rate has steadily risen over time, whereas rural saving has been more volatile but was considerably higher in recent years compared with the early 1990s. However, urban households account for three-fourths of total household consumption and so are instrumental in the overall increase in aggregate saving.

In addition to their high and rising saving rate, the failure of households to show income growth to keep pace with GDP growth has also been a major factor helping to explain the decline in the consumption ratio (Figures 7.3 and 7.4). From the early 1990s to 2009, urban household per capita income dropped from nearly 90 percent of GDP per capita to just under 70 percent. As discussed in Chapter 6, the fact that household income has fallen as a share of GDP over time is an important factor for explaining the decline in private consumption as a share of GDP.

Figure 7.1
Consumption in China and Selected Countries

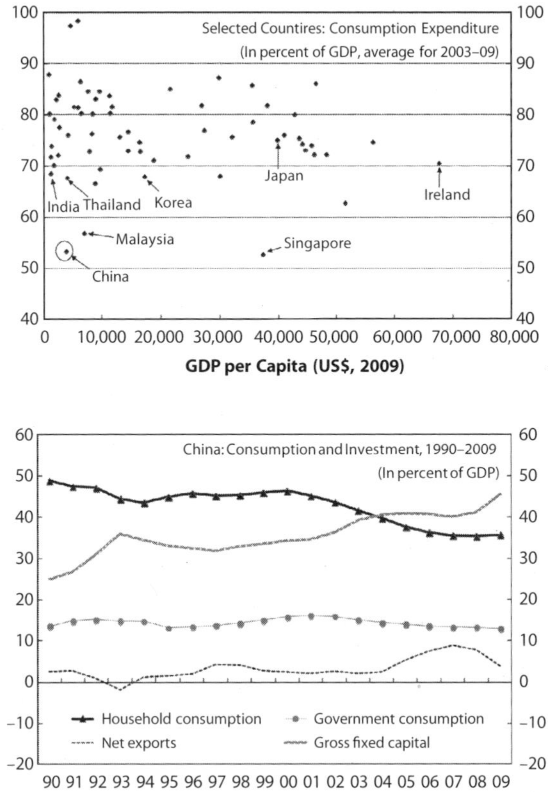

Sources: CEIC Data Co. Ltd.; and IMF staff calculations.

Figure 7.2
China: Urban and Rural Saving Rates, 1991–2009
(In percent of income)

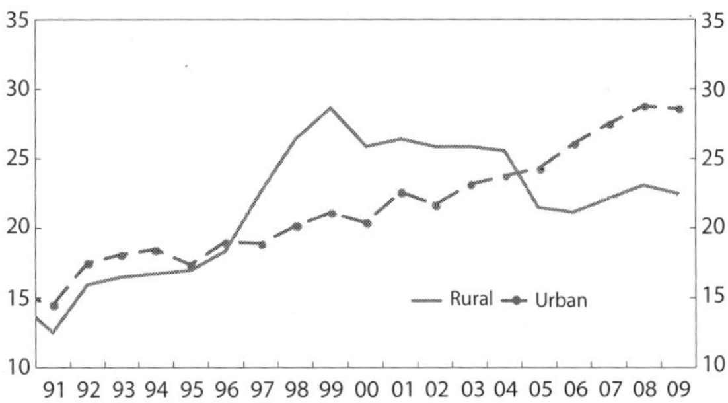

Sources: CEIC Data Co. Ltd.; and IMF staff calculations.

Figure 7.3
China: Urban and Rural Income, 1991–2009
(In percent of GDP per capita)

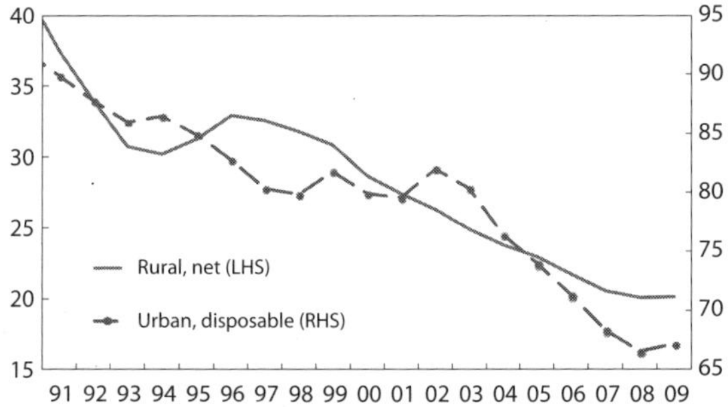

Sources: CEIC Data Co. Ltd.; and IMF staff calculations.

REDUCING PRECAUTIONARY SAVING: A ROLE FOR PUBLIC SPENDING?

This section examines whether increases in government spending on health and education have an impact on saving in China. Provincial data are pooled to exploit variations in provincial spending on health and education and differences in saving rates. Data from 1994–2007 are used, but a smaller sample of 2003–07 is also employed to check robustness and control for the possibility of structural changes.

The analysis looks at urban and rural households separately. As noted above, the trends in their saving behavior differ as do their income levels, making it likely that their responses to increases in government spending would not be the same. Ideally, therefore, the government spending variables used—for education and health spending—would break down spending into two areas: that undertaken in urban areas and that undertaken in rural areas. However, the provincial government spending data do not distinguish between these types of spending. As a result, the differences in results for urban and rural behavior should be regarded with some caution, since they could merely reflect differences in how government spending has been allocated.

Urban Households

The results suggest a statistically significant relationship between health spending and urban saving (Table 7.1). The parameter estimate is highly statistically significant and fairly stable across the two samples and remains so with the inclusion of education spending. The estimate is around -2, which suggests that each 1 yuan of government health spending results in a 2 yuan decrease in saving—or, equivalently, a 2 yuan increase in consumption. This is a strong impact, as it would imply that an increase in government health spending of just 1 percent of GDP would boost private consumption by 2 percent of GDP and could yield a total demand effect of up to 3 percent of GDP.

Figure 7.4
China: Indicators of Urban and Rural Consumption and Income, 1991–2009

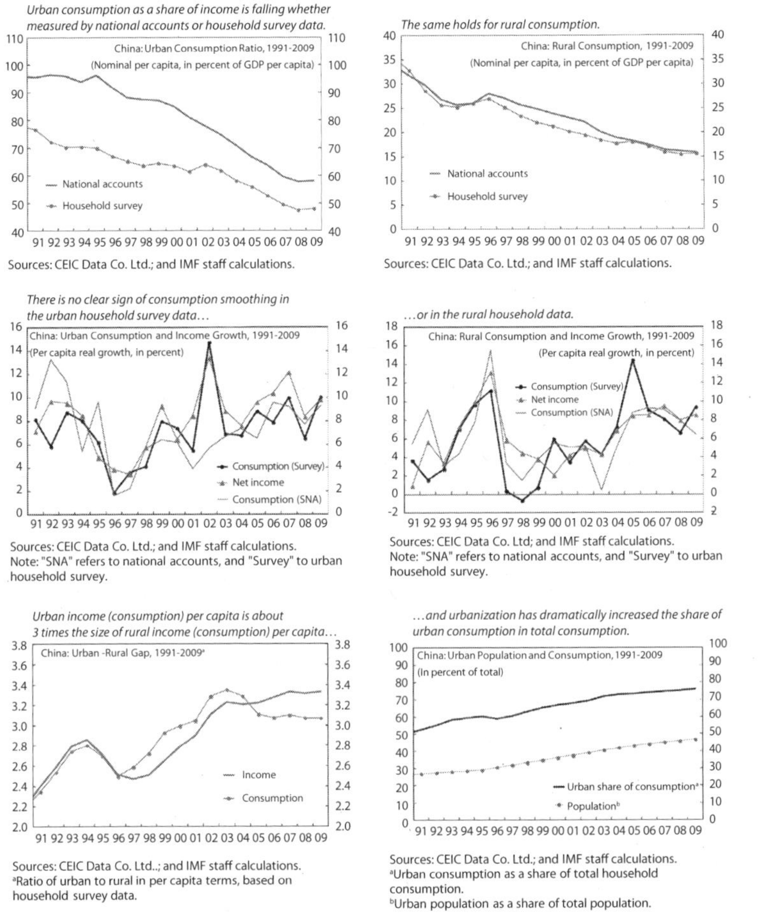

Sources: CEIC Data Co. Ltd.; and IMF staff calculations.

Sources: CEIC Data Co. Ltd.; and IMF staff calculations.

Sources: CEIC Data Co. Ltd.; and IMF staff calculations.
Note: "SNA" refers to national accounts, and "Survey" to urban household survey.

Sources: CEIC Data Co. Ltd; and IMF staff calculations.
Note: "SNA" refers to national accounts, and "Survey" to urban household survey.

Sources: CEIC Data Co. Ltd..; and IMF staff calculations.
[a]Ratio of urban to rural in per capita terms, based on household survey data.

Sources: CEIC Data Co. Ltd.; and IMF staff calculations.
[a]Urban consumption as a share of total household consumption.
[b]Urban population as a share of total population.

The impact of government health spending on saving is larger than might have been expected. In this first step, government health spending simply substitutes for private health spending, which would cause the saving rate to increase. That is, for each extra yuan the government spends on health, individuals could spend 1 yuan less, freeing up that 1 yuan to be allocated to additional saving and consumption. However, the net impact would be an increase in the saving rate, provided that at least part of the freed-up income is saved. The negative sign, therefore, indicates that government spending is not substituting for private spending and suggests that it is instead reducing the need for saving. That is, higher government health spending seems to reduce the need for precautionary saving and frees up households' ability to spend on other goods and services.

TABLE 7.1

Urban Households in China: Saving and Government Spending[a]

	Sample: 1994–2007				Sample: 2003–07			
	(1)	(2)	(3)	(4)	(5)	(6)	(7)	(8)
Health								
Estimate	−2.10	...	−1.92	...	−1.94	...	−2.06	...
(Standard error)	(0.72)	...	(0.86)	...	(0.60)	...	(0.58)	...
[P-val]	[0.00]	...	[0.03]	...	[0.00]	...	[0.00]	...
Education								
Estimate	...	−0.78	−0.44	...	...	0.42	0.66	...
(Standard error)	...	(1.10)	(1.07)	...	...	(1.20)	(1.07)	...
[P-val]	...	[0.48]	[0.68]	...	...	[0.73]	[0.54]	...
Health & education								
Estimate	...	...	...	−0.90	...	...	...	−0.41
(Standard error)	...	...	...	(0.63)	...	...	...	(0.89)
[P-val]	...	...	...	[0.16]	...	...	...	[0.64]
R-squared	0.24	0.22	0.25	0.24	0.19	0.18	0.19	0.18
# Obs.	285	304	285	285	150	150	150	150

Sources: CEIC Data Co. Ltd.; and IMF staff estimates.

[a]All variables are in first differences. The dependent variable is the saving rate, and government spending variables are per capita spending expressed as a share of per capita urban disposable income (lagged one period). Pooled Provincial data are used, with fixed and time effects.

There is some evidence that increased government spending on health care may have freed up resources of urban households for other spending or saving. Urban health care spending (from the household survey) fell by more than ½ percent of urban household consumption over the past five years, as government spending on health care increased sharply (Figure 7.5). However, national accounts data show no obvious trend in spending on health care by urban households. Rural health care spending increased as a share of rural household consumption over the past four to five years.

The econometric results for education are quite different, however. There is little evidence that higher government education spending decreases household saving. The coefficient is never statistically significant, and the sign actually switches between negative in the full sample to positive in the latter period. The lack of a statistically significant relationship could reflect the fact that much of the increased government spending has been for primary and secondary education, whereas the saving is more targeted toward higher education. Moreover, the increase in government education spending may not have kept pace with the rise in expected household education spending. Education spending per capita is more than two times higher than health spending and has grown rapidly over the past three years.

Rural Households

For rural households, there is little evidence that higher health spending reduces precautionary saving (Table 7.2). The estimated coefficient on health is never

Figure 7.5
China: Health and Education Spending, 2000–09

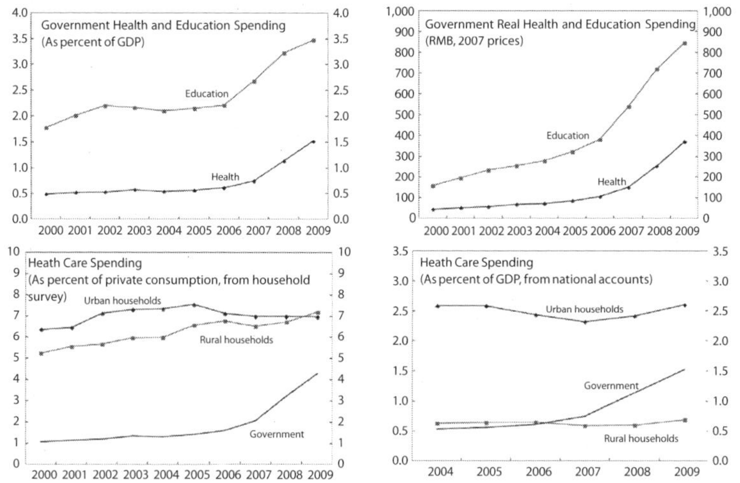

Sources: CEIC Data Co. Ltd.; and authors' estimates.

TABLE 7.2

Rural Households in China: Saving and Government Spending[a]

	Sample: 1996–2007				Sample: 2003–07			
	(1)	(2)	(3)	(4)	(5)	(6)	(7)	(8)
Health								
Estimate	0.51	...	0.22	...	0.37	...	0.06	...
(Standard error)	(0.59)	...	(0.58)	...	(0.67)	...	(0.64)	...
[P-val]	[0.39]	...	[0.70]	...	[0.58]	...	[0.93]	...
Education								
Estimate	...	0.45	0.49	...	...	0.91	0.90	...
(Standard error)	...	(0.36)	(0.38)	...	...	(0.61)	(0.54)	...
[P-val]	...	[0.22]	[0.20]	...	...	[0.14]	[0.10]	...
Health & education								
Estimate	...	...	...	0.39	...	...	...	0.53
(Standard error)	...	...	...	(0.29)	...	...	...	(0.47)
[P-val]	...	...	...	[0.18]	...	...	...	[0.27]
R-squared	0.36	0.37	0.36	0.36	0.31	0.32	0.32	0.32
# Obs.	285	304	285	285	150	150	150	150

Sources: CEIC Data Co. Ltd.; and IMF staff estimates.

[a] All variables are in first differences. The dependent variable is the saving rate, and government spending variables are per capita spending expressed as a share of per capita urban disposable income (lagged one period). Pooled Provincial data are used, with fixed and time effects.

statistically significant and is always positive, which would suggest that higher government health spending actually increases saving. This may reflect the fact that many rural households are subsistence consumers and would be expected to save a substantial part of the resources freed up by the government providing more health care coverage. It could also be that rural areas are receiving a smaller share of provincial health spending, which is therefore having much less effect than in the urban areas, or else that the increase in public spending has been small relative to expected rural health spending needs.

Likewise, there is little evidence that an increase in education spending has any impact on rural household saving. The coefficient is always positive, and while it is not statistically significant at conventional levels, it is quite close to being significant in the 2003–07 sample. This would be consistent with an increase in government education spending simply substituting for private spending—and the coefficient of near unity would suggest a nearly one-for-one impact.

Robustness Checks

The coastal provinces in China have developed faster than the inland region, have higher income per capita, and tend to be more urbanized. The regressions are repeated, allowing the impact to be different in the eight highest-income provinces.[1] This helps check the robustness of the results more generally but also examines whether there are systematic differences among the highest-income provinces.

The results for *rural* households suggest that government health spending in high-income provinces, unlike spending for the whole sample, is associated with a decline in rural household saving. The magnitude, moreover, is similar to the -2 found in the urban regressions reported above. This could reflect a variety of factors, including the fact that rural households in high-income provinces are wealthier (and thus resemble urban households elsewhere) or that they are a larger beneficiary of government health spending.

The results for urban households, however, do not provide strong evidence that the impact of health spending differs in higher-income provinces. The interaction term is not usually statistically significant, although it is always negative, which would suggest that the impact could be marginally stronger in higher-income provinces.

Finally, the results for the impact of government health spending on urban household saving hold up to other robustness checks. Different explanatory variables are included to gauge the impact on the statistical significance and magnitude of the parameter estimate on health spending. Variables that are added, in various combinations, include real income growth, inflation, and unemployment. The results (not reported) did not change substantially in either the whole sample or the 2003–07 sample.

Baldacci and others (2010) reach similar conclusions about the impact of public health spending on household consumption in China, although they use

[1]These are Beijing, Fujian, Guangdong, Jiangsu, Shangdong, Shanghai, Tianjin, and Zhejiang.

a completely different methodology. They estimate a model of the impact of social spending on household consumption for a panel of OECD countries. They then apply the model estimates to Chinese data and find that 1 percent of GDP in additional health spending would increase household consumption by 2.1 percent of GDP. We find this same quantitative impact for urban households using Chinese provincial data. In contrast to our findings, however, their model also suggests that 1 percent of additional spending on education would boost household consumption by 0.7 percent of GDP.

CONCLUSION

The main finding of this chapter is that higher government health spending reduces urban household saving. This suggests that broadening coverage of public health care could have an important effect on household precautionary savings. The magnitude of the impact, moreover, is quite large and appears robust to variants in specification. The results suggest that each additional 1 yuan in government health spending boosts urban household consumption by 2 yuan.

However, for rural households, with the exception of those in the higher-income provinces, we were unable to find evidence of a relationship between government health spending and saving. There was also no evidence that higher government education spending has an impact on either urban or rural saving. This is not entirely surprising, since the precautionary saving motives are likely to be much higher for health than for education. In both cases, an increase in government spending has competing effects on saving. First, it could increase saving by substituting public for private provision of services, thereby freeing up household resources, of which some would be saved. To reduce saving, government education or health spending would need to have an additional effect, such as reducing precautionary saving motives. Given that a large part of the saving is being generated by older generations, who are more likely to need to save for health care costs than for educating their family members, it is sensible to expect that improvements in public health care are likely to have a more potent effect on household saving behavior than expanding publicly provided education.

Although past rural health care spending appears to have had little impact on consumption, the government's new health reform strategy for 2009–11 has the potential to improve health outcomes and raise rural consumption. The government has given priority to the health sector, along with other social sectors, such as education and social protection, in its 11th five-year plan. A comprehensive study by Wangstaff and others (2009) suggests that while progress is being made to improve China's rural health system, including by marching quickly toward universal coverage for rural areas, a number of challenges remain. Importantly, the study notes that the inequalities in China's health system reflect, at least in part, inequalities in government health spending. It notes that government health expenditure disproportionately benefits the better off. This reflects the fact that over half of general government health spending supports urban insurance schemes, whose members are disproportionately from higher-income groups, even within urban areas. The reorientation of government spending toward the poorer rural areas and increased efficiency in the delivery of public health care will be key factors in improving health outcomes and impacting consumption behavior.

In recent years, China has made significant progress in expanding health coverage in rural areas and in reaching near-universal coverage in urban areas (IMF, 2010). Recent reforms have included building hospitals and community health centers, subsidizing health insurance premiums, and expanding the number of health care workers. The authorities' priorities going forward include investing in primary and community care facilities, working toward universal coverage (particularly for rural and migrant workers), and reducing out-of-pocket expenses. Moreover, the government plans to increase budget spending on health by 850 billion yuan (2¼ percent of annual GDP) during 2009–11, which, based on the estimates in this chapter, could provide a significant boost to household consumption.

REFERENCES

Aziz, J., and L. Cui, 2007, "Explaining China's Low Consumption: The Neglected Role of Household Income," IMF Working Paper No. 07/181 (Washington: International Monetary Fund).

Baldacci, E., G. Callegari, D. Coady, D. Ding, M. Kumar, P. Tommasino, and J. Woo, 2010, "Public Expenditures on Social Programs and Household Consumption in China," IMF Working Paper No. 10/69 (Washington: International Monetary Fund).

Blanchard, O., and F. Giavazzi, 2005, "Rebalancing Growth in China: A Three-Handed Approach," MIT Department of Economics Working Paper No. 05-32 (Cambridge: Massachusetts Institute of Technology).

Chamon, M., and E. Prasad, 2010, "Why are Saving Rates of Urban Households in China Rising?" *American Economic Journal: Macroeconomics*, Vol. 2, No. 1, pp. 93–130.

International Monetary Fund (IMF), 2007, "China's Difficult Rebalancing Act," *IMF Survey Online,* September 12, 2007 (available via Internet at http://www.imf.org/external/pubs/ft/survey/so/2007/CAR0912A.htm)

———, 2010, *People's Republic of China: 2010 Article IV Consultation—Staff Report,* IMF Country Report No. 10/238 (Washington).

Wangstaff, A., M. Lindelow, S. Wang, and S. Zhang, 2009, *Reforming China's Rural Health System* (Washington: World Bank, July).

CHAPTER 8

Access to Finance and Household Saving

MARCOS CHAMON AND SONALI JAIN CHANDRA

INTRODUCTION

In many Asian economies, the share of household consumption in GDP is low by international standards (Figure 8.1). The share of consumption in GDP in several of the major countries in the region has been declining in recent years; consumption in emerging Asia has declined by 2 percentage points of GDP relative to the 1990s.

There is an extensive literature on the need to boost the share of domestic demand in emerging Asia. In the case of China, consumption has been limited both by a low household income share in GDP to begin with, as well as by high saving rates. It has often been argued that the high level of household saving has resulted from enhanced risks faced by households and precautionary saving resulting from an absence of public provision of social services (Chamon and Prasad 2010). Accordingly, boosting spending on social safety nets would reduce the need for some of the precautionary saving. Against the background of this extensive literature, we focus on a complementary set of reforms, those related to financial market development and its effect on household consumption.[1]

More specifically, this chapter examines how different levels of financial development and, in particular, household access to financing affect household consumption and saving decisions. Financial liberalization involves various aspects, some of which may boost consumption. For instance, liberalization that increases household access to consumer credit or housing finance may lead to lowering household saving. Reform measures can encapsulate various dimensions, including removal of a credit ceiling and directed credit, improvements in banking supervision, removal of entry barriers, and removal of interest controls, privatization, and securities market reform.

[1]It is possible that some rebalancing of consumption will occur naturally, as some of the saving may be due to one-off events (e.g., the housing reform). More generally, as China transitioned to a more market-oriented economy, households had to increase their saving in order to quickly build up a buffer stock adequate for the new economic environment (which may have caused saving rates to overshoot their new steady state).

Figure 8.1
Private Consumption Expenditure at Constant Prices

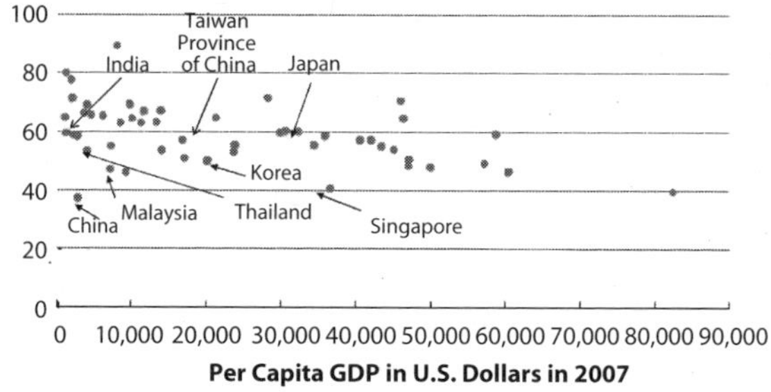

Source: IMF, WEO database.

Financial reform and the resulting changes in access to financing are closely related to a household's decision on the level and timing of saving. There are several channels through which access to finance can affect saving decisions. The availability of consumer loans has a direct impact on consumption by helping households to purchase lumpy goods and big-ticket items. The availability of loans can also help households cope with adverse shocks, reducing the need to save for precautionary motives. For example, households accumulate saving in order to protect themselves against shocks to their income (such as unemployment spells) or unexpected expenditures (such as a family member getting sick).

If households have limited access to financing, they must self-insure against these shocks, which leads to inefficiently low consumption. For example, if only one out of ten households will actually experience an adverse shock, nine out of ten will have saved too much *ex post*, while the one actually experiencing the shock will wish it had saved more. If insurance against such shocks were available, aggregate consumption would increase, since risk would be pooled and only an amount commensurate to the expected aggregate shock would need to be saved. Many of these shocks are difficult to insure, even in developed financial markets. But the ability to borrow in the aftermath of an adverse shock would still yield a more efficient outcome than pure self-insurance, helping to raise aggregate consumption.

While we start from the assumption that financial development should boost consumption, in theory the effect could be ambiguous. For example, in a more liberalized financial market, households might have easier access to finance and so need to save less, since precautionary saving motives become less pressing for the reasons described above. At the same time, in a more liberalized financial market, interest rates may rise, inducing households to save more. Similarly, changes in access to mortgage financing can have an ambiguous effect on consumption, depending on the starting point. Lowering down-payment requirements from a high to a moderate level can induce more saving, since households that previously could never meet that high down payment may now save to meet the lower requirement. But further declines in down-payment ratio may eventually lower saving by reducing the amount of consumption forsaken in order to meet that requirement. Given the starting level of financial development for loans to households in China, it is reasonable to assume that more development should contribute to higher consumption.

This chapter approaches the question of how financial sector development and reform can affect households' consumption decisions by estimating an empirical relationship between household consumption as a share of GDP and measures of financial sector development as well as indices of financial reform across countries. While these comparisons are useful, we are mindful of their limitations. We complement the results by analyzing whether more specific measures related to the financial sector could improve household access to credit and boost consumption in China through a narrative approach and a discussion of case studies from Brazil and Korea.

THE EFFECT OF FINANCIAL SECTOR REFORM ON HOUSEHOLD CONSUMPTION: AN EMPIRICAL INVESTIGATION

Data and Methodology

We test the hypothesis that the extent of financial development affects households' saving decisions by estimating a panel regression based on a cross-country database, similar to the exercise in Chapter 4.

We estimate an econometric relationship between the share of household consumption in GDP and financial sector development and reform over time for a number of emerging markets.

Data on household final consumption expenditures are available in the national accounts for virtually all countries, and that is the measure we focus on in our regressions. Data on the share of household disposable income in GDP are available for far fewer countries, but given the importance of this variable for understanding consumption, we chose to include it, restricting the sample to 24 advanced and emerging economies since 1980.

The regression controls for other possible determinants of consumption, including the log of per capita GDP measured in PPP terms and a host of variables related to the financial sector that have been used in previous studies of household savings, including these: private sector credit/GDP, M3/GDP, the real interest rate, and inflation (all available through the World Bank's World Development Indicators).[2] We also use different measures of financial reform constructed by Abiad, Detragiache, and Tressel (2008). These include indices for entry barriers (such as

[2]For an overview of how a broader set of controls (including demographics and fiscal policy variables) affects private saving on a panel of countries, see Loayza, Schmidt-Hebbel, and Serven (2000).

Figure 8.2
Financial Reform Index, 2005

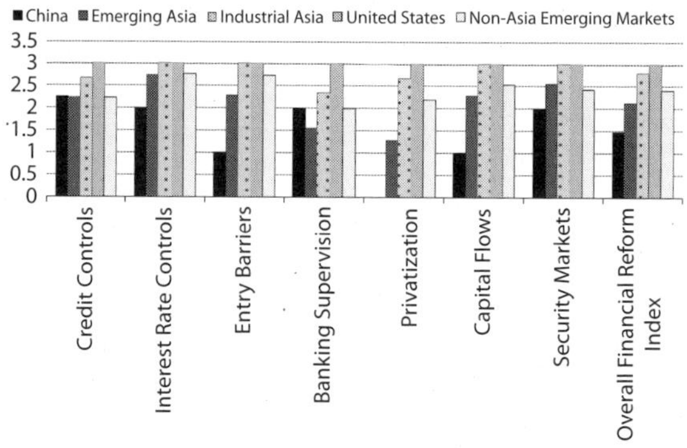

Source: Abiad, Detragiache, and Tressel (2008).

licensing requirements and limits in the participation of foreign banks), interest and credit controls, privatization in the financial sector, international financial transaction restrictions, and operational restrictions on security markets and banking supervision, as well as their overall financial reform index (Figure 8.2).

Figure 8.3 compares some of the main variables of interest across a group of emerging markets. The level of household consumption as a share of GDP tends to be lower in Asia, with China being a large outlier (top-left chart). Asian countries tend to have very high private sector credit/GDP ratios, and China's is very large, particularly if one takes into account its income level (top-right chart). But China has a relatively low value for the overall financial reform index described above (bottom-left chart). The development of China's mortgage credit market seems broadly in line with its level of income (bottom-right chart). China's high saving rates contribute to the high level of credit, since much of that credit is driven by the ample supply of saving. But its financial sector allocates a relatively small share of that credit for consumer loans and for household loans in general.

Results

Table 8.1 reports results from an OLS regression.[3] We chose not to use country fixed-effects, since this would capture much of the variation in the variables of interest. That is, while fixed-effects would capture unobserved cross-country variability (which is fixed over time), it would not allow us to trace the effects on consumption of the large differences in cross-country means of the financial variables and of the share of household income in GDP back to those variables.

[3]The results report robust standard errors.

Figure 8.3
Household Consumption, Credit, and Financial Reform in Comparator Countries

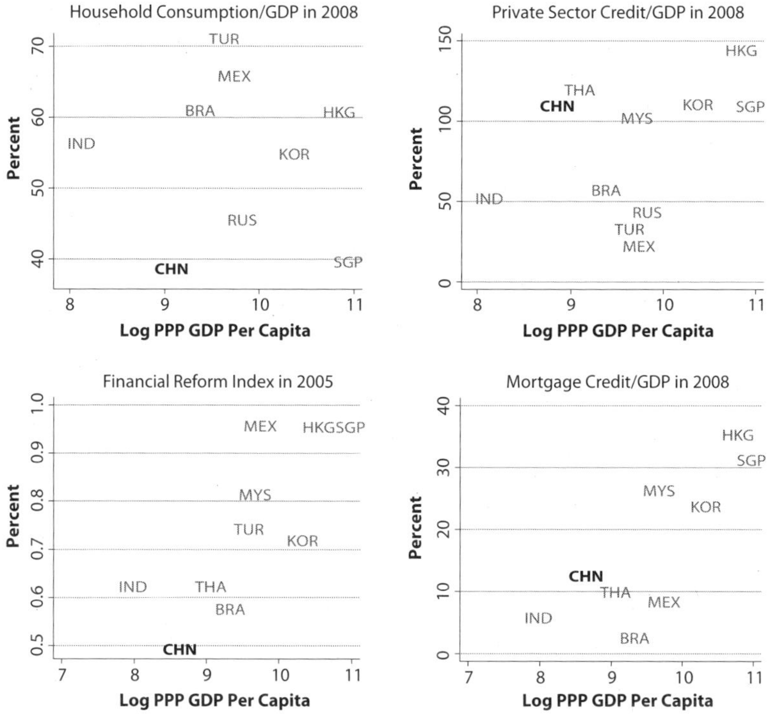

Sources: UNSTAT, World Development Indicators; Abiad, Detragiache and Tressel (2008); and national sources.

Measures of financial depth, such as the private sector credit to GDP and M3/GDP, have opposite signs (likely due to the noisiness in the estimates coming from their high correlation).[4] But taken at face value, the estimates on private sector credit to GDP suggest that a 1 percentage point increase in that ratio would raise consumption by 0.05 percent of GDP. The point estimates suggest that a 1 percentage point increase in the real interest rate would raise consumption by 0.1 percent of GDP (although in theory the effect is ambiguous due to competing income and substitution effects). The fitted values from that regression suggest that China's household consumption should have been 46 percent of GDP in 2008 instead of the actual 37 percent. Note that this estimate already controls for China's very low household disposable income as a share of GDP (less than 60 percent in 2008).

[4]In some cases, a high credit/GDP ratio may reflect the supply of saving and a reliance on bank financing, rather than the depth or sophistication of the financial sector.

TABLE 8.1

Cross-Country Determinants of Household Final Consumption Expenditure/GDP[a]

Explanatory Variables	1	2	3	4	5	6	7	8	9	10
Household Disposable Income/GDP	0.739*** [0.037]	0.676*** [0.033]	0.703*** [0.036]	0.704*** [0.037]	0.652*** [0.035]	0.747*** [0.033]	0.706*** [0.040]	0.717*** [0.035]	0.699*** [0.035]	0.701*** [0.038]
Log PPP GDP Per Capita	0.789 [0.496]	−0.738 [0.480]	0.464 [0.518]	0.426 [0.526]	−0.793 [0.497]	0.227 [0.436]	0.505 [0.551]	0.292 [0.464]	−0.048 [0.491]	−0.009 [0.621]
Private Sector Credit/GDP	0.050*** [0.007]	0.028*** [0.008]	0.038*** [0.008]	0.041*** [0.008]	0.046*** [0.007]	0.038*** [0.007]	0.041*** [0.007]	0.024*** [0.009]	0.039*** [0.008]	0.046*** [0.008]
Real Interest Rate	0.109*** [0.026]	0.097*** [0.019]	0.133*** [0.025]	0.131*** [0.025]	0.056*** [0.021]	0.090*** [0.020]	0.100*** [0.024]	0.102*** [0.023]	0.097*** [0.022]	0.106*** [0.025]
M3/GDP	−0.076*** [0.008]	−0.047*** [0.008]	−0.059*** [0.009]	−0.061*** [0.009]	−0.066*** [0.008]	−0.057*** [0.007]	−0.064*** [0.009]	−0.051*** [0.008]	−0.065*** [0.008]	−0.068*** [0.008]
Log (1+Inflation)	−13.455* [7.326]	13.701 [8.465]	−2.456 [8.811]	−2.323 [8.904]	−2.391 [7.584]	2.539 [6.688]	−6.006 [8.519]	−9.951 [7.140]	−4.896 [7.979]	−7.003 [8.462]
Financial Reform Indices										
Financial Reform Overall		10.648*** [1.536]								
Directed Credit			0.879*** [0.305]							
Credit Controls				0.834*** [0.317]						
Interest Rate Controls					2.041*** [0.328]					
Entry Barriers						2.132*** [0.272]				
Banking Supervision							0.576** [0.228]			
Privatization								1.271*** [0.231]		
International Capital Markets									1.398*** [0.372]	
Security Markets										1.079** [0.527]
Constant	4.231 [6.442]	13.769** [6.009]	6.593 [6.584]	6.959 [6.615]	19.143*** [6.261]	3.303 [5.972]	7.76 [6.921]	8.314 [6.058]	11.070* [6.174]	11.089 [7.026]
Observations	421	401	401	401	401	401	401	401	401	401
R-squared	0.654	0.711	0.67	0.669	0.699	0.721	0.667	0.688	0.676	0.667

Source: IMF staff estimates.

[a]Robust standard errors in brackets. *, ** and *** denote statistical significance at the 10, 5, and 1 percent level, respectively. Financial Reform Overall Index ranges from 0–1 while each sub-index ranges from 0–3 (in both cases, index coded so that the higher the index the more developed the financial market).

While most attention is focused on China, given its unusually low consumption share, India's consumption is also relatively low. Based on the regression model for consumption used here, India's consumption level was about 9 percent of GDP lower than its fitted value. However, its consumption share stood at 56 percent of GDP in 2008, which is almost 20 percentage points higher than China's share.

Moving to the financial reform variables (specifications 2–11, Table 8.1), the results suggest that financial reform is indeed associated with a higher household consumption share in GDP. The overall financial reform index in specification 2 ranges from 0 to 1, and its value for China in 2005 was 0.49. Regression 2 suggests that if China's index was to increase to 0.71, the level of Korea, household consumption would have increased by 2.4 percent of GDP, while raising that index to the maximum level would have raised consumption by over 5 percent of GDP. While this would represent a substantial improvement, a large gap would remain between China's consumption level and the international norm (which would call for a consumption level of about 50 percent of GDP). In the case of India, raising its financial reform index in 2005 to the level of Korea would have only increased consumption by 1 percent of GDP.

Due to the correlation of the financial reform indices among themselves, we only consider one reform indicator at a time. The results are reported in specifications 3–11 (Table 8.1). Each subindex ranges from 0 to 3, and the effect of a change in any particular subindex, all else equal, implies a weaker effect on consumption than the one estimated for the overall index. (Raising China to the highest level of the index would increase consumption/GDP by as little as 0.6 percentage points in the case of banking supervision and by 4.3 percentage points in the case of entry barriers).

These results suggest that while financial reforms could help raise consumption in China by improving households' access to the country's vast supply of credit, bringing China's consumption in line with international norms would likely require tackling the root causes of that low consumption. Those causes include the low household income share in GDP and large precautionary savings, which are compounded by a limited social safety net. In fact, our estimates suggest that raising China's share of household disposable income in GDP from 60 percent to 70 percent, which would be broadly in line with international standards, would have increased its consumption by 7 percent of GDP. If China's financial sector inefficiently allocates too much credit to capital-intensive industries, financial development that helps allocate more credit towards labor-intensive sectors could help increase the share of household disposable income in GDP and, as a result, could indirectly contribute to higher consumption.

While financial development is not a silver bullet with which to solve the low consumption problem, these efforts should still be pursued, helping complement other initiatives. In particular, policy makers should identify the low-hanging fruit, that is, policies that could boost consumption at the margin without contributing to systemic risks. We discuss in detail below a number of possible initiatives.

CASE STUDIES

We examine here some case studies of countries that have introduced reforms to raise access to finance, and review their implications for both lending behavior and household decisions. Three case studies are considered:

- Consumer loans using public sector wages as collateral in Brazil
- Development of mortgage markets in Korea, and
- Development of credit cards in Korea.

We also discuss the role auto loans could play, given the growing demand for cars in China (see Box 8.1).

Case Study 1. Payroll Loans: Lessons from Brazil

Access to consumer financing remains limited in Brazil. The average real interest rate on loans to individuals was well above 50 percent per year during much of the last decade, and interest rates on credit cards and bank overdraft charges can easily run into triple digits. Despite these exorbitant rates, loans to individuals account for about 35 percent of private sector credit (this figure excludes housing loans, which account for only 9 percent of private sector credit).

Policy Change and Impact

The very large loan spreads in Brazil remain a puzzle. Concerns about credit risk certainly contribute to the high spreads, although taxes, high reserve requirements, directed credit, and limited competition in the banking sector also contribute to those high spreads. A rapidly growing segment of the individual credit market is payroll loans. In these types of loans, an individual can pledge a share of his or her future wages (or pension) as collateral for the loan. That allows the bank to automatically deduct the loan repayments from the wage/pension payments. For example, if an individual receives $1,000 every month and has to repay $50 as part of the payroll loan, the bank would automatically deduct that amount from the pay check, and only $950 would be deposited into the borrower's account. This can in theory remove default risk from the loan, except for cases where there is a loss of job (which affects only private sector workers) and longevity risk (affecting mainly retirees). Payroll lending existed in Brazil since the beginning of the 1990s, but it was restricted to government personnel and its operation was limited to "peculium institutions" which could act as trusts before public administration agencies. In the late 1990s, banks saw profitable opportunities in that market and started acquiring those peculium institutions. But payroll loans only took off following a September 2003 law that regulated the possibility of salary consignation for the private sector (formal workers) and for private and public retirees (from the publicly administered pay-as-you-go pension system).

Within two years, payroll loans accounted for 20 percent of all loans to individuals, and at present these loans correspond to about 3½ percent of GDP. There has been a market expansion since 2004 in payroll loans as well as other loans to individuals and in housing loans (Figure 8.4). The average interest rate on payroll loans is about 30 percent per year, which is much lower than the average interest in comparable individual loans. Some of that gap is due to differences among the types of borrowers, the terms, and the amount of the credit. Rodrigues and others

BOX 8.1

The Potential for Automobile Loans in China

Chamon, Mauro, and Okawa (2008) draw on a panel of countries to document a remarkably stable relationship between income and car ownership. Car ownership remains low at per capita income levels below $5,000, but then takes off very rapidly. China is currently at the cusp of that takeoff. Although traffic jams occur in major cities, car ownership remains relatively low at about 3 cars per 100 people. But if past international experience is any guide, an explosion in car ownership is about to occur.

Given China's low initial level of income, only a relatively small tail of rich households can afford to own a car. But as incomes grow, more and more households will cross the income threshold at which car ownership is attainable. Assuming a threshold of RMB 35,000 for the per capita income level at which households contemplate buying a car, the share of the population above that threshold will increase from 20.6 percent in 2008 to 27.0 and 34.7 percent in 2011 and 2014, respectively.[a] Based on the estimates from Chamon, Mauro, and Okawa (2008), the number of cars in China was projected to increase from about 20 million in 2005 to over 50 million by 2010 and to 87 million by 2015. The increase could be even more dramatic if auto financing becomes more readily available and complements this surge in demand.

Banks were initially the main providers of auto loans, but many withdrew from the car loan market due to high nonperforming loan ratios on those loans. Since 2004, auto companies have been allowed to finance auto purchases, which has helped fill the gap left by banks. In theory, auto financing should be relatively safe to the lender, given the presence of collateral (the car being purchased). But in practice, the creditworthiness of that collateral depends on an effective title and registration system, which makes it difficult for someone to default on the loan while keeping the car, as well as the costs involved in claiming that collateral. As the auto loan market has matured and become less risky, banks have renewed their interest in it.

The projected increase in car ownership is sufficiently large to make a difference in China's aggregate consumption, but this explosion in car ownership will have a number of other policy implications, including infrastructure needs and urban planning and environmental concerns. Thus, while cars are a promising way to boost consumption, and a sign of China's affluence, policies aimed at developing auto finance should bear in mind the timing of other complementary policies that need to be in place to accommodate this expansion. For example, given the high population density in major cities, traffic considerations alone may suggest caution before pursuing policies that would stimulate car ownership.

---

[a] In order to construct these estimates, we use data from the IMF, *World Economic Outlook*, and assume that household disposable income is equal to 57 percent of GDP per capita. We then assume a log-normal income distribution and a Gini coefficient of 45.

Figure 8.4
Brazil: Volume of Credit to Individuals and Housing, 2004–09

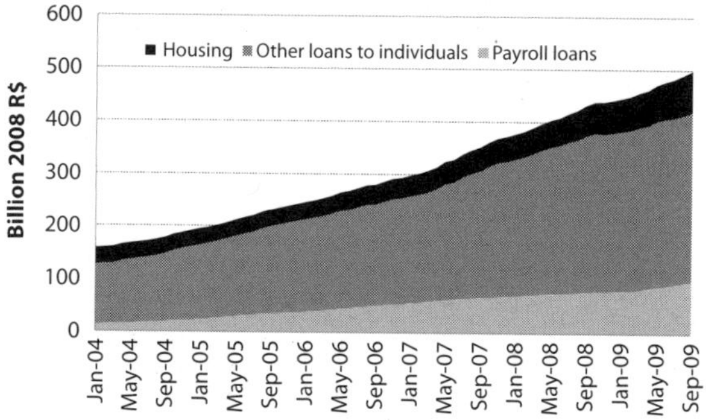

Source: Banco Central do Brasil.

(2006) use loan-level data to estimate the impact of payroll collateral on spreads. In their December 2003 sample, the average difference in interest between payroll loans and comparable individual loans was 25 percent. After controlling for a host of borrower and loan characteristics (such as term and amount of loan), they conclude that the payroll collateral lowered interest rates by 13 percentage points. Payroll loans have remained popular, despite court rulings that have called into question the bank's ability to attach wages in the event of default if the borrower litigates (Costa and De Mello, 2006).

Relevance for China

Could payroll loans help China boost consumption? Conditions in China are very different from those in Brazil, where household savings are actually quite low due to a high propensity to spend. But even if there is limited demand by Chinese households to take on payroll loans to finance consumption expenditures, these loans could still play an important role in reducing precautionary savings. If the introduction of payroll loans makes it easier for households to deal with unexpected shocks, the loans could provide an alternative to self-insurance, reducing precautionary saving motives. For example, someone who is saving more because he or she is afraid that an elderly parent could get sick (and incur large medical expenses) could save less if he or she knew that it was possible to quickly and easily borrow against future wages if needed. Note that in such a case, just the possibility of borrowing against future wages could induce more consumption, even if in the end no borrowing actually took place. Depending on the extent of payroll lending allowed, it could also help households meet somewhat large expenditures, such as housing construction or weddings, reducing the need for savings.

While the introduction of payroll loans is likely to have a limited effect on consumption, the cost of creating such a program (in terms of risk to the financial system) is very small, so it is likely worth pursuing. A natural strategy could be to start with public sector workers, where the government is in a good position to control the wage stream. Public sector workers face less uncertainty than workers in state-owned enterprises and in the private sector, and therefore are likely to have lower precautionary saving. But to the extent that it is common for public sector workers to be married to workers in other sectors, the potential effect of the availability of payroll loans on precautionary saving should not be underestimated. The effect could become larger if we consider other relatives, such as children and parents. In principle, the government could provide payroll loans itself, for example, in the form of salary advances that charge an interest rate. There are also benefits in allowing banks to administer the loans, which could help financial development.

Extending the scheme to workers in other sectors could be difficult, since the future income stream is not as certain. For example, borrowing against future wages is not useful if one is saving precisely because one is afraid of losing the job. But by providing clear rules, the government could allow banks to judge, on a case-by-case basis, how appropriate future wages are as collateral. In the limit, the government could also allow some borrowing against funded pension accounts. A natural way to proceed could be to start with a pilot program for public sector workers, which in a second pilot round could be carefully expanded to workers in state-owned enterprises and in the private sector.

Case Study 2: Mortgage Market Reforms in Korea

Mortgage markets in Asia have expanded significantly since the mid 1990s, although the expansion has been uneven across countries. Mortgage markets in a number of Asian countries are more than 30 percent of GDP, including Hong Kong SAR, Singapore, Korea, and Malaysia. However, while in China and India the pace of expansion of mortgage debt has been impressive, there is considerable scope to increase the size of the mortgage market, which currently stands at around 10 and 5 percent of GDP respectively (Figure 8.5).

Asian mortgage markets are mainly characterized by adjustable rate products, average loan-to-value of between 70 and 80 percent, and typical length of contracts between 10 and 20 years. Previous work using cluster analysis has shown that differences in mortgage contract arrangements are not noteworthy among Asian countries with more and less developed mortgage markets (Zhu, 2006). Rather, the literature has shown that countries with stronger legal rights for borrowers and lenders, deeper credit information systems, and a more stable macroeconomic environment have more developed and deeper housing finance systems (Warnock and Warnock, 2008). In some countries, reliable systems to register property rights are missing and their development would be valuable. Importantly, across most of the region secondary mortgage markets remain underdeveloped.

Figure 8.5
China and Selected Asia: Size of Mortgage Markets—Average 2003–08
(As percent of GDP)

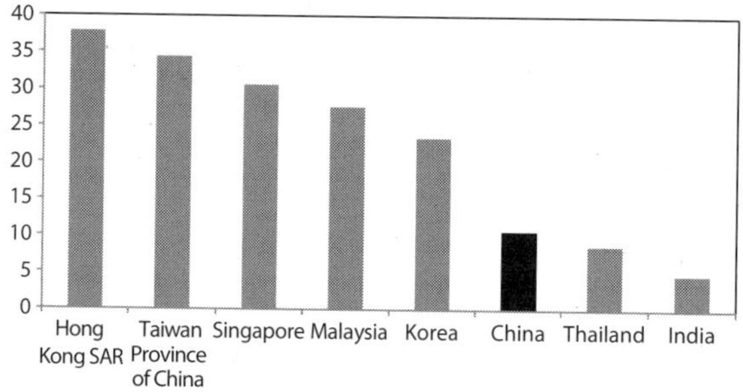

Source: CEIC Data Co. Ltd.

Policy Change and Impact

In the 1990s, Korea's housing finance system was gradually deregulated, including interest rate liberalization and financial deregulation. After the Asian crisis, financial sector reform, including housing finance reform, took center stage when the Korea Housing Bank, the dominant mortgage provider (with a 75 percent market share in 1995), was privatized in 1997. Commercial banks, which historically focused on corporate lending, began to provide mortgages. Furthermore, mortgage banks and other special finance companies were created. These changes made the housing finance industry more competitive.

The set of reforms started in 1999 focused on the development of the secondary mortgage market with the creation of the Korea Mortgage Corporation, which was set up to securitize loans. The government also passed a comprehensive asset-backed-securities law to support all asset-backed securities, including mortgages, which led to the rapid development of the secondary mortgage market. In addition, the Mortgage-Backed Securities Company Act was passed. The establishment of the Korea Housing Finance Corporation in 2004 was a key event in the development of long-term, fixed-rate mortgages and MBS in Korea.

These efforts to develop mortgage markets were complemented by policies to curb the rise in house prices and prevent speculation. The policies included the following:[5]

- Lengthening the minimum holding period for tax exemption
- Altering the house price ceiling for tax exemption
- Increasing property taxes
- Designating speculation zones in which the resale of new apartments was to be restricted (2002)

[5] Chung, 2009

- Introducing a maximum loan-to-value of 60 percent that was tightened further (2002)
- Restricting multiple mortgages (2005), and
- Increasing loan loss provisioning against mortgage loans (2007).

With the slump in property prices following the 2008 global recession, some of these measures have been reversed. Regulatory changes have altered the composition and maturity of mortgage loans. Until recently, short-term mortgage loans represented the majority of mortgages, and three-year bullet-type mortgages were the most popular. Mortgage lenders also typically allowed low loan-to-value ratios in the past. In recent years, however, regulators have allowed higher loan-to-value ratios for longer-term mortgages to encourage a move away from the three-year bullet loans. Loan-to-value ratios vary from 50 percent for three-year mortgages in designated speculation zones to 70 percent for longer-term 10-year mortgages. As a result of these regulatory changes, the 10-year-plus maturity share reached almost 60 percent in 2008 (Figure 8.6). In addition, most housing loans are originated as floating-rate products, with fixed-rate mortgages constituting just 5 percent of the total. This leaves households vulnerable to sharp and unanticipated increases in interest rates and may lead to higher default rates down the road.

As the mortgage market has deepened significantly, the consumption share of GDP has risen in tandem in Korea. Despite the low loan-to-value requirements in Korea, the incentive to save for the down payment has not led to a rise in household saving. On the contrary, the consumption share of GDP has risen to almost 55 percent, one of the highest in emerging Asia (Figure 8.7).

Relevance for China

While the mortgage market has grown rapidly in China, there is substantial opportunity for further development. Empirical work based on a benchmark model for the OECD suggests that, relative to the underlying socioeconomic and financial conditions, the mortgage market should be much larger (Ben-Shahar and others, 2009).[6] One limiting factor is that the mechanisms to share mortgage lending risks have not been fully developed. The links between the housing market and capital markets are not well developed, so the risks are held by the housing finance institutions. With greater reliance on capital markets, the availability of mortgage finance will likely be enhanced. Securitization is one way to integrate mortgage markets with capital markets and could lead to market deepening and

[6]Their paper estimates a benchmark model for OECD countries and relates mortgage activity to domestic financial system, real economic variables, and demographics. The dependant variable is total outstanding mortgage volume and the explanatory variables are household size, interest rate spread, urbanization rate, new housing completions, housing stock, ratio of financial assets to GDP, and the savings rate. A calibration of the model for China suggests that it has a smaller volume of mortgages outstanding (as a percent of GDP) compared to the predictions of the benchmark model.

Figure 8.6
Mortgage Loans by Maturity, 2004–08

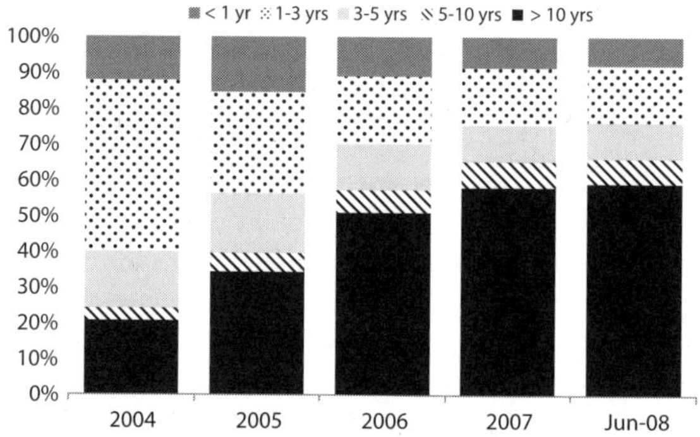

Source: Financial Supervisory Service.

Figure 8.7
Korea: Mortgages and Consumption, 2004–08

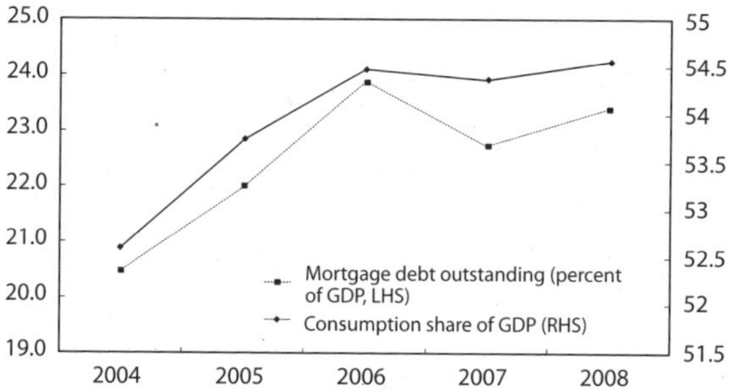

Source: CEIC Data Co. Ltd.

access to a wider pool of saving to finance mortgages. China issued its first mortgage-backed security in 2005, and while adequate safeguards have to be built in to safeguard financial stability, there is vast potential to deepen this market.

Some of the large household saving can be traced to the need to meet housing down-payment requirements, particularly among younger households (Chamon and Prasad, 2010). Lowering down-payment requirements would reduce these saving motives, but again at the cost of some additional credit risk to banks and adding pressure to an already overheated market. An alternative could be to facilitate borrowing for finishing owner-occupied apartment units. It is common (at least in major cities) for the builder to sell only the shell of the apartment, with the buyer incurring substantial costs to finish the unit, which typically is not included in the mortgage. The regulation of housing loans could allow for the cost of that finishing to be included as part of the loan, provided the down payment and amount spent on finishing the unit meet the minimum down payment for a home value that includes both the shell and the finishing.

Another option for households to borrow against wealth would be to allow households to borrow against their illiquid housing wealth, such as through the home equity lines of credit available in some countries. Most urban households own their dwellings and have a sizable equity position in them, particularly the dwellings that were bought as part of the housing reform process. Households could save less for precautionary reasons if they could more easily use their home equity as collateral for a loan in the event of an adverse shock, or refinance their mortgages in order to cash-out part of that equity. This would require a proper regulatory framework so that no two creditors could have a claim against the same housing asset. While in the same spirit of the payroll loans, this strategy is more likely to create systemic risks in the banking system, since property loans would become less resilient as home equity is drained from them.

Case Study 3: Credit Card Boom and Bust in Korea

Policy Change and Impact

A number of regulatory changes contributed to the boom in credit cards in Korea from 1999 to 2002, which eventually led to a bust in 2003 and placed stress on financial stability. These regulatory changes (IMF, 2003) included the following:

1. The government removed the ceiling on cash advances in May 1999.
2. A tax deduction was introduced, equal to 20 percent of credit card purchases in excess of 10 percent of gross income.
3. Authorities abolished the limit on leverage on credit card issuers and maintained a low capital requirement for issuers.
4. To bring merchants into the value-added tax net, the government initiated a lottery for credit card users in 2000, with one lottery ticket assigned to each purchase (so as to induce credit card use and improve value-added tax compliance).

In addition, ample liquidity and low interest rates led banks to search for new avenues for profits, including consumer lending. Credit card companies used aggressive marketing and little income verification in an attempt to capture market share. They tried to contain risks by obliging consumers to settle monthly balances. However, consumers acquired multiple credit cards and began to revolve credit across cards or "kiting." As a result, Korean credit card usage grew rapidly, leading to the average Korean having four credit cards by end-2002. Exacerbating the boom was a limited credit reporting infrastructure, as the coverage was inadequate in terms of both customer base and types of data collected

(BIS). These factors led to heightened risks that eventually resulted in financial stress.

In 2002, delinquencies began to rise, and credit bureaus started to recognize that consumer debt was often spread across multiple cards. Responding to these developments, the authorities began to tighten prudential regulations and banned aggressive marketing tactics. Credit card companies became wary of extending credit to the riskier borrowers, and more generally started to contract credit to bolster their balance sheets. This resulted in a vicious cycle of credit contraction and deteriorating asset quality. Investors were troubled by an accounting scandal at SK Global in 2003, leading to a freeze in the market for credit card company bonds. Later on in the year, LG Card lost access to capital markets, prompting the government to step in to rescue it.

Relevance for China

The boom and bust episode in Korea provides a cautionary tale, namely, that rapid increase in indebtedness, although bolstering consumption, may create issues for financial stability. The lessons learned include these two: (1) the necessity of putting in place infrastructure to mitigate information asymmetries between credit card issuers and borrowers. A sophisticated credit information sharing, providing comprehensive information on borrowers' debt, is essential to safely expand consumer credit. Indeed, in the aftermath of this episode, three competing private credit bureaus began operating in Korea. (2) It is also necessary to put in place appropriate prudential and supervisory measures and policies to mitigate risks from consumer lending.

CONCLUSION

International experience suggests that the development of consumer finance could help boost consumption (but not without risks). That would help China rebalance its economy, although a large gap would still remain between China's consumption share and that of comparable countries. Fully bridging that gap would likely require attacking the root causes of China's low household consumption, which include too small a share of households in total income and precautionary saving motives stemming from rising uncertainty and the limited social safety net.

While this chapter has focused on access to credit, other types of financial development could also help boost consumption. China's credit market may inefficiently allocate too much credit to capital-intensive industries. If financial development were to result in credit being shifted from capital-intensive to more labor-intensive sectors, that would tend to increase the ratio of households' disposable income to GDP. That in turn should contribute to higher consumption. The development of insurance markets should also increase consumption. Theoretical models of consumption suggest that much of the precautionary saving might be driven by the need to protect against low-probability events that imply large loss of consumption (such as unemployment spells, health expenditures, disability). As such, even modest improvements in the social safety net, possibly complemented by private insurance products, could have an appreciable impact on consumption. The health care reform being implemented is an important step in that direction.

Some of the financial development measures with the largest potential to boost consumption are those related to housing markets, such as developing secondary mortgage markets, lowering collateral, and allowing households to borrow against their illiquid housing wealth. However, these also carry some of the largest risks to the financial system. A more cautious approach could focus on pursuing other policies, such as the payroll loans described in this chapter. While the impact on consumption would be more modest, the added risks to the financial system would be minimal if the program were properly designed. A balance must be struck between the competing objectives of stimulating consumer loans and protecting the financial system from additional risks. Nevertheless, financial development and liberalization remains a worthwhile long-run objective to pursue.

REFERENCES

Abiad, A., E. Detragiache, and T. Tressel, 2008, "A New Database of Financial Reforms," IMF Working Paper No. 08/266 (Washington: International Monetary Fund).

Ben-Shahar, D., C. Ka, Y. Leung, and S. Ong, 2009, *Mortgage Markets Worldwide* (Oxford: Blackwell Publishing).

Chamon, M., P. Mauro, and Y. Okawa, 2008, "Mass Car Ownership in the Emerging Market Giants," *Economic Policy*, April, pp. 243–96.

Chamon, M., and E. Prasad, 2010, "Why Are Saving Rates of Urban Households in China Rising?" *American Economic Journal: Macroeconomics*, Vol. 2, No. 1, pp. 93–130.

Chamon, M., K. Liu, and E. Prasad, 2010, "Income Uncertainty and Household Savings in China" (unpublished).

Chung, C., 2009, "The Evolution of Mortgage and MBS Markets in Korea" (unpublished).

Costa, A. and J. M. De Mello, 2006, "Judicial Risk and Credit Market Performance: Micro Evidence from Brazilian Payroll Loans," in *Financial Markets Volatility and Performance in Emerging Markets*, ed. by Sebastian Edwards and Márcio Garcia (Cambridge, Massachusetts: National Bureau of Economic Research).

Guo, K., and P. N'Diaye, 2010, "Determinants of China's Private Consumption: An International Perspective," IMF Working Paper No. 10/93 (Washington: International Monetary Fund).

International Monetary Fund (IMF), 2003, *Korea—Selected Issues*, IMF Staff Country Report No. 03/80 (Washington).

Loayza, N., K. Schmidt-Hebbel, and L. Servén, 2000, "What Drives Private Saving Across the World?" *Review of Economics and Statistics*, Vol. 82, No. 2, pp. 165–81.

Rodrigues, E., V. Chu, L. Alencar, and T. Takeda, 2006, "O Efeito da Consignação em Folha nas Taxas de Juros dos Empréstimos Pessoais," *Trabalhos para Discussão*, No. 108 (Brasília: Central Bank of Brazil).

Warnock, V., and F. Warnock, 2008, "Markets and Housing Finance," *Journal of Housing Economics*, Vol. 17, No. 3, pp. 239–51.

Zhu, H., 2006, "The Structure of Housing Finance Markets and House Prices in Asia," *BIS Quarterly Review* (December).

About the Authors

Vivek Arora is an Assistant Director in the IMF's Asia and Pacific Department where he reviews the department's regional research and leads the country team on the Philippines. Mr. Arora joined the IMF in 1992. His country assignments have included China, the United States, Canada, Korea, South Africa, and others. He served as the IMF's Senior Resident Representative in Beijing, China from 2006 to 2010. He has a Ph.D. in economics from Brown University and received his undergraduate education at St. Stephen's College, Delhi.

Steven Barnett is a Deputy Division Chief in the Asia and Pacific Department of the IMF.

Ray Brooks is the IMF's Mission Chief for Australia and New Zealand. His responsibilities also include oversight of IMF work on Fiji, Papua-New Guinea, Samoa, Timor Leste, and Tuvalu. Mr. Brooks has worked for the IMF since 1991, and was previously the IMF's Senior Resident Representative in Beijing, China. Prior to joining the IMF, he worked at the Reserve Bank of New Zealand and studied at the University of Essex.

Roberto Cardarelli heads the Regional Studies Division in the IMF's Asia and Pacific Department. Before this, he worked in the World Economic Studies Division of the IMF's Research Department. Mr. Cardarelli holds a Ph.D. from Cambridge University.

Marcos Chamon is a Senior Economist in the Research Department at the International Monetary Fund.

Kai Guo is an Economist in the IMF's Strategy, Policy, and Review Department.

Sonali Jain-Chandra is an Economist in the IMF's Asia and Pacific Department.

Adil Mohommad is a Research Assistant in the Regional Studies Division of the IMF's Asia and Pacific Department.

Malhar Nabar is an Economist in the IMF's Asia and Pacific Department.

Papa N'Diaye is a Senior Economist in the IMF's Asia Pacific Department.

Nathan Porter is an Economist in the IMF's Strategy, Policy, and Review Department. Previously, he worked in the IMF's Asia and Pacific Department covering China.

Murtaza Syed is the IMF's Deputy Resident Representative in Beijing, China. Prior to joining the IMF, he worked at the Institute for Fiscal Studies in London and taught at Oxford University.

Olaf Unteroberdoerster is a Senior Economist in the Regional Studies Division of the IMF's Asia and Pacific Department.

Index

Note: Page references followed by *"f,"* *"t,"* and *"b"* denote figures, tables, and boxes respectively.